BCh - 3rd ed

THE THIRD CHILD

FIRST REPORT IN THIS STUDY

Family Growth in Metropolitan America, by Charles F. Westoff,
Robert G. Potter, Jr., Philip C. Sagi, and Elliot G. Mishler

PUBLISHED FOR THE OFFICE OF POPULATION RESEARCH
PRINCETON UNIVERSITY

The Third Child

A STUDY IN THE
PREDICTION OF FERTILITY

By CHARLES F. WESTOFF
ROBERT G. POTTER, Jr.
and PHILIP C. SAGI

PRINCETON, NEW JERSEY
PRINCETON UNIVERSITY PRESS
1963

TO FRANK NOTESTEIN
for his faith in this research

Foreword

Ten years ago a work conference sponsored by the Milbank Memorial Fund initiated plans for a new study of urban fertility in the United States. The resultant project, centered at the Office of Population Research, has had the benefit of invaluable help from outside Princeton—financial support from the Milbank Fund, the Carnegie Corporation, and the Population Council, and intellectual assistance from many colleagues at other institutions, including an expert steering committee.

In 1961, the Princeton University Press published *Family Growth in Metropolitan America*, setting forth the results of the first phase of this research—an interview with 1,165 couples who had recently borne a second child in one of the large metropolitan areas of the United States. That book necessarily emphasized fertility performance in the early phases of family formation, and attitudes toward further increases in family size at a stage that most recently married American couples reach. In the present book, the emphasis is on fertility behavior (in terms of contraceptive practice, the occurrence of pregnancy, and the duration of interpregnancy intervals) in the three and a half years following the second birth. It is based on a second interview with 905 couples (of the original 1,165) three years after the first.

The design of the study has made it possible to discover how actual performance is related to previously expressed attitudes and preferences, and to extend by more intensive questioning insights gained from the first interview. The value of this design is indicated by the numerous findings presented in the final chapter.

The authors of this book collaborated fully at every stage of their research, although the first draft of each chapter was an individual responsibility. Chapters II, III, V, VI, and VII were drafted by Potter; Chapters IV, XIII, and XIV by Sagi; and Chapters I, VIII, IX, X, XI, and XV by Westoff. Chapter XVI was written jointly by the three authors. Clyde V. Kiser of the Milbank Memorial Fund and the Office of Population Research wrote Chapter XII.

ANSLEY J. COALE, *Director*
Office of Population Research
Princeton, New Jersey

Preface

One intrinsic feature of a longitudinal study is that a large number of persons inevitably contribute in one way or another. Eight years have elapsed from the initial formulation of the research to publication of this second report during which we have had the benefit of the best professional advice available. This advice has come in many forms—in conferences of a special committee established specifically to guide the early development of the study, in numerous personal consultations with other social scientists working in the same field, and through the medium of professional meetings where progress reports or partial results of our research have occasionally been presented. The Steering Committee whose advice was sought in the beginning of the study and whose suggestions helped determine the ultimate design and much of the content and thus the shape of the analyses reported in the present volume consisted of:

Frank W. Notestein, Chairman—The Population Council, Inc.
Ansley J. Coale   —Office of Population Research, Princeton University
Ronald Freedman   —University of Michigan
Philip M. Hauser   —University of Chicago
Dudley Kirk   —The Population Council, Inc.
Clyde V. Kiser   —Milbank Memorial Fund
Frank Lorimer   —Princeton University
Donald G. Marquis   —Social Science Research Council
Frederick Osborn   —The Population Council, Inc.
Lowell J. Reed   —Johns Hopkins University
P. K. Whelpton   —Scripps Foundation for Research in Population Problems, Miami University

Elliot Mishler, now with the Massachusetts Mental Health Center, actively participated in the first phase of the study and thus helped to formulate many of the decisions which determined the future direction of the research. Our colleague Ansley Coale has been in more or less constant contact with the study and his suggestions have invariably been helpful. Ronald Freedman of the University of Michigan and P. K. Whelpton of the Scripps Foundation at Miami University have been in close contact during the entire duration of the study and we have benefited continually from their experience gained in the Growth of American Family Study done in collaboration with Arthur Campbell of the Scripps Foundation. We have continued to benefit from the experience of Whelpton and Campbell in the second phase of their study. A note of appreciation is also due David Goldberg of the University of Michigan whose work in the Detroit Area Study has been another resource of research suggestions.

Special acknowledgment is due Norman Ryder of the University of Wisconsin who read through both manuscripts prior to publication and who gave generously of his time and advice. His numerous suggestions and criticisms have contributed greatly to the improvement of both volumes.

The operational aspects of this phase of the study as in the first phase were again shared with National Analysts, Inc., of Philadelphia. This organization conducted the interviewing and much of the coding and punching operations. The quality of their work evidenced in the first phase was again consistently maintained. Although many persons in National Analysts contributed their special skills in the field work operations, our main debt of gratitude is owed to Jean Szaloczi (now with the Social Security Administration) who again assumed responsibility for directing and coordinating the project. This involved assistance in construction of the interview schedule, interviewer training, the editing of completed interviews, coding and punching stages. Sidney Binder was also especially helpful in the early stages of planning tabulations.

At various times during the data-processing stages we have been able to count on the knowledge and help of Roald Buhler of Educational Testing Service at Princeton whose work with computers and skill in writing special programs was invaluable.

In addition to the large volume of calculations programmed for electronic computers, the second phase involved many forms of analyses and computations expertly performed by Erna Härm and Wanda Pieslak.

During the summer of 1961 Patricia Backman worked on several special analyses with characteristic zeal and enthusiasm. One of her main responsibilities was the rather unrewarding analysis of the association between personality characteristics and fertility.

The heavy load of clerical work and general bookkeeping

services was borne by Hazel Chafey who patiently and thoroughly coped with the endless details and who successfully mastered the problems inherent in having to work with three authors.

A special note of appreciation is due Patricia Collins for her painstaking proof-reading of the entire manuscript and for her helpful editorial suggestions.

Our thanks must also go to the 71 interviewers who worked on the second phase of this study and finally to the 905 interviewees who made the study possible.

CHARLES F. WESTOFF
ROBERT G. POTTER, JR.
PHILIP C. SAGI

Contents

Tables

⟨ *xix* ⟩

⟨ *xxi* ⟩

Appendix Tables

PART I
INTRODUCTION

Chapter I. Background, Sample, and Objectives

BACKGROUND

In the first few months of 1957 we interviewed a sample of 1,165 women all of whom had given birth to their second child about six months earlier. One of the questions we asked concerned the number of children they wanted to have. We also collected information on contraceptive practice, desired spacing of children, length of birth intervals, and on a wide variety of background information, attitudes, and behavior. A basic interest then was to learn the kinds of factors relevant to the number of children American couples want to have. Accordingly it was possible to analyze a wide array of social and psychological factors in relation to desired family size, birth intervals, and fertility-planning success. The interrelations of spacing attitudes, desired family size, birth intervals, and contraceptive practice were also explored in greater detail than had been possible in previous studies. These analyses resulted in the publication of a volume entitled *Family Growth in Metropolitan America.*[1]

In early 1960, three years later, we interviewed the same women again. Three and a half years had now elapsed since their second child was born. Again we completed a lengthy interview with the woman, collecting data on her fertility over the three-year period as well as on changes in the social and economic status of the couple. This longitudinal feature of our study design also permitted us to include questions reflecting new leads gained from the analysis of the first interviews. The primary objective of this second phase of the study is to explain why some couples stopped at two children while others went on to have a third and even a fourth child during this interval of time. Thus the analysis of data collected in the second round of interviews was focused on trying to account for fertility since the second birth. A report of this second phase of the study is the task of the present volume.

SAMPLE AND STUDY DESIGN

The original panel of 1,165 respondents was subject to eligibility criteria aimed at producing a sample of urban, native white couples with two children whose marriages so far had been uncom-

---

[1] Charles F. Westoff, Robert G. Potter, Jr., Philip C. Sagi, and Elliot G. Mishler, *Family Growth in Metropolitan America*, Princeton University Press, Princeton, N.J., 1961.

plicated by death, divorce, separation, or extensive pregnancy wastage. Full details of the sample design are included in the book describing the first phase.[2] A probability sample, stratified by metropolitan area, was drawn from the seven Standard Metropolitan Areas (exclusive of Boston)[3] with populations of at least 2 million persons. Accordingly suburbs as well as central cities are represented in the sample. Nor were any direct restrictions placed on social class or religion, though the composition of the sample in these respects is affected indirectly by the restrictions of race, nativity, and residence. To be considered eligible, both spouses had to be once-married and still living together with no stillbirths and no more than one miscarriage experienced before the second birth. In addition the second birth must have occurred during the same month (September 1956)[4] for every couple. Other eligibility criteria included no infant deaths, adoptions, or plural births.

The goal of the second round of field work has been to interview every woman still eligible. Defined as ineligible for reinterview are wives who have become widowed, divorced, or permanently separated from their first husband. Also regarded as ineligible were 13 wives who reported a sterilizing operation at the first interview.

As before, all field work has been done by the professional interviewing staff of National Analysts. The details of steps taken to contact respondents for reinterview are described in Appendix B. Altogether, out of the original panel of 1,165 wives, 42 proved ineligible for one reason or another, 125 could not be contacted, and 93 refused the second interview. The remaining 905 were successfully interviewed a second time. Results of the second phase of field work are summarized in Appendix Table B-1.

Not surprisingly the 905 respondents are a selected group within the total panel of 1,165. A detailed comparison of the 905 respondents with the 260 nonrespondents (Appendix Table B-2) shows that at first interview the respondents had higher income, more education, more white-collar jobs, and a barely higher proportion of successful family planners than the respondents not included in the second phase. The 905 respondents include disproportionately many Jews and disproportionately few Catholics. As the most marked contrast, 87 per cent of the respondents returned mailed

---

[2] *Ibid.*, Chapter 2.

[3] Boston was excluded only because birth order was not recorded in their vital statistics, which made the location of eligible couples impracticable.

[4] The selection of this month had no significance other than being six months prior to the time the field work was ready to begin.

questionnaires after the first interview, compared with 57 per cent of the nonrespondents. Nevertheless, many contrasts proved statistically insignificant. For example, nonsignificant differences were found in connection with the size of family desired by wife, interval between marriage and second birth, age of husband, Standard Metropolitan Area, and number of residential changes since marriage.

Because the respondents are a selected group, means, proportions, and percentage distributions based on their responses must be interpreted with caution. However, there is little evidence that correlations yielded by this subsample differ materially from the correlations that might have been obtained with a more ideal sample predicated on no refusals and no failures to contact eligible persons. It is clear (Appendix Table B-3) that with respect to all possible correlations among 31 variables collected in the first interview, the total sample and subsample of 905 respondents reinterviewed yield very similar results.

Procedures for interviewer training and coder training, along with measures taken to control the quality of coding, punching, verifying, and preliminary tabulation, are closely modeled after those utilized in the first phase of the study, and for details the reader is referred to Chapter III of the earlier book.

Basic Organization

The same basic organization of chapters is followed in this monograph as in the previous one relating to the first phase of the study. Two sets of substantive chapters follow the introductory material. In the present volume Chapters II–VII deal with some of the interconnections among family-size preferences, spacing preferences, birth and pregnancy intervals, fertility since second birth, and contraceptive practice. A second set of substantive chapters (Chapters VIII–XV) focuses on the relationships between a wide array of social and psychological factors and selected indices of fertility, most notably fertility since the second birth.

Most American couples try to limit their family size as well as exercise some control over their birth intervals. Of course the degree of fertility control actually achieved varies from couple to couple and usually falls well short of perfection. Even if a majority of United States couples succeed in having the number of children they want—an assertion not above dispute—their regulation of child spacing appears much weaker. The next chapter (Chapter II) reviews previous research relating to family growth in the United States. Its main theme is that efficient control of family size appears far more common than does close regulation of birth intervals. This state of affairs implies a strong trend toward more efficient contraception as desired family size is neared or else an unprecedented amount of sterilization utilized for purposes of family limitation.

The following five chapters will focus on this problem of fertility control, the central question being: to what extent do the number and spacing of births in the present sample reflect clear-cut preferences rather than accidental factors. To this end, family growth is viewed as a process through time in which the number and spacing of births are much influenced, though rarely wholly determined by, family-size and spacing preferences, and these preferences themselves may have a complicated history. Vagueness of spacing preferences, fallible contraception, pregnancy wastage, and slowness to conceive are all examined as barriers to precise regulation of birth spacing. A particular effort is made to gauge the extent of improvement in contraception, and to gain insight into the mechanisms of its improvement as desired family size is approached and attained. Some of the implications of these inquiries for short-range predictions of fertility are also considered.

More specifically, Chapter III deals with conceptive delays, that is the number of months waited for conception either in the absence of contraception or following its deliberate interruption. In the first phase of this study, conception delays were shown to be a very important element in the variation of birth intervals. To answer the question of how often couples try to hurry conception and how effective are their efforts, conceptive delays are considered in relation to coital frequency, knowledge about the timing of ovulation within the monthly cycle, and use or nonuse of this knowledge.

Two chapters (Chapters IV and V) relate to the improvement of contraceptive practice as desired family size is approached. The mechanisms of this improvement, such as reduction of chance-taking and choice of method, are explored in Chapter V.

Chapter VI is aimed at trying to understand the basis of the inverse association between desired family size and the length of the interval between second birth and next pregnancy. The issue posed is whether this relation depends mainly on a tendency for mothers desiring larger families to prefer shorter birth intervals or to practice less effective contraception.

The final chapter of the section, Chapter VII, examines the interrelationships of several variables measuring different aspects of fertility with emphasis on their capacity to predict the number of pregnancies occurring since the second birth. Particular attention is devoted here to evaluating desired family size as a predictor of fertility performance during the three-year interval. A great deal of recent research[5] in fertility has depended upon the validity of such predictions. Other variables in that analysis include length of birth intervals, preferred intervals, and fertility-planning success from marriage to the second birth.

The following section includes chapters on religion and religiousness, reactions to change in general economic conditions, socioeconomic status, social mobility, the structure of familial relationships, age and sex composition, residence and migration, and is concluded with a summary multivariate analysis. With the exception of two chapters on concepts and hypotheses and personality characteristics the topics parallel those included in the first book. No chapter is devoted to concepts and hypotheses as such, partly because this would mean a certain amount of redundancy but mainly because questions of theoretical significance are tied directly into the analyses as they appear.

A discussion of personality characteristics has been eliminated for quite different reasons, however. Readers of the first volume will recall that the correlations found between the number of children desired or fertility-planning success and measures of six personality characteristics[6] were all discouragingly low. The pessimism voiced then has been justified in view of the low correlations again uncovered, this time in connection with variations in actual subsequent fertility. For all intents and purposes no significant associations of any kind[7] have been disclosed. Although as we concluded in the first book the measurement of personality may be at fault, there is no apparent justification for devoting further attention to these variables in this study.

There is one chapter included here which does not have a predecessor in the first book, Chapter XI, "Reactions to Change in General Economic Conditions." The economic recession of 1957–58 occurred between the two sets of interviews providing us fortuitously with a kind of natural social experiment. In the second interview we included a question on the effects of the recession, as well as one on the steel strike which occurred in 1959. We were then able to

[5] For a review of this research, see Philip C. Sagi and Charles F. Westoff, "An Exercise in Partitioning Some Components of the Variance of Family Size," in *Emerging Techniques in Population Research*, New York Milbank memorial Fund, 1963.

[6] They are: generalized manifest anxiety, nurturance needs, compulsiveness, ambiguity tolerance, cooperativeness, and need achievement.

[7] We examined the associations both with number of pregnancies and fertility-planning success. The tests used permitted nonlinear associations to appear. We also examined the discriminating power of persons at the highest and lowest scale positions.

classify couples according to type of economic effect and examine the implications for their fertility during that period of time.

Throughout the second section of this book the main dependent variable is the number of pregnancies that occurred during the three-year interval since the first interview. Another dependent variable frequently of interest is desired family size as reported in the second interview which is the best available single index of completed family size. Although the measurement of fertility-planning success is beset by serious problems of unreliability, a matter analyzed and discussed in Appendix C, this variable is also frequently viewed as a dependent variable.

Although our ultimate objective is to account for as much as possible of the variation of fertility, the particular analyses are organized around individual themes and lines of theoretical interest based upon previous research. The early work incorporated in the Indianapolis Study is of course the primary progenitor of this entire study. Similarly the work of Freedman, Whelpton, and Campbell has provided us with numerous leads and bases for comparison. Since *The Third Child* is the second report of a longitudinal study, most of the theoretical organization of course has been supplied by the lines of interest drawn in our first book. In many respects the analyses contained in the present volume may be regarded as behavioral tests of hypotheses confirmed with attitudinal data in the first phase. This means that the interest we had in the number of children desired as it related to religion or socio-economic status is now to be reexamined in the light of actual fertility over the succeeding three-year period. The general themes involve religion and religiousness, socio-economic status, social mobility, and various aspects of family relationships and composition.

The influence of religion and religiousness on fertility was the focus of a great deal of attention in the first phase in which we concluded that religion was the best single predictor of the number of children desired. Does this association persist with actual fertility? Does education in Catholic schools still provide a good basis for predicting Catholic fertility? What kinds of perceptions do American women have of their religion's views on family planning and family size? Do such perceptions have any influence on their fertility? Other avenues of interest pursued in Chapter VIII are on the fertility of mixed marriages and the role of ethnic background in explaining internal variations in the fertility of the religious groups.

The chapter on socio-economic status (Chapter IX) pursues several themes. The major aim is to compare the influence of occupation, income, and education on the fertility of the different religious groups. The influence of a rural culture as it affects the socio-economic factor in the fertility of the present generation is also examined for each religious category. The chapter also includes an analysis of a number of attitudes, aspirations, and perceptions associated with the socio-economic area.

A heavy investment was made in the first phase of this study in the hypothesis that social mobility, or aspirations for upward mobility, are related to fertility. Since the findings were largely negative, emphasis on this hypothesis has been reduced somewhat in the present analysis. The chapter devoted to this topic (Chapter X) includes analyses of the relation of fertility to changes in occupation within and across generations, changes in income, and various measures of levels of aspiration.

As in the volume based upon the first phase of the study, the present report also contains a chapter (Chapter XII) on the relation of migration and residence to fertility. The analysis focuses on the relation of the advent and timing of the third birth to migration during the three years between interviews and to character of residence. The longitudinal design of the study lends itself particularly well to an examination of the impact of suburban residence on fertility. Previous investigations have always been complicated by the problem of disentangling the sequence of suburban moves and increases in family size.

In the areas of the wife's adjustment to marriage, to work, to children, and to the role of mother, the analysis follows themes developed in the earlier volume. Here the parallel ends for two reasons. First, such new variables as problems with the first two children, husband-wife agreement in different areas of family-decision making, urban-rural background, and visiting patterns were introduced. Second, the analysis could now focus on factors affecting fertility subsequent to the second birth. The rationales for the new variables come from studies recently published as well as elaborations of notions suggested by data collected in the first interview. For example, "extent of visiting relatives" as compared with "visiting friends" was found to be associated with larger families and the number of urban generations appears to reflect the degree of assimilation of urban-associated values of family planning and family size. These analyses are pursued in Chapter XIII.

The second interview also provided the opportunity for collecting additional data on the parental family's size, sex composition, and birth order of the respondent and her husband. This continues (Chapter XIV) the investigation of the relationship between family sizes of successive generations.

Some Further Connections with the First Book

We noted above that the subject of personality and a specific chapter on concepts and hypotheses have been excluded from this report. Also excluded are a chapter on methodology as such and the details of index construction. Little if any methodological innovation has been advanced in the present analysis and there is no reason to repeat the discussion of the correlational, multivariate, and scaling techniques employed. The reader who is interested in the content of the scales and indexes used should consult Appendix C in the first book where each item with its distribution of responses is presented. The present set of appendices, however, does include the interview schedule used for the second interview.

PART II

FERTILITY AND FERTILITY CONTROL

Chapter II. Current Fertility and Fertility Control in the United States: A Review

Among the values characterizing the postwar family of the United States are the following three: a preference for marrying young, a striking consensus on two, three, or four as the ideal number of children, and a desire to have these children at a controlled rate—not as fast as biologically possible, but fast enough to compress most of the childbearing into the first half of the reproductive period.

To put the following six chapters into perspective, an idealized description is attempted here of the process of family growth that has developed in response to the above three values. Some of the surface features pertaining to marriage age, birth spacing, and total children born may be documented from publications of the Census Bureau and the National Office of Vital Statistics. However, to learn anything about the dependence of these overt fertility patterns upon spacing and family-size preferences, as mediated by efforts at fertility control, it is necessary to draw upon a few special sample surveys such as the Indianapolis Study,[1] the 1955 Growth of American Families Study (hereafter abbreviated simply as the GAF Study),[2] certain of the Detroit Area Studies,[3] and the present study. At many points the picture of contemporary fertility and fertility control in the United States is incomplete. It is hoped that succeeding chapters will partially fill a few of these gaps. Given at the end of this chapter is a list of specific questions that the subsequent five chapters are intended to answer.

Marriage and Natality Patterns

Four features of contemporary marriage and natality in the United States are especially noteworthy in the present context. First is the predominantly young age of brides entering first marriage. For comparison with the 1,165 wives of the present study, the most relevant birth cohorts are those of 1925–29 and 1930–34,

[1] P. K. Whelpton and C. V. Kiser, eds. *Social and Psychological Factors Affecting Fertility*, Milbank Memorial Fund, New York, 5 vols., 1946–58.

[2] Ronald Freedman, P. K. Whelpton, and Arthur Campbell, *Family Planning, Sterility and Population Growth*, McGraw-Hill, New York, 1959.

[3] See D. Goldberg, H. Sharp, and R. Freedman, "The Stability and Reliability of Expected Family Size Data," Milbank Memorial Fund *Quarterly*, 37 (October 1959) pp. 369–385 and R. Freedman, D. Goldberg, and H. Sharp, " 'Ideals' About Family Size in the Detroit Metropolitan Area: 1954," Milbank Memorial Fund *Quarterly*, 33 (April 1955) pp. 187–197.

representing women aged 30–34 and 25–29 years in 1959. Ninety-five per cent of the women of both cohorts had married by 1959 and among these ever married women, the median age at first marriage was 20 years in both cohorts, with 75 per cent marrying by 23 and 22 years, and 85 per cent by 25 and 24 years of age[4] in the earlier and later cohort respectively. Incidentally, a similar pattern of marriage is found for the 1,165 wives of the present study. Roughly one-quarter, one-half, and three-quarters married by their 18th, 20th, and 22nd years.

A second noteworthy feature is the large proportion of families ending their childbearing with a total of two to four births. Ever married white women aged 40–44 in 1959 show 30 per cent childless or with one child, 12 per cent with five or more children, and therefore a majority of 58 per cent with two to four children ever born.[5] The next younger group, aged 35 to 39 in 1959, may produce an even greater concentration of families with two to four children since currently only 25 per cent have fewer than two births, 63 per cent have two to four births, and the remaining 13 per cent have five or more. The prospect for ever married white women 30–34 years in 1959 is less certain. The proportion finishing with two to four births may not be greater than 60 per cent because, although the proportion of women either childless or with one child is already below 25 per cent, the proportion bearing five children or more is expected to exceed 13 per cent possibly by a sizable margin.[6]

A third feature is the degree to which childbearing is compressed into the first ten years of marriage, or into those years before the wife reaches 30. The most direct data come from the Census Bureau's Current Population Survey for April 1954. The results of greatest interest relate to white, once-married women living with husbands whose children are all alive and present in the household at time of survey.[7] Among all second, third, and fourth births to

---

[4] "Marriage, Fertility, and Childspacing: August 1959," *Current Population Reports,* Series P-20, No. 108 (July 1961), Bureau of the Census, Washington, D.C., p. 22. See also Paul C. Glick, *American Families,* John Wiley & Sons, New York, 1957, p. 54.

[5] *Current Population Reports,* p. 17.

[6] According to the vital statistics of 1959, based on a 50 per cent sample of births (*Vital Statistics of the United States 1959,* Section 13, "Live Births by Age of Mother and Birth Order," U.S. Dept. of Health, Education and Welfare, Washington, D.C., Table 39A, p. 249) 14 per cent of all births in 1959 were of parity 5 or higher. However, this proportion still depends heavily on contributions from wartime marriages and therefore does not properly reflect any trend in favor of larger families among couples married after the war.

[7] "Child Spacing as Measured from Data Enumerated in the Current Population Survey: United States, April 1950 to April 1954," *Vital Statistics-Special Reports,* U.S. Dept. of Health, Education and Welfare, Vol. 47, No. 3 (October 1958), p. 94.

such women during the years 1950–54, 89, 71, and 54 per cent respectively occurred to wives married less than ten years. The corresponding proportions of second-, third-, and fourth-order births, to wives 29 years or younger were 77, 62, and 55 per cent. If one accepts these proportions at face value one has to conclude that a large majority of all second and third births and half or so of all fourth births occur within the first ten years of marriage or on the average before the mother's 30th birthday.

Actually these proportions are subject both to downward and upward biases. The requirement that all children be living and present in the household selects against high-parity couples and as a result may introduce a downward bias in the proportions of births occurring before age 30 or in the first ten years of marriage. This bias arises because, as will be shown later, a larger size of completed family means shorter intervals on the average between marriage and any specified order of birth. On the other hand, upward bias exists because the births associated with short marriage durations and ages below 30 stem mainly from postwar marriage cohorts, which are larger than the wartime and prewar cohorts furnishing most of the births identified with longer marriage durations and ages over 30.

The net balance of these opposing biases is conjectural. However, less direct data suggest that the above results are not unreasonable. Among couples married in 1935–39 and therefore having time to complete virtually all of their childbearing by 1959, the initial ten years of marriage accounted for 96 per cent of all first births, 85 per cent of all second births, and 67 per cent of all third births.[8] These proportions would be somewhat higher if births produced in remarriages could be excluded. Significantly, too, recent marriage cohorts are having their first and second babies sooner after marriage than did the prewar cohort.[9] Thus again the evidence points to a large majority of second- and third-order births and an appreciable fraction of fourth ones occurring in the first ten years of marriage. Indirect data also confirm a comparable concentration of childbearing before age 30.[10]

[8] *Current Population Reports*, p. 28. A proportion cannot be given for fourth births since they are not separated from births of higher order.

[9] *Ibid.*, pp. 6–7.

[10] Vital registration data for native-white women, based on a 50 per cent systematic sample of the nation, show that 73 per cent of all 1959 births were born to women 29 years or younger and these births included 70 per cent of all third births and 55 per cent of all fourth births. See *Vital Statistics of the United States 1959*, Section 13, "Live Births by Age of Mother and Birth Order," U.S. Dept. of Health, Education and Welfare, Table 39A, p. 249. Again care must be exercised in the interpretation of such figures. Births to the age group 35–39 depend primarily on first marriages centered on

Partly because they represent first marriages contracted mostly in the last ten years, the 1,165 women of the present sample had their first and second babies sooner after marriage than did the 1935–39 cohort. For example, 80 per cent of the present sample had their second birth within seven years of marriage as compared to two-thirds for the cohort. (Table 1).

TABLE 1
Duration between Marriage and Second Birth of Couples, from the *Family Growth in Metropolitan America* Study

Interval (months)	Frequency	Cumulative Percentage
Under 24	65	6
24–35	235	26
36–47	236	46
48–59	158	60
60–71	134	71
72–83	91	79
84–101	101	88
102–125	76	94
126 and over	69	100
Total	1,165	100

A fourth noteworthy feature of contemporary marriage and natality is the tendency for larger families to associate with shorter birth intervals. Doubtless this association is a general characteristic of completed fertility, though it is interesting that it remains so marked in populations exercising extensive control over family size. Documented some years ago for Great Britain,[11] this association has only recently been validated in detail for the United States. One of its expressions is appreciably longer intervals between marriage and any birth when that birth is the last child born as compared to

the period 1940–44, while births to the age groups 30–34 and 25–29 depend most heavily on first marriages contracted in the years 1945–49 and 1950–54 respectively. Owing to the unequal sizes of different marriage cohorts, births to the 30–34 age group are somewhat inflated while those to the 35–39 age group are understated. To some extent these two biases cancel each other out in the estimate of childbearing completed before age 30. If the postwar cohorts are going to have higher fertility in their middle and late thirties than the wartime cohorts, then the estimate of 73 per cent as the proportion of total childbearing before age thirty may be slightly high. However, the estimates of 70 and 55 per cent for third and fourth births before age 30 are much less affected by this consideration since such high proportions of third and fourth births occur prior to age 35.

[11] D. V. Glass and E. Grebenik, *The Trend and Pattern of Fertility in Great Britain: A Report on the Family Census of 1946*, H.M.S.O., London, 1954, especially Chapter VII of Part I.

when that birth is followed by one or more additional ones. (See Table 2 for illustration.)

TABLE 2

Median Intervals between Marriage and Births of Specified Order, for White Women First Married in 1935–39

| | Median Intervals in Months | | |
| | Specified Birth Is Last Birth | Specified Birth Is Followed by Additional One(s) | |
Interval			*Difference*
Marriage to first birth	37.4	19.3	18.1
Marriage to second birth	85.0	51.0	34.0
Marriage to third birth	119.1	79.1	40.0

SOURCE: *Current Population Reports*, Series P-20, No. 108, Bureau of the Census, Washington (July 12, 1961) pp. 41–43.

To summarize thus far, most postwar brides are entering marriage in their late teens or early twenties. About one-fifth of the women will reach the end of their reproductive period childless or with one child only and quite likely this proportion will be under one-fifth for wives whose first marriages remain intact until menopause. A majority of wives will end their reproductive careers with two to four children born, though more than 13 per cent will complete their childbearing with five births or more. How many more than 13 per cent remains an intriguing question for the future to settle. Most second and third babies and roughly half of the fourth babies will be born before the mother is 30, and in the first ten years of marriage. Also to be expected is a marked inverse correlation between average length of birth interval and completed size of family.

FAMILY-SIZE AND SPACING PREFERENCES

Data on family-size preferences have come mainly from a few special sample surveys listed already. On the basis of such studies, Freedman has generalized that since the war there has developed "a remarkable consensus in the American population on a moderate size family of 2 to 4 children, whether the measure of values used is desired, ideal or expected number of children."[12]

[12] R. Freedman, "American Studies of Factors Affecting Fertility," mimeographed paper prepared for International Population Conference, 1961, p. 4. See also his analysis, "Social Values about Family Size in the United States," *International Population Conference*, Vienna, 1959, pp. 173–83.

"Three-fourths of the women interviewed expect to have 2 to 4 children, 85 per cent said they would have 2 to 4 if they could live their lives over again, and 91 per cent consider 2 to 4 children ideal for the average American family. Most of the women expecting less than 2 children are subfecund while a substantial number of those expecting 5 or more children don't want them."[13]

In addition, nearly all wives want to space their children rather than have them as rapidly as biologically possible, unless of course they perceive themselves as slow to conceive or especially prone to pregnancy wastage. So general is the use of contraception for spacing purposes, that nonuse of contraception after a first birth usually connotes either religious conviction or subfecundity. For instance, in the GAF Study, 88 per cent of the "relatively fecund" couples married five to nine years and 92 per cent of those married longer than ten years are ever users of contraception.[14] In the present study, with the incidence of subfecundity reduced by eligibility criteria, 83 per cent of the total sample utilize contraception before their second birth; and of the 11 per cent still not practicing contraception after a second birth, two-thirds give religion or subfecundity as their principal reason. Indeed, only 21 women, or less than 3 per cent of the total sample, explain their nonuse of contraception on the basis of wanting three children as quickly as possible or else being indifferent about their spacing.[15]

Though she wants her babies spaced, the postwar mother is not usually interested in long birth intervals, say longer than four years. The only direct data on spacing attitudes for the postwar period come from the present study. Asked to assess their own past birth intervals, wives of the present study more often than not accept as "just right" any interval of 18 to 48 months.[16] Such a wide range of tolerated birth spacing suggests that no narrow band of interval length is perceived as peculiarly advantageous while all other lengths are deemed too short or too long. More will be said later about vague spacing standards in connection with fertility control. The wives were also asked to define an ideal spacing between second and third births. Over half preferred intervals of two and a half years or less, while 85 per cent favored intervals of four years or less.[17]

[13] R. Freedman, "American Studies . . . ," p. 11.

[14] Freedman, Whelpton, and Campbell, *Family Planning, Sterility and Population Growth*, p. 65.

[15] Charles F. Westoff, Robert G. Potter, Jr., Philip C. Sagi, and Elliot G. Mishler, *Family Growth in Metropolitan America*, Princeton University Press, Princeton, N.J., 1961, p. 72.

[16] *Ibid.*, pp. 120–121

[17] *Ibid.*, p. 126.

It was also found in the present study that women who desire larger families tend to seek shorter birth intervals, as measured by length of contraceptive practice among women successful in their contraception or not practicing it because the next baby is wanted as soon as possible. The correlation between desired family size and interval intended between marriage and first birth was −.19, and

TABLE 3

Per Cent of Wives Considering Timing of Second Child as "Too Soon," "Just Right," "Too Late," or "Didn't Matter," by Length of Interval between First and Second Births

Length of Interval First to Second Birth	Number of Wives	Timing Too Soon (per cent)	Timing Just Right (per cent)	Timing Too Late (per cent)	Timing Didn't Matter (per cent)	Total (per cent)
12 months or less	57	58	37	2	4	100
13 to 18	222	40	55	—	5	100
19 to 24	205	12	81	1	4	100
25 to 30	155	5	90	5	1	100
31 to 36	131	2	82	15	1	100
37 to 48	149	—	68	31	1	100
49 to 60	94	1	38	59	2	100
61 to 84	77	—	19	78	3	100
85 and over	75	—	9	89	1	100
Total	1,165	13	61	22	3	100

SOURCE: Westoff *et al.*, *Family Growth in Metropolitan America*, Table 29, p. 120.

with interval intended between first and second birth, −.35.[18] Further analysis of the latter correlation revealed that it depends primarily on the fact that most of the mothers wanting their second baby right away also wanted families of four children or more. This result is paralleled by another. The minority of wives who explain their nonuse of contraception after first birth on the basis of either indifference to spacing or religious conviction also tend to want larger than average numbers of children.

This tendency to seek or to tolerate short birth intervals when a large family size is wanted, together with the unpopularity of birth intervals longer than four years, helps to explain the concentration of childbearing in the first ten years of marriage. In addition, approximately half the couples do not try to delay their first born at all after marriage, though, to be sure, some of these marry when the bride is already pregnant. This figure of roughly 50 per cent not

[18] *Ibid.*, p. 124.

using contraception between marriage and first pregnancy was obtained in the GAF Study as well as the present one.[19]

CONTROL OF FAMILY SIZE

The evidence reviewed so far indicates that in the postwar United States, and more particularly among urban whites, couples typically want two to four children so spaced that most or all of their childbearing is accomplished within the first ten years or so of marriage. Obviously one of the challenges of fertility control posed by these objectives is to maintain a desired family size achieved rather early in marriage against the risk of additional pregnancies and births.

Elsewhere it has been estimated that among couples whose first marriages remain intact until the wife reaches menopause, a proportion of 9 to 18 per cent is thwarted from reaching intended family size by sterility or subfecundity.[20] This rough estimate is based on the assumption that equal numbers of couples are seeking two, three, and four children while none aim for a number outside this range.[21] The estimate rests further on the assumption of early marriage since the incidence of fecundity impairments rises with increasing age.

Besides this fraction thwarted by fecundity impairments from reaching family-size objectives, at least another fifth of the couples whose first marriages remain intact until menopause will exceed their intended number of pregnancies. Of 509 GAF respondents married fifteen years, 22 per cent reported unwanted last pregnancies, while the proportion was 26 per cent among the 214 "relatively fecund" wives of this marriage duration. Among 695 respondents aged 35–39, the proportion of unwanted last births was 17 per cent, and 21 per cent for the 324 relatively fecund members of this

[19] *Ibid.*, p. 73, and Freedman, Whelpton, and Campbell, *Family Planning, Sterility and Population Growth*, pp. 62–63.

[20] R. G. Potter, Jr., "Some Physical Correlates of Fertility Control in the United States," to be published in the Proceedings of the International Population Conference, 1961.

[21] The number of children which a respondent is aiming for, and perhaps expects to have, is sometimes less than the number she reports as desired and might have sought under more favorable conditions. For instance, in the GAF Study, the proportion of married white women expecting fewer children than desired is 23 per cent for the whole sample and 32 per cent for women aged 35–39. However, the authors suspect that some of the subfecund women are reporting interest in more children than they would be prepared to have if physical barriers were removed. Also, the reasons for expecting fewer children than preferred include economic and other nonphysical considerations, since, of the 23 per cent, only .71 are classified as subfecund or sterile. Cf. Freedman, Whelpton, and Campbell, *Family Planning, Sterility and Population Growth*, pp. 260–262.

age group.[22] Hence, in this investigation at least, roughly four-fifths of the respondents late in their reproductive period—three-quarters for those still relatively fecund—claim to have limited family size successfully. A similar result was obtained for the prewar period in the Indianapolis Study.[23]

One can think of a number of reasons why these alleged incidences of successful family limitation may be exaggerated. A few of the respondents will have additional pregnancies, since they had not all completed their periods of pregnancy risk by the time of interview. Some respondents may have forgotten last pregnancies which conveniently ended in spontaneous abortion; others are concealing pregnancies which they had to end by induced abortion. Still others, who came to accept an originally unwanted infant long before its arrival, quite sincerely have forgotten the initial period of chagrin. Indeed, if the unintentional pregnancy occurred while the couple were still trying to make up their minds whether or not they wanted another child, it is not even clear how they *should* classify the pregnancy.

Obviously, then, the proportion of white couples who successfully control their family size during a first marriage that remains intact is not known with any precision and depends heavily on what definitions are adopted. With a tolerant definition of success and optimistic assumptions about subfecundity and accuracy of reporting, one can raise the estimated incidence of successful control to as high as 70 per cent. Under a less tolerant definition and more pessimistic assumptions, the estimated frequency of successful control is reduced to 60, or even 50 per cent. Nevertheless, it remains plausible that a large majority of the couples under discussion is going to approach their family size objectives fairly closely: that is, will neither be deprived by fecundity impairments from having most of the children they want nor burdened with more than one unwanted birth by gross failure of family limitation. This last premise is reinforced by the expectation, documented earlier, that 60 per cent or so of the 1945–49 and 1950–54 marriage cohorts will finish their childbearing with two to four births.

CONTROL OF SPACING

If a majority or near majority of couples realize their intended family size, many fewer regulate the spacing of their births with any

[22] For a discussion of these data, see R. G. Potter, Jr., "Some Comments on the Evidence Pertaining to Family Limitation in the United States," *Population Studies*, 14 (1960) pp. 40–41.

[23] *Ibid.*, p. 41.

precision. Of course, by practicing no contraception at all, most couples could meet one goal, namely to reach desired family size within the first ten years of marriage. However, precise control of birth-spacing requires that each pregnancy be delayed as long as desired, that conception follow closely upon interruption of contraception, and finally that pregnancy end in a live birth.

Only a minority of couples can claim to be "number and spacing planners," that is, deliberate interruptors of contraception before each pregnancy. In the GAF Study the proportion is 16 per cent for relatively fecund women married fifteen years or more, and 10 per cent for all women of this marriage duration.[24] For shorter durations, the proportions are of course higher. At the time of their second birth, 28 per cent of the couples of the present study are in the category of number and spacing planners and the proportion rises to 40 per cent if not practicing contraception in order to have the next baby as soon as possible is also defined as successful spacing behavior. An identical percentage of 28 per cent was found for the "relatively fecund" couples of the Indianapolis Study, where the couples were married twelve to fifteen years.[25]

Effectiveness of contraception is not impressive during the initial birth intervals. Based on data from the Indianapolis Study and the present one, the average pregnancy rate during contraception appears to exceed .025 pregnancies per month of exposure, or 30 pregnancies per 100 years, when the experience of each couple is weighted equally so as to obtain a simple mean of individual accident rates.[26] A corresponding rate cannot be computed for the GAF sample, but the one-third frequency with which contraceptive practice ends in accidental pregnancy is the same as that encountered in the present study for the interval between marriage and second birth.[27]

Besides high rates of accidental pregnancy, there are several other signs to indicate that many couples in the present study were not motivated to try to practice the most efficient contraception. For example, barely half of the wives reported reliability as a main reason for preferring their current method. In addition, there is very little association between shifting or not shifting from a method and

[24] Freedman, Whelpton, and Campbell, *Family Planning, Sterility and Population Growth*, p. 97.

[25] P. K. Whelpton and C. V. Kiser, "The Planning of Fertility," in Kiser and Whelpton, eds., *Social and Psychological Factors Affecting Fertility, op.cit.*, II, p. 254.

[26] R. G. Potter, Jr., "Some Comment on the Evidence Pertaining to Family Limitation in the United States," *op.cit.*, pp. 47–51.

[27] Freedman, Whelpton, and Campbell, *Family Planning, Sterility and Population Growth*, p. 209, and C. F. Westoff *et al.*, *Family Growth in Metropolitan America*, pp. 92–93.

prior experience with it. Among 50 couples persisting with a method despite two previous failures with it, 11 acknowledged that both failures resulted from omissions of contraception, 17 were devout Catholics avowing loyalty to the rhythm method, while 12 of the remaining 22 reported knowledge of more efficient methods but had not yet bothered to take them up.

Such perfunctory practice of contraception during the early birth intervals suggests that many women are not seriously concerned by the prospect of experiencing a desired pregnancy sooner than intended. This impression is borne out, in the present study, by the respondents' assessments of their own first two birth intervals (between marriage and first birth, and first and second birth). As noted earlier, these women were inclined to accept a rather wide range of interval length as "all right." Even the interval first to second birth had to be extremely short—one year or less—to be usually considered as too short, or else longer than four years to be considered by a majority as too long. If this experience is representative, then no narrow band of interval length commands special acceptance. There appear to be no sharp priorities among interval lengths of 18, 24, 30, or 36 months.

Thus a mother might easily reach the position, some months after the last childbirth, when she has not quite made up her mind to interrupt contraception, yet would not be dismayed to find herself pregnant. At such times she may, by omitting contraception, take chances that she would have resisted a few months earlier. In other instances, the penalty of a short interval may seem too trivial to justify going to any real bother about contraception, such as adopting a more effective method or perhaps even commencing contraception at all. One hypothesis, then, to explain why close control over child-spacing is not more common is that spacing values are often vague and of low intensity, thereby resulting in a half-hearted practice of contraception, or sometimes dispensing with it altogether.

Additional barriers weaken still further the regulation of birth intervals. Even when desired, conception occurs only after a delay of variable length. Then, too, a minority of birth intervals are prolonged by pregnancy wastage or by temporary separations, especially in connection with military service. Accordingly, one cannot realistically expect a high correlation between spacing preferences and actual birth intervals. This point was dramatized in the present study by an analysis of the first two birth intervals which showed that purposive postponement of pregnancy, as measured by length of contraceptive practice, accounted for not quite half of the variance of birth intervals. The larger portion was accounted for by such extraneous factors as conceptive delays, separations, and delays added by pregnancy wastage.[28] Interestingly enough, the respondents recognized this weak association between spacing preferences and actual intervals. Barely half of the mothers desiring a third birth expected to have it about the time they wanted it.[29]

CONTRACEPTIVE PRACTICE AND DESIRED FAMILY SIZE

It was noted earlier that contemporary couples are completing a large part of their total childbearing in the first ten years of marriage. The fraction of all desired children born in this duration is necessarily even higher. Also noted was the fact that this concentration of childbearing in the first half of the reproductive period depends partly on a prejudice against long birth intervals, but also is abetted by delayed use and half-hearted practice of contraception. When such a pattern of childbearing is combined with an early age at marriage, desired family size is attained when the wife is yet in the vicinity of 30 years, if not younger. If, in addition, her first marriage endures until menopause, then she faces a period, averaging around ten years or so, during which she must protect herself against the risk of additional pregnancies and births.

The point has been argued elsewhere[30] that if such women relied exclusively on contraception and if that contraception were no more effective than that observed during the initial one or two birth intervals, then several excess pregnancies would be common experience. Yet such an outcome is flatly contradicted by what wives in their late 30's are saying about their success at controlling family size, as well as by total births registered for the last few cohorts to complete their fertility.

Part of the explanation lies in the increase in fecundity impairments as age increases. Judging from societies practicing little or no family limitation, the proportion of couples becoming infertile begins to climb rapidly after the mid-30's so that age of mother at last birth averages in the vicinity of 40 or 41 years. At the same time, among couples remaining fertile, speed of conception declines with advancing age, though at too slow a rate to make this the main factor.[31]

---

[28] *Ibid.*, pp. 105–107.

[29] *Ibid.*, p. 128.

[30] R. G. Potter, Jr., *op. cit.*, pp. 51–53 and R. G. Potter, Jr., "Some Physical Correlates of Fertility Control in the United States," pp. 8–10.

[31] L. Henry, "La Fécondité Naturelle: Observation-Théorie-Résultats," *Population*, 16 (October–December 1961) p. 631. Averaging the experience of six European groups practicing little or no family limitation, Henry computes age–specific fertility rates of

Another part of the explanation lies in sterilization. The GAF Study has shown that the incidence of sterilizing operations steadily increases with advancing age until, among wives 35–39, the frequency is 17 per cent, though what proportion is dictated by motives of family limitation rather than medical reasons is not known.[32] Induced abortion also figures in the picture but useful statistics do not exist to gauge the magnitude of its role. In the end, unless one is willing to hypothesize very high orders of unreported sterilization and induced abortion, the principal explanation must lie with contraception. That is, a great improvement in the practice of contraception must take place once desired family size is reached.

That such an improvement might occur seems plausible enough. Presumably once desired family size is attained, the penalties of accidental pregnancy become much greater. Hence one expects more diligent contraception when it is being practiced to prevent unwanted births rather than merely to delay a desired baby. Moreover, if most methods of contraception are highly efficient when regularly used, as also seems plausible,[33] so that the principal reason for contraceptive failures is omission of contraception and willingness to take chances, then increased motivation, expressed in greater contraceptive vigilance, could well produce the large improvement in contraceptive effectiveness being hypothesized.

In fact, the trend toward improved contraception might well start before total fertility goals are reached. Family-size preferences, like spacing preferences, are not always definite and unambiguous. In the present study, 345 of 1,165 women gave "either/or" responses or otherwise indicated uncertainty about their total fertility desires. A couple may know from the beginning of their marriage that they want at least two children but long remain uncertain about whether they want a third or not. For such couples an unplanned pregnancy might have consequences intermediate between

---

couples who bear at least one birth in a later quinquennium thereby demonstrating their continued fertility. The fertility rates of these couples for ages 20–24, 25–29, 30–34, and 35–39 stand in a 100, 97.5, 89.5, and 78.5 relationship to each other. Thus between ages 20–24 and 35–39, birth intervals increase by roughly 25 per cent. However, the relative increase in conceptive delays could be 50, or even 75 per cent if, for example, two-thirds of the total birth interval were composed of pregnancy and postpartum amenorrhea and if both these lengths were independent of age. Presumably an increased incidence of pregnancy wastage is also contributing to the 25 per cent lengthening of birth intervals. In sum, Henry's results suggest that by ages 35–39 the average conception rate during menstrual exposure is somewhere between .50 and .75 of its value at ages 20–24.

[32] Freedman, Whelpton, and Campbell, *Family Planning, Sterility and Population Growth*, p. 28.

[33] This topic is discussed in detail in Chapter VII.

those felt by couples definitely eager for or definitely set against an additional child. If so, then the effectiveness of contraception practiced in this situation might also be intermediate. Another fairly common situation is one in which the couple disagrees over the desirability of another child: one spouse wants it, the other does not. The contraception practiced here, too, might tend to be intermediate in its effectiveness since if one partner is deeply committed to avoiding another pregnancy, the other is less so. In sum, it is a reasonable expectation that contraceptive practice should prove strikingly more efficient after attainment of desired family size than before, and also that some improvement should be noted with a close approach to the number of children wanted.

Some Unanswered Questions

The highly idealized description of American fertility just given raises a number of unanswered questions. Four sets of these are taken up in the next five chapters.

First of all, slowness to conceive may be quite as much a barrier to close regulation of birth spacing as vagueness about what constitutes a best interval and any resultant irregularity of contraceptive practice. The extent to which conception delays are subject to voluntary control is considered in Chapter III.

Second, to what extent does practice of contraception improve as desired family size is approached and reached; and if such an improvement is documented, what are its primary mechanisms? To these two basic questions Chapters IV and V are directed.

Third, there is the question of the relative importance of the various elements underlying the undoubted inverse association between completed family size and average length of birth interval. These elements include: (1) differential fecundity wherein couples thwarted by subfecundity from having all the children they want are for the same reason slow on the average to bear the one or two births they do have; (2) an interrelationship among fertility preferences such that couples desiring large families tend to seek shorter than average birth intervals; and (3) a linkage between contraceptive practice and desired family size whereby couples desiring large families tend to practice less effective contraception during the initial birth intervals. In the present sample, eligibility criteria render the first-mentioned element, namely differential fecundity, unimportant. However, the relative importance of the second and third bases may be tested with respect to the interval between second birth and next pregnancy. This opportunity is exploited in Chapter VI.

A final set of questions concerns short-range prediction of fertility. Adapted to the design of the present study, this means prediction of fertility over a three-year period starting half a year after the second birth. If it is true that contraception improves as desired family size is approached, and becomes highly efficient after desired family size is attained, then not only total family-size preferences measured in the first interview, but also marriage duration and family-planning success up to the second birth should be useful predictors of fertility over the three-year period. This expectation is tested in the final chapter of this section, Chapter VII.

Chapter III. Voluntary Factors in the Speed of Conception[1]

One reason why couples do not succeed in regulating their birth spacing more closely is the uncertain success of conception in any given menstrual cycle, even when conception is desired. Even when sought, conception ensues only after a variable delay. The importance of these delays in the total variation of birth intervals has been stressed in the previous chapter. The main objective of this chapter is to investigate the extent to which speed of conception is subject to voluntary control.

The very fact that conceptive delays are so variable indicates that control over them is partial at best. Nevertheless it may be possible to exercise such control as to shorten conceptive delays appreciably, and thus to avoid much of the inconvenience of unwanted delay.

Unfortunately, it is necessary in this chapter to adopt a rather narrow definition of voluntary acceleration of conception, namely, any deliberate increasing of coital frequency at times of the month believed to be particularly fertile. The role played by medical treatment in reducing conceptive delay must be ignored since systematic data have not been collected on this topic.

The degree to which members of the present sample shorten their delays of pregnancy will be investigated as a function of three variables. First is the general bearing of coital frequency upon speed of conception; second is the proportion of couples actually trying to hasten conception; and third is the accuracy of their ideas about when to increase coital frequency above normal rates. Broadly speaking, the first factor determines the potentialities of voluntary acceleration as it is being defined in this chapter, while the second and third factors dictate the extent to which this potentiality is being realized. Obviously, if the proportion of couples trying to hurry conception is low, and if many of them are handicapped by inaccurate views of the monthly cycle, then the possibilities of reducing conceptive delays by voluntary action are being exploited only in small part.

With regard to the first factor, it is generally believed that under

[1] Sections of this chapter and Chapter V appear in R. G. Potter, Jr., P. C. Sagi, and C. F. Westoff, "Knowledge of the Ovulatory Cycle and Coital Frequency as Factors Affecting Conception and Contraception," Milbank Memorial Fund *Quarterly*, 40 (January 1962), pp. 46–58.

usual conditions a higher coital frequency means quicker conception on the average. Only during a relatively short period, approximately in the middle of the menstrual cycle, does a woman have an appreciable chance of conceiving. The average duration of this "fertile period" is not known precisely but almost certainly averages under 48 hours.[2] Since the period is this brief, level of sexual activity has a bearing on conception ease, and this bearing is the more assured because of evidence, furnished primarily by the studies of MacLeod and Gold,[3] indicating that coital frequency may be increased without jeopardizing virility, except possibly in cases where the increase is to very high levels or the male is of low sperm count.

Thus the central concern of this chapter may be reduced to two main questions. First, what is the proportion of couples trying to hasten conception and what is the proportion of this group having accurate knowledge of the ovulatory cycle? Second, with correct information about the menstrual cycle, how effective are efforts to hurry conception? Data relevant to the first question are now considered.

EXTENT AND CALIBER OF EFFORTS TO ACCELERATE CONCEPTION

Beliefs about the Ovulatory Cycle

A series of questions were used in the reinterviews to elicit opinions about the timing of the fertile period within the monthly cycle. After preliminary queries about typical flow and cycle length, each respondent was asked to indicate, on a chart representing her typical monthly cycle, the days she believed to be especially fertile. Often more than one fertile period was alleged and each of these periods might include one day or several.

All responses have been classified into one of three categories: "correct," "incorrect," and "don't know." The "correct" category has been leniently defined to include any reply stating a single fertile period approximately in the middle of the month.[4] Doubtless

[2] See C. Tietze, "Probability of Pregnancy Resulting from a Single Unprotected Coitus," *Fertility and Sterility*, 11 (September–October 1960), pp. 485–488 and R. G. Potter, Jr., "Length of the Fertile Period," Milbank Memorial Fund *Quarterly*, 39 (January 1961), pp. 132–162.

[3] Of special relevance, among several pertinent articles by these authors, is J. MacLeod and R. Z. Gold, "The Male Factor in Fertility and Infertility: Semen Quantity in Relation to Age and Sexual Activity," *Fertility and Sterility*, 4 (January–February 1953), pp. 10–33. For brief comment on this work and the related work of E. J. Farris, see R. G. Potter, Jr., "Length of the Fertile Period," p. 140, n.18.

[4] More specifically, this fertile period had to overlap with at least one of the three most fertile days as judged by the Ogino-Knaus or Farris rhythm calculations, predicated on the cycle length which the respondent reported as most typical for her.

some of the wives answering "don't know" had opinions about the fertile portions of the menstrual cycle, but lacked confidence in them.

Altogether, 49 per cent of the replies have been labeled as "correct," 24 per cent as "don't know," and 27 per cent as "incorrect." Thus about half the sample have a realistic view of the ovulatory cycle; another quarter hold inaccurate opinions; and the remaining quarter disclaim any confident knowledge. Class-religious differentials exist, as Table 4 indicates. Persons of higher socio-economic

TABLE 4
Information about the Positioning of the Fertile Period by Class and Religion

Class and Religion	Number of Couples	Knowledge about the Fertile Period			
		Correct	Incorrect	Don't Know	Total (per cent)
White-collar Catholic	179	60	21	18	100
White-collar Protestant	191	54	23	24	100
Jewish	110	48	21	31	100
Blue-collar Catholic	244	45	32	23	100
Blue-collar Protestant	181	41	32	27	100
Total	905	49	27	24	100

status possess more knowledge on the average than those of lower status while, within class, the Catholics have an advantage over non-Catholics. This religious difference is related to the Catholics' greater emphasis upon the rhythm method. As will be seen in Chapter V, disproportionately many users of rhythm have correct opinions about the timing of the fertile period.

Use of Information about the Ovulatory Cycle

Only 18 per cent of the sample report ever trying to hasten pregnancy by deliberately increasing coital frequency during particular times of the month. A higher proportion had been expected and several conjectures are advanced later to explain this low incidence of control effort. No significant socio-economic differentials are found. Couples who deliberately interrupt contraception in order to conceive are slightly more inclined to try to hasten pregnancy than couples who do not use contraception at all during the interval. In addition, efforts to shorten pregnancy delays are barely more common among users of rhythm than among users of other methods of contraception.[5]

[5] Successful contraceptors seek to hurry 14 per cent of their first conceptions as compared to 6 per cent for noncontraceptors, with the subsamples large enough so that

Not surprisingly, couples who report past problems in relation to becoming pregnant are much more likely to say that they have tried to hurry at least one pregnancy. About half of these latter couples

TABLE 5

Proportions Trying to Hasten Conception, by Perception of Pregnancy Problems in the Past and Order of Pregnancy

Perception of Pregnancy Problems	*Frequency of Efforts to Hasten Conception*		*Proportion Ever Trying to Hasten Conception*	
	First Pregnancy	Second and Subsequent Pregnancies		
Yes	47% (49)	38% (39)	48% (88)	
No	6 (856)	9 (817)	15 (1,126)	
Total	8 (905)	10 (1,165)	18 (905)	

TABLE 6

Proportion Ever Trying to Hasten Conception, by Length of Longest Conception Delay

Longest Conception Delay (Months)	Number of Couples	Percentage Ever Trying to Hasten Conception
No delay[a]	91	—
0–6	452	14
7–23	219	25
25 and over	143	31
Total	905	18

[a] All the pregnancies of these couples resulted from lapses or failures of contraception.

have sought to hasten a conception (Table 5), as compared to only 15 per cent among the remainder who remember no pregnancy problems. In Table 6, couples are classified according to their longest conceptive delay and it is clear that the frequency of attempts to

this difference is significant at the .005 level. With reference to the second pregnancy, the difference is in the same direction though reduced in size to 17 versus 11 per cent (significant at about the .05 level). Doubtless this reduction of difference is related to the increased proportion of subfecund couples found among the noncontraceptors after first birth. Apparently those who take contraceptive action to delay pregnancy are a little more inclined also to take action to accelerate conception when it is wanted. The tendency is not strong, however. Among the 107 couples who report interrupting contraception before every pregnancy preceding second birth, only 21, or 20 per cent, also report action taken to hasten pregnancy.

The tendency for users of rhythm to try to hasten conception more often than do users of other methods of contraception is barely significant statistically, in part because it is weakened by the greater frequency with which use of rhythm terminates in an accidental pregnancy, thereby obviating the need for any efforts to speed conception.

speed conception increases regularly as the longest conceptive wait increases. However, the experience of a long conceptive delay is no assurance that an effort to hurry conception will be made. Even among those having conceptive delays of two years or more, two-thirds recall no such endeavor. Nor is a long conceptive wait the only reason for such efforts, since a small proportion of the prompt conceivers also reports attempts to reduce pregnancy delay.

Interestingly enough, the 18 per cent who report trying to hasten pregnancy are no better informed about the ovulatory cycle than are the remainder of the sample. The ratios of incorrect and uncertain opinions to correct ones are virtually the same in the two subsamples. In other words, the wives who take action proceed on whatever information they happen to possess at the moment and apparently make no special effort to check their ideas or acquire more certain information about the monthly cycle if they are doubtful. This failure to secure better information raises questions about how sustained and intensive are many of the reported efforts to increase coital frequency above normal levels. Unfortunately, since the question about trying to hasten pregnancy required only a yes or no answer, nothing can be inferred about degree of effort.

A Minority Pattern

The above data show that only a minority of the present sample has made special efforts to speed conception and half of these have been handicapped by uncertain or incorrect knowledge of the ovulatory cycle. To be sure, subfecund couples are under-represented in the present sample owing to the eligibility requirement of two live births as well as the restrictions against pregnancy wastage prior to second birth. In addition, not all the respondents have completed their desired childbearing so that a few additional members will discover a slowness to conceive. Nevertheless, Table 6 makes it clear that even in a sample more heavily weighted toward subfecundity, well under half the couples would be likely to report deliberate increases of sexual activity at certain times of the month in order to facilitate conception. This kind of attempted control appears to be a minority pattern.

Why attempts to hasten pregnancy are reported by so few of the respondents can only be conjectured since attitudinal data on this topic have not been collected. Perhaps many of the mothers have never felt a strong need to speed conception. Some have had all their pregnancies as the result of lapses or failures of contraception. Moreover, in the present sample, a majority of conceptive delays has lasted 6 months or less and a large majority 12 months or less.[6] Many mothers may not have become seriously upset about their slowness to conceive until the delay approached a year or so. This supposition fits with the thesis, developed in the previous chapter, that child-spacing standards are often vague. Couples who have practiced contraception irregularly and thereby risked having a desired pregnancy several months early might also prove tolerant of a several months' delay.

Others among the respondents may have wanted to hasten one or more pregnancies but were dissuaded for one reason or another from the particular form of attempted acceleration under consideration here. For instance, some may have reacted to their need by going to their physician and receiving specific treatment. Presumably, in complicated ways, a couple's willingness and capacity to increase coital frequency above customary levels at chosen times of the month is related to their sexual adjustment. In the present sample such willingness is demonstrably related to opinions about the ovulatory cycle. Only half as many respondents answering "don't know" about the ovulatory cycle report efforts to hasten conception as do respondents with correct or incorrect opinions about the monthly cycle. A few of the couples may have even blamed their slowness to conceive on too high a coital frequency, so that if they took any action at all, it was to reduce sexual activity. Finally it is possible that some who increased their coital frequency for a brief period have in the meantime forgotten these temporary efforts.[7]

Thus it follows that in the selectedly fecund sample under study, only a minority of couples reports ever trying to hasten conception and many of these are hampering their efforts with unsound or uncertain knowledge of the menstrual cycle. Clearly the possibilities of reducing conception delay by voluntary action are being realized

[6] Eighty per cent of the conceptive delays following interruption of contraception are recalled by the respondents as 6 months or less, 90 per cent as 12 months or less. Corresponding proportions are 64 and 80 per cent for delays of first conception when contraception is not practiced until after first pregnancy. Cf. Westoff *et al.*, *Family Growth in Metropolitan America*, pp. 54–57.

[7] This last speculation can be extended. It is well known that many women hold a stereotyped view of their menstrual cycles as being quite regular, contrary to what a written record of cycle lengths might show. Ability to conceive within the first month or two of trying may be another such stereotype, which, if it exists, would favor memories of short conceptive delays achieved without any special efforts. One reason for suspecting this latter stereotype is the fact that delays of first conception recalled by respondents as following interruption of contraception are so much shorter—averaging 5 months instead of 10—than delays of first conception obtained by differencing marriage and first pregnancy dates when contraception is not started until after the first pregnancy. Cf. Westoff *et al.*, *op. cit.*, pp. 57–61.

only in small part. Just how good these possibilities are is the next topic considered.

Effectiveness of Voluntary Acceleration

Rather than proceeding directly to an analysis of conceptive delays as influenced by efforts to accelerate them, it is useful first to review the coital frequencies reported by the present sample of respondents and then to examine the manner in which these frequencies correlate with prior conceptive delays.

Frequency of Marital Intercourse

The coital frequencies reported by the respondents are tabulated in Table 7.[8] As evident in other studies, these frequencies decline

TABLE 7

Coital Frequency at Time of Second Interview

Rate per Week	Frequency
Less than once per week	48
Once	140
One to two times	142
Twice	254[a]
Two to three times	81
Three times	117
Three to four times	60
Four times	37
More than four times	26
Total	905

[a] 31 indeterminate frequencies are assigned to this modal category.

with advancing age. The correlation with wife's age is $-.21$, to be compared with a corresponding correlation of $-.35$ obtained by Terman.[9] Within an age control, the present data correspond fairly well to results from the female sample of Kinsey et al.[10] Another point of agreement with the latter study is the absence of significant class-religious differences with respect to coital rates, a result also obtained by Terman.[11]

[8] Roughly one-third of the women indicated monthly frequencies and these frequencies were multiplied by $\frac{7}{23}$ to convert them to a weekly rate. Twenty-three days was viewed as a typical intermenstrum—i.e., 28 days minus 5 days for flow. No strong bias appears to have resulted from this procedure inasmuch as a nonsignificant difference is found between the distributions of converted frequencies and those not requiring conversion.

[9] L. M. Terman, *Psychological Factors in Marital Happiness*, McGraw-Hill, New York, 1938, p. 271.

[10] A. C. Kinsey, W. B. Pomeroy, C. E. Martin, and P. H. Gebhard, *Sexual Behavior in the Human Female*, W. B. Saunders, Philadelphia, 1953, p. 394.

[11] *Ibid.*, pp. 355, 360 and Terman, *op.cit.*, p. 275.

Bearing on Conceptive Delay

If the fertile period is less than 48 hours, then doubling coital frequency at mid-cycle, say from two to four times per week, should reduce mean conceptive delay by a factor of one-third to one-half, except perhaps in the case of husbands of low sperm count.[12] In a previous study by Stix,[13] the empirical relationship between coital frequency and conceptive delay does approach this theoretical standard. A strong association is also found by MacLeod and Gold, although their data are presented in a form which precludes precise comparison with Stix's results.[14] In a third study by Stix and Notestein,[15] the relationship between reported coital frequency and conceptive delay proved negligible for reasons that are not entirely clear.

TABLE 8

Mean Conceptive Delay as Related to Coital Frequency, by Pregnancy Interval and Contraceptive Status

| | First Conception | | Second and Third Conception[a] | |
| | No Contraception Used During Interval | Contraception Deliberately Interrupted | No Contraception Used During Interval | Contraception Deliberately Interrupted |
Weekly Coital Frequency				
Under 2 times	11.0 mos. (158)	7.1 (111)	21.7 (91)	7.0 (185)
2 to 3 times	7.1 (144)	4.5 (122)	19.8 (82)	5.2 (197)
3 times or more	6.6 (106)	4.4 (85)	12.9 (49)	5.8 (146)
Total	8.5 (408)	5.4 (318)	19.0 (222)	6.0 (528)

[a] All these third conceptions preceded second births.

The results of the present study are tabulated in Table 8. Care has been taken to distinguish first conceptions from subsequent ones and within these two classes, to separate delays following deliberate interruption of contraception from those occurring before first use of contraception. Thus four trials of the relationship are provided. Nine classes of coital frequency are combined into three to give more stability to the mean conceptive delays. A consistent tendency for conceptive delay to shorten as coital frequency increases is evi-

[12] R. G. Potter, Jr., "The Length of the Fertile Period," pp. 149–156.
[13] R. K. Stix, "Birth Control in a Mid-Western City, I." Milbank Memorial Fund *Quarterly*, 17 (January 1939), p. 82.
[14] J. MacLeod and R. Z. Gold, "The Male Factor in Fertility and Infertility," *op.cit.*, p. 2 9.
[15] Regine K. Stix and Frank W. Notestein, *Controlled Fertility*, Baltimore, The Williams and Wilkins Co., 1940, p. 11.

dent in three of four trials, though the associations are weaker than the one observed in Stix's data.

Doubtless one factor operating to weaken relationships in the present sample is the reporting of coital frequency at a time point several years after the conceptive delays being correlated with it. Unfortunately there is no ready way to gauge the importance of this factor.[16]

Theoretical Effectiveness

It is worth considering the relationship between coital frequency and conceptive delay in greater detail for its implications for the effectiveness of voluntary efforts to reduce pregnancy delay. Table 8 leaves no doubt that higher coital rates generate shorter conceptive delays *on the average*. Nevertheless the linear correlation between conceptive delay and reported coital frequency is very low. The four correlation coefficients corresponding to the data of Table 8 are all in the region of −.10.

We may offer some speculations to explain this low correlation. It is convenient to think of each couple as having, in the absence of contraception, a typical monthly chance of conception, or fecundability. This fecundability is responsive to level of sexual activity and may be raised during a single pregnancy interval if, for instance, the couple suddenly embark on special efforts to hasten pregnancy. However, the level of a couple's fecundability is also affected, and perhaps primarily determined, by a host of other, mostly physiological, factors.[17] For example, let us imagine that because of reproductive impairments (such as partially occluded tubes, cystic ovaries, etc.) a particular group of couples have only one chance in twenty of conceiving any month, given their customary coital frequencies. By augmenting their sexual activity at mid-month, they manage to double their fecundability from .05 to .10. Yet they still remain at a disadvantage with respect to the majority of couples

[16] The conceptive delays occurring since second birth are the most concurrent and for that reason might be expected to yield the highest correlation with reported coital frequency. However there are only 46 completed pregnancy intervals since second birth in which no contraception was practiced. In another 146 pregnancy intervals since second birth, contraception was deliberately interrupted but the ensuing conception delays are strongly selected for brevity, only 6 showing durations greater than 6 months.

[17] Evidence that fecundabilities vary widely among couples is afforded by two models designed to reproduce a criterion series of conception delays: C. Tietze, "Differential Fecundity and Effectiveness of Contraception," *The Eugenics Review*, 50 (January 1959), pp. 231–237; and R. G. Potter, "Length of the Observation Period as a Factor Affecting the Contraceptive Failure Rate," Milbank Memorial Fund *Quarterly* 38 (April 1960) pp. 141–144.

whose fecundabilities are well above .10. Furthermore, individual conceptive delays are subject to chance variation, the magnitude of which tends to increase as fecundability decreases.[18] Thus it is plausible to think that coital frequency is only moderately correlated with fecundability which in turn is only moderately, perhaps only weakly, correlated with individual conceptive delays.

If the above argument is sound, then deliberately increasing coital frequency at mid-cycle should have a definite albeit limited effectiveness toward reducing pregnancy delay. If the rate of marital intercourse is increased around mid-cycle for as many cycles as necessary, then fecundability is raised and average conceptive delay reduced, but prompt conception is not thereby assured. The couple remain subject to a chance factor, all the larger if their initial fecundability was low.[19]

Observed Effectiveness of Deliberate Efforts

The comparison of conceptive delays with and without efforts to accelerate is given in Table 9. Contrary to what one might first

TABLE 9

Mean Conceptive Delay as Related to Deliberate Efforts to Hasten Pregnancy, by Pregnancy Order and Contraceptive Status

Efforts to Hasten Pregnancy	First Conception		Second and Third Conception[a]	
	No Contraception Used During Interval	Contraception Deliberately Interrupted	No Contraception Used During Interval	Contraception Deliberately Interrupted
Yes	30.9 (23)	11.3 (46)	34.0 (23)	9.1 (90)
No	7.1 (384)	4.4 (272)	17.3 (199)	5.3 (438)

[a] All these third conceptions preceded second birth.

expect, couples who strive to speed pregnancy take longer on the average to conceive than those who report no special efforts. According to Table 9, this unexpected relation holds in the initial as well as in the following two pregnancy intervals (all preceding second birth) irrespective of whether contraception is deliberately interrupted or not used at all. In three out of four instances, the relationship is significant at beyond the .005 level despite heavy

[18] This point is justified mathematically by reference to the geometric distribution. Cf. R. G. Potter, Jr., "Some Physical Correlates of Fertility in the United States," to be published in the Proceedings of the International Population Union Conference, 1961 graphed Paper No. 12, IPU Conference, 1961.

[19] Some couples may be using basal body temperature charts to date their ovulation more precisely. However, such charts are an uncertain aid since the drop in temperature more often follows ovulation than coincides with or precedes it.

losses of information entailed by the choice of significance test.[20] Obviously this outcome is related to the fact, documented earlier, that women who have experienced trouble conceiving are much more likely to take action to hasten pregnancy. Doubtless many of these couples did not initiate their special efforts to conceive until several months without pregnancy had elapsed.

Given this selective process, it is impossible to measure directly the effectiveness of deliberately increasing sexual activity as a device to hasten pregnancy. However, women reporting such efforts may be classified according to the correctness of their present opinions about the timing of the fertile period and a check made whether accurate information on this score bestows an advantage. The dif-

TABLE 10

Mean Conceptive Delay among Couples Trying to Hasten Pregnancy, by Pregnancy Interval and Accuracy of Information about the Fertile Period

Information about the Fertile Period	First Conception		Second and Third Conception[a]	
	No Contraception Used During Interval	Contraception Deliberately Interrupted	No Contraception Used During Interval	Contraception Deliberately Interrupted
Correct	17.4 (9)	9.4 (32)	29.0 (8)	6.4 (50)
Incorrect	40.9 (9)	21.4 (8)	30.4 (10)	11.1 (24)
Don't Know	39.5 (14)	8.2 (6)	49.2 (5)	14.6 (16)

[a] All these third conceptions precede second birth.

ferences contained in Table 10 do suggest such an advantage. Special attention has been paid to a comparison of conceptive delays between women possessing correct and incorrect information, with respondents claiming no knowledge set aside. Although all differences are in the expected direction, the number of cases involved is so small that only two of the four relationships are significant beyond the .05 level.[21]

SUMMARY

Conceptive delays are an important source of variation in birth intervals. This chapter has treated the extent to which pregnancy delays are reduced when frequency of coitus is deliberately increased at times of the month believed to be particularly fertile.

[20] To cope with the highly skewed distributions of conceptive delay, an extension of the median test based on chi square was utilized. Cf. S. Siegel, *Nonparametric Statistics*, McGraw-Hill, New York, 1956, pp. 179–184.

[21] The Mann-Whitney U-test has been used. See S. Siegel, *op.cit.*, pp. 116–126. One-third of the four tested relationships proved statistically significant at between .1 and .2.

This kind of voluntary acceleration appears to have had very limited effectiveness in the present sample for two main reasons.

First of all, only one-fifth of the respondents report ever trying to hasten conception by this means; and only half of these have correct information about the ovulatory cycle. Since the information level of those who did not try to hasten pregnancy is just as high, it would seem that those who acted did so on whatever information they happened to have and did not make any special efforts to acquire further information about the monthly cycle. This lack of enterprise raises questions about how extensive and sustained were reported efforts to increase sexual activity at chosen times of the monthly cycle.

A second main reason for the limited effect of control efforts is the means being employed. Indirect evidence suggests that coital frequency is only moderately correlated with fecundability which in turn is only moderately correlated with individual conceptive delays. Theoretically, then, by increasing coital frequency at mid-cycle, a group of couples may reduce their average wait for conception but cannot typically assure themselves a prompt conception. The effectiveness of deliberate efforts to speed conception cannot be measured directly because it is subfecund couples who are most apt to make such efforts. However, when control efforts are guided by correct information about the monthly cycle, they appear to lead to shorter delays than when guided by inaccurate information.

Chapter IV. Contraceptive Effectiveness as a Function of Desired Family Size[1]

It is a well-known fact that among married couples there is variation in willingness to use contraception, in the faithfulness with which contraception is used, and in the effectiveness of contraception in preventing pregnancy. Beebe and others have explained such variations in terms of the inclusive notion of method acceptability.[2] Where couples reject a method or fail to use a method faithfully or well, the method is described as not acceptable. Various factors affecting method acceptability have been alleged, such as religious convictions, ignorance and fear, interference with pleasure, "messiness," inconvenience, and the like. Quite naturally, efforts have been made to develop more acceptable methods by overcoming these objections. Implicit is the assumption that the objections relate materially to the nonuse and the ineffectual use of contraception.

In this presentation, an attempt is made to account for varying contraceptive failure rates in terms of the number of children couples desire in conjunction with their actual fertility. Stated differently, where actual fertility approaches the desired number of children, contraceptive efficiency improves.[3] Conceptually, this notion rests on prior assumptions—that motivation to control the spacing of births is weaker than the motivation to limit numbers, and that, in general, given adequate motivation it is safe to suppose that any harmless method is acceptable or, given little motivation, the only acceptable techniques of contraception are those that involve minimal inconveniences.

[1] A condensed version of this chapter was read at the 1961 meetings of the Population Association of America, and subsequently published under the title of this chapter in *Population Studies*, 4 (March 1962), pp. 291–296.

[2] Gilbert Wheeler Beebe, *Contraception and Fertility in The Southern Appalachians*, The Williams and Wilkins Co., Baltimore, 1942. See especially pp. 244–245 for the definition of acceptability. Other illustrations of the use of the concept are: Regine K. Stix and Frank W. Notestein, *Controlled Fertility*, The Williams and Wilkins Co., Baltimore, 1940; C. Tietze *et al.*, "A Family Planning Service in Rural Puerto Rico," *American Journal of Obstetrics and Gynecology*, Vol. 81, No. 1 (January 1961), pp. 174–182; Charles F. Westoff, *et. al.*, "The Use, Effectiveness and Acceptability of Various Methods of Fertility Control," *Social and Psychological Factors Affecting Fertility*, Milbank Memorial Fund, New York, 5 vols., 1946–58, IV, pp. 885–951.

[3] Similar propositions are advanced in Westoff *et al.*, *op.cit.*, p. 893; H. V. Muhsam and Clyde V. Kiser, "The Number of Children Desired at the Time of Marriage," *Social and Psychological Factors Affecting Fertility, op.cit.*, V, p. 1311, and Ronald Freedman, "Summary of American Studies of Factors Affecting Fertility," to be published in the Proceedings of the International Population Union Conference, 1961.

Data[4] brought to bear on this thesis are of two types: those having to do with the relative frequency of use and nonuse of methods of contraception, and those dealing with efficacy of contraception. In order to bring out the effect of heightened motivation to use contraception, frequencies and rates are considered by successive pregnancies and by the number of children desired by the wife as expressed at the time of the first interview (six months after the birth of the second child). The analysis is strengthened by the fact that the last pregnancy interval information pertains to the interval between interviews and was picked up three years after the first statement of family-size preferences. Thus, these data can be examined from the point of view of their predictive value as well.

The first hypothesis that can be tested is that as the number of children a couple desires is approached or achieved, the proportion of couples attempting fertility control increases. Relevant data are in Table 11 where we report the per cent *not* practicing contraception, by pregnancy interval, and by number of children desired. These data are unusually well behaved. The percentages double as we go across any row from two to four or more children desired and increase roughly threefold as we go up any column from the third interval to the first. It may be well to point out that suspected subfecundity accounts for 58 per cent of the few nonusers in the third interval of those wanting only two children. The relative frequency of this reason declines sharply to 24 and 19 per cent among those

---

[4] In addition to information on birth dates and pregnancy wastage, which were utilized in computing months of exposure with due allowances made for temporary separation as well as for gestation, five questions dealing with contraceptive practice were repeated for each pregnancy reported. For the second pregnancy these were modified to read:

"Did you or your husband ever use any of these methods during the time between your first and second pregnancy?"

"Which method or methods did you use most frequently before your second pregnancy?"

"Under which *one* of these circumstances did your second pregnancy occur?

1. "While we were actually using some method and didn't want a pregnancy just then."
2. "When we took a chance and didn't use a method."
3. "After we deliberately stopped using a method in order to have a child."
4. "Some other circumstance. (SPECIFY)"

If took a chance: "Why did you take a chance and not use a method?"
If no method used: "What is the main reason that you did not use any method before your second pregnancy?"

A further question on current contraceptive practice was included as well. Number of children desired by the wife was obtained from responses to the following two items: "How many children do you want to have altogether, counting those you have now?" "Do you feel sure that (number given) is the number you want or do you feel that you might want more, or that you might want fewer?"

wanting additional children. Religion for the former group and religion plus desired short intervals account for most of the remaining reasons for nonuse. Thus when the desired number is achieved, unless it is a matter of religious conviction or suspected subfecundity, all but the rare exception revert to contraception.

TABLE 11
Number and Per Cent Not Practicing Any Form of Birth Control, by Interval and by Number of Children Desired

| | NUMBER OF CHILDREN DESIRED | | | | | |
| | 2 | | 3 | | 4 or more | |
INTERVAL	N	%	N	%	N	%
Marriage to first pregnancy	66	31	82	41	240	59
First to second pregnancy	27	13	39	20	106	26
Since second live birth	19	9	29	15	74	18

The second hypothesis is that the success with which fertility is controlled improves as fertility approaches the desired number. Failure rates presented in Table 12 are in agreement with this last

TABLE 12
Contraceptive Failure Rates[a], by Pregnancy Intervals and by Number of Children Desired[b] for Wives Practicing Some Form of Contraception in Each of Three Intervals

| | Number of Children Desired | | | |
Interval	2	3	4 or more	Total
Marriage to first pregnancy	30.5	37.3	59.6	42.9
First to second pregnancy	13.4	22.9	32.2	22.8
Since second live birth	3.7	14.7	22.4	13.5
All intervals	14.5	23.5	35.8	24.7

[a] Distribution of months of contraceptive exposure truncated at 12 months and failure rates computed according to Number of Unplanned Pregnancies × 1200/Total Months of exposure = Failure Rate per 100 years exposure.

[b] Number of children desired by the wife as expressed 4–6 months following the birth of the second child. In this and all subsequent tables, wives responding "two or three children" desired were held out from the analysis in order to simplify and make unambiguous the notion of the number of children wanted by the couple.

assertion. In this analysis, however, the effects of experience, motivation, and methods employed are confounded. However, comparisons within rows control, at least crudely, on experience (all couples have used contraception since marriage) and thereby display the effect of motivation and method differences. That differences within a row represent primarily motivational factors is supported by comparisons along the diagonals indicated. In other words, as couples approach the number of children desired, *whatever number* that might be, contraceptive failure rates tend to converge to a common minimum value, while the rate of convergence is a function of the number of children desired. In order to rule out the variation due to method differences, the subsample was further refined to include

TABLE 13

Contraceptive Failure Rates[a] in Each of Three Intervals among Couples Using Condom, Diaphragm, or Coitus Interruptus since Marriage, by Number of Children Desired

| | Number of Children Desired | | | |
Interval	2	3	4 or more	Total
Marriage to first pregnancy	21.1	26.6	45.9	29.8
First to second pregnancy	7.8	13.7	16.3	11.6
Since second live birth	2.6	16.5	13.4	9.4
All intervals	9.5	18.7	24.5	16.1

[a] These failure rates are variously based on approximately 500–1,000 months of exposure. Thus sampling variabilities are large. However, inflating the number of months of exposure by truncating, say, at 24 months instead of 12 months, merely increases problems of interpretation and comparability. See Robert G. Potter, Jr. and Philip C. Sagi, "Some Procedures for Estimating the Sampling Fluctuations of a Contraceptive Failure Rate," in *Research in Family Planning*, Clyde V. Kiser, ed. Princeton University Press, Fall 1962.

TABLE 14

Number and Per Cent Using Douche and Safe Period among Those Practicing Birth Control in All Intervals, by Total Number of Children Desired[a]

| | NUMBER OF CHILDREN DESIRED | | | | | |
| | 2 | | 3 | | 4 or more | |
INTERVAL	N	%	N	%	N	%
Marriage to first pregnancy	32	23.5	22	21.6	60	40.5
First to second pregnancy	26	19.1	20	19.6	54	36.5
Since second live birth	26	19.1	26	25.5	46	31.1

[a] Number of children desired as expressed by the wife 4–6 months following the birth of the second child.

only condom and diaphragm users. With exceptions, the row-column pattern persists. Here it should be noted that sampling variability is large due to small sample size. Table 13 compared to Table 12 shows some improvement in rates with the shift to methods thought more reliable. In the next table, Table 14, we obtain some indication of the magnitude and timing of shifts in the use of methods on an aggregate basis. With one cell excepted, couples shift from less reliable to more reliable methods as their fertility approaches the number desired, though the amount of shifting is small.

It is apparent that contraceptive performance improves with time and parity. A portion of this improvement is due to a shift to more reliable methods though the greater portion of the improvement, we suspect, is due to increased contraceptive vigilance. Turning to Table 15, we can see that vigilance as inferred from reports of "chance-taking and getting caught" increases with parity in a pattern closely resembling that revealed for contraceptive failure rates.

TABLE 15

Per Cent of Couples Failing in Contraception Attributing Conception to "Taking a Chance," by Pregnancy Interval and by Number of Children Desired

| | Number of Children Desired | | |
Interval	2	3	4 or more
Marriage to first pregnancy	20.8	20.5	27.5
First to second pregnancy	14.8	21.2	20.9
Since second live birth	4.7	14.1	18.9
Current practice[a]	25	32	36

[a] Current practice refers to the proportion of couples reporting nonfaithful use of method. This row is not comparable to the preceding since the latter represents only those incidents of nonuse that resulted in conception. There is also the suspicion that chance-taking is not independent of knowledge of the ovulatory cycle. Some chance-taking would be, therefore, nonuse during infertile days.

Unfortunately, these data are insufficient to warrant a decisive conclusion. The failure rates are based on anywhere from 300 to 1,500 or so months of exposure, depending on the cell. Also, the factor of religious belief enters into the choice of contraception (use or method) between those wanting few and those desiring many children. Any attempt to refine the analysis and hold religion constant further reduces the already meager data. However, despite these weaknesses, comparisons along diagonals support the notion that these rates—while perhaps influenced by the aforementioned weaknesses and the progressive sophistication of the couples—do respond importantly to the discrepancy between desired and actual fertility. This tendency appears established.

The consistency of these results, despite mentioned weaknesses in the quality and quantity of the data, invite a series of *speculative* propositions. To list a few:

1. The maximum use-effectiveness of rhythm as well as other techniques is approached only as couples near and achieve desired

TABLE 16

Failure Rates for Rhythm Technique of Contraception, by Desired Number of Children and Pregnancy Interval for Those Using Rhythm in All Prior Intervals

	NUMBER OF CHILDREN DESIRED					
	2		3		4 or more	
INTERVAL	Rate	N	Rate	N	Rate	N
Marriage to first pregnancy	47	(9)	86	(12)	87	(39)
First to second pregnancy	20	(6)	15	(7)	37	(30)
Since second live birth	0	(5)	0	(4)	36	(19)

TABLE 17

Contraceptive Failure Rates[a], by Religion, Pregnancy Interval, and Number of Children Desired

	Number of Children Desired			
	2	3	4 or more	Overall rates
Protestants				
Marriage to first pregnancy	37.6	53.9	64.5	50.2
First to second pregnancy	21.4	39.5	44.4	34.2
Since second live birth	8.4	14.8	20.5	14.8
Catholics				
Marriage to first pregnancy	23.8	31.8	67.6	46.1
First to second pregnancy	10.2	26.0	42.2	31.3
Since second live birth	5.3	19.3	33.7	25.0
Jews				
Marriage to first pregnancy	34.4	15.2	17.1	23.1
First to second pregnancy	7.1	9.9	8.2	8.2
Since second live birth	3.0	14.0	8.7	7.8
All Religions				
Marriage to first pregnancy	33.6	35.7	57.7	43.0
First to second pregnancy	15.5	28.9	39.3	29.2
Since second live birth	6.5	16.6	27.1	18.6
Overall rates	16.0	25.0	36.5	27.9

[a] Months of exposure distribution truncated at 12 months. Rates are expressed in terms of failures per 100 years exposure. Rates are variously based on approximately 200 to 17,000 months of exposure. Also, rates are based on all persons using a method of birth control in the intervals specified. Hence rates reported here are somewhat higher than rates based on couples practicing birth control in all intervals.

fertility. It follows, therefore, that estimates of efficacy based on a random sample of fecund couples, without regard to number of children desired, reporting contraceptive use are bound to underestimate the protective values of methods. Limited data presented in Table 16 are suggestive on this point. Equally suggestive are data in

Table 17, wherein religious differences, granting differential distributions of methods used among religions, are not great once desired size of family is controlled.

2. The preceding generalization (1), as Ronald Freedman[5] has pointed out, reconciles the published figures of high failure rates with, for example, the successful limitation of families during the depression without the need to posit extraordinary sterilization or abortion rates. Further, the ominous implications of high failure rates such as those observed in the initial two intervals for ultimate family size will not be realized.[6]

3. Many of the reported differences among methods are due in large measure to an association between desired number of children and contraceptive technique employed. The more children desired, the less imperative becomes the choice of a dependable method and the less vigilant is the couple in using the method chosen.

4. Chance-taking or occasional nonuse is as much a way of having a deliberately unplanned pregnancy as it is a measure of method acceptability. Psychologically, chance-taking is a convenient way of having a child while sharing responsibility with fate.

5. High reported failure rates even among sophisticated American urbanites with definite notions regarding the number of children they want and the benefits of spacing suggest a reason for high rates of failure and nonuse among less sophisticated populations. That reason is the minor importance attached to the precise spacing of births. The more children anticipated, the less is the importance attached to spacing.[7]

[5] Professor Freedman's comment was made in his role as a discussant during the 1961 meetings of the Population Association of America.

[6] Robert G. Potter, Jr., "Some Relationships between Short Range and Long Range Risks of Unwanted Pregnancy," Milbank Memorial Fund *Quarterly*, 38 (July 1960), pp. 255–263.

[7] This inference is directly supported by analysis of preferred birth intervals in Charles F. Westoff, Robert G. Potter, Jr., Philip C. Sagi, and Elliot G. Mishler, *Family Growth in Metropolitan America*, Princeton University Press, Princeton, N.J., 1961, pp. 115–135.

Chapter V. Improved Contraception and Its Mechanisms

In Chapter II we emphasized that the level of contraceptive control observed for urban white couples early in marriage is so inefficient that if it is not improved or supplemented by other means of family limitation by the time desired family size is reached, the number of excess pregnancies resulting will far exceed those acknowledged by respondents who are currently near the end of their reproductive period. Roughly three-quarters of these respondents claim successful family limitation. Quite likely this claim is optimistic, though it would be surprising if as many as half these couples failed to keep their families within intended bounds. Nor is it known at all precisely how much credit to grant induced abortion and sterilization, as opposed to improved contraception, in accounting for the family limitation that is achieved.

The previous chapter has provided the first direct evidence that contraception improves markedly as family-size objectives are approached and realized. It has also presented evidence suggesting that greater regularity of contraceptive use is more important in explaining this improvement than either changes in method preference or increases of skill accruing from a longer experience with contraception.

This chapter has two purposes. The first is to estimate how much initial contraception must be improved in order to achieve specified standards of family limitation without dependence on induced abortion or sterilization. The improvements of contraception actually observed so far for FGIMA couples then may be compared with these theoretical requirements. Secondly, additional evidence is adduced for the hypothesis that increased regularity of contraception goes far toward explaining the more effective contraception seen later in marriage.

CONSEQUENCES OF NO IMPROVEMENT

As a start, it is useful to consider how many unwanted pregnancies the present couples might have if they did not improve their contraception after the first birth interval. The original analysis, given in full detail elsewhere, will merely be summarized here.[1]

[1] R. G. Potter, Jr., P. C. Sagi, and C. F. Westoff, "Improvement of Contraception During the Course of Marriage," *Population Studies*, 16 (November 1962), pp. 160–174.

As a first step, a simple waiting time model is used to derive a curve describing the pregnancy risks of FGIMA couples during their initial interval of contraception. The resultant L-shaped curve is depicted in Figure 1. The main simplifying assumption involved in this derivation is that each couple has a typical monthly risk of accidental pregnancy which remains fixed throughout an interval of exposure, while, among couples, these typical risks are distributed as a Type III curve. For later steps of the analysis, it is assumed that upon attaining desired family size, each couple faces a ten-year "risk period" during which they must protect themselves against excess fertility. It is also assumed that following each unwanted conception is an 18-month "immunity period" of pregnancy and post-partum amenorrhea during which reimpregnation is impossible. Finally, attention is restricted to couples whose first marriages remain intact until menopause and who have no sterilizing operations.

Under these simplified conditions, it is estimated that if FGIMA couples failed to improve their contraception after the first birth interval, they would average two excess pregnancies, with only 40 per cent succeeding in their family limitation and a third experiencing three unwanted pregnancies or more. These estimates of excess fertility are subject to opposing biases. On the one hand, the estimates are conservative in view of the long immunity periods being posited as well as the ten-year risk period which probably underestimates the average duration of risk for contemporary first marriages lasting until menopause. On the other hand, the estimates of excess fertility are inflated by the selectively fecund character of the present sample and by a failure to allow for the decline in fecundability that takes place during risk periods.

IMPROVEMENT NEEDED

Inquiry is also made into the increases of contraceptive efficiency necessary to meet three standards of family limitation. The high standard, modeled after the claims of respondents, is defined as 75

TABLE 18
Three Standards of Family Limitation

STANDARD	PROPORTION SUCCESSFULLY LIMITING FAMILIES	AVERAGE NUMBER OF EXCESS PREGNANCIES (*Per Ten Year Risk Period*)	
		Unsuccessful Couples	All Couples
High	75%	1.33	0.33
Medium	67	1.50	0.50
Low	50	2.00	1.00

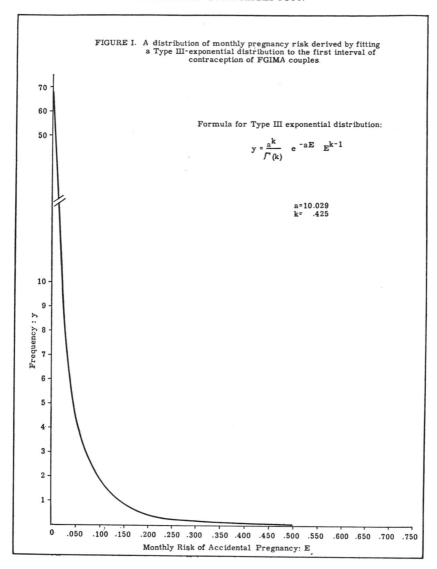

FIGURE I. A distribution of monthly pregnancy risk derived by fitting a Type III-exponential distribution to the first interval of contraception of FGIMA couples.

Formula for Type III exponential distribution:

$$y = \frac{a^k}{\Gamma(k)} \; e^{-aE} \; E^{k-1}$$

a=10.029
k= .425

Frequency : y

Monthly Risk of Accidental Pregnancy: E

per cent successfully limiting family size. The medium and low standards are taken as 67 and 50 per cent successful, respectively. Corresponding mean excess fertilities are one-third, one-half, and one excess pregnancy per couple. (For convenience of reference, these three standards are enumerated in Table 18.) Again immunity periods are assumed to be 18 months and risk periods ten years.

The need for surprisingly large improvements of contraception is indicated. For example, if it is assumed that all couples are reducing their risks of accidental pregnancy by the same amount, then it turns out that an improvement factor of 13 is required to produce a high standard of family limitation. That is, initial risks must be divided by a factor of 13 to bring the proportions successfully limiting their families up to 75 per cent. Improvement factors of 8 and 3 are demanded for medium and low standards of family limitation (see top row of Table 19) wherein 67 and 50 per cent successfully limit their families.

TABLE 19

Average Improvement Factor Required to Give High, Medium, and Low Standards of Family Limitation, by Manner of Change from Initial Pregnancy Risk E to Reduced Risk E', Assuming a Ten-Year Risk Period

Relationship of Initial Risk E to Reduced Risk E'	Average Improvement Factor $\left(\text{Mean Value of } \dfrac{E}{E'} \text{ Ratios}\right)$ Number of Excess Pregnancies Per Couple		
	$\frac{1}{3}$	$\frac{1}{2}$	1
$E' = E/n$	13.1	8.1	3.2
$E' = \dfrac{E}{1 + RE}$	7.4	4.8	2.3

Actually the assumption that all couples are increasing their contraceptive efficiency by the same factor is not very realistic. Couples who start with an effective method and practice it carefully and regularly have minimal scope for improvement, whereas couples initially accident-prone because of irregular practice of contraception may increase their efficiency many times. Hence it is likely that couples having high initial risks tend to improve the most. To give an extreme expression to this tendency, the following assumption may be made, namely initial monthly risks

$$E' = E/(1 + RE) \qquad (R > 0)$$

where E designates the initial monthly risk of accidental pregnancy and E' designates the reduced risk prevailing after desired family size is attained.

Here a larger initial risk E means automatically a larger factor of improvement E/E', thereby insuring a strong positive correlation between the two sets of elements. Even on this basis it is found that improvement factors must average around 7.5 to provide a high standard of family limitation and nearly 5.0 to provide a medium standard (second row of Table 19).

If the analysis just reviewed is at all valid, then quite clearly the present couples must reduce their early risks of contraceptive failure by a factor of several times; otherwise they cannot hope to attain even a medium standard of family limitation without depending upon abortion or sterilization to a considerable extent.

IMPROVEMENT OBSERVED

How do the improvements actually observed for FGIMA couples compare with the theoretical requirements just derived? Usefully complete information is available only for 220 mothers who reported wanting two children at first interview.[2] Their histories are worth reviewing. During the first 12 months of marriage, 69 per cent practiced contraception, exhibiting a rate of 33.6 accidental pregnancies per 100 years. In contrast, during the year following second birth, 91 per cent used contraception, with 14 of the 28 non-users reporting a sterilizing operation. Furthermore, in this later interval, the pregnancy rate among contraceptors was only 6.5 per 100 years of exposure. According to a rough calculation, this rate of 6.5 corresponds almost to a medium standard of family-size control with two-thirds succeeding in their family limitation. Because the rate of 6.5 is subject to appreciable sampling error and biases, the possibility that this segment of the total sample is presently practicing contraception of such caliber as to promise a low or a high standard of family limitation cannot be excluded without more data. Nevertheless, there can be little doubt that they have substantially reduced their initial risks of accidental pregnancy, fairly surely by a factor in excess of three times.

TWO SECONDARY FACTORS

Attention now turns to the possible factors underlying this marked improvement in contraception. Evidence from the previous chapter indicates that changes in method choice have played only a secondary role. For instance, the relationship between contraceptive effectiveness and distance from desired family size remains strong when the analysis is confined to experience with the three most effective methods, namely, condom, diaphragm, and coitus interruptus. Then, too, changes in method composition have remained small, in part because the Jewish and white-collar Protestant couples have relied heavily upon condoms and diaphragms from the first interval,

[2] Of the 220, 211 were interviewed twice and the remaining 9 were declared ineligible for reinterview because they reported a sterilizing operation at first interview.

while the Catholic members have maintained a fairly high level of emphasis upon rhythm.[3]

A secondary role may also be ascribed to factors associated with aging. To be sure, mean fecundability declines with increasing age, but this decline is apparently quite slow as long as most of the mothers are still in their 20's or early 30's.[4] Moreover, from results to be given later, it is clear that a small decline in coital frequency, associated with aging, will little affect risks of accidental pregnancy.

REGULARITY OF USE

Thus the marked increase in contraceptive effectiveness observed for FGIMA couples desiring two children must rest almost entirely on their improved practice of contraception, rather than upon a wholesale shift in methods used or a rapidly declining fecundability. Furthermore, it is likely that this improved practice depends primarily on increased regularity of contraceptive use rather than on increases in skill accruing from longer experience with contraception.

Substantiation for this latter hypothesis is found in two of the previous chapters. In Chapter II several lines of evidence were reviewed to indicate that many couples are not fully motivated to achieve efficient contraception during the initial one or two birth intervals. It also seems reasonable to suppose that as desired family size is approached, and particularly after it is attained, the penalties of accidental pregnancy become much higher, with the result that contraceptive vigilance progressively increases. This last expectation is borne out by the results of Chapter IV showing that risks of accidental pregnancy decrease sharply as family-size objectives are approached and reached. Just as important, the inverse relationship between contraceptive effectiveness and number of additional children wanted remains strong when examined within groups of couples practicing contraception for the same number of pregnancy intervals. By this restriction, length of contraception is being partially controlled, and with it any skill elements that may depend on length of practice. Thus contraceptive effectiveness appears to be much more sensitive to the stage of family building than to duration of contraceptive practice.

[3] C. F. Westoff, R. G. Potter, Jr., P. C. Sagi, E. G. Mishler, *Family Growth in Metropolitan America*, Princeton University Press, Princeton, N.J., 1961, pp. 80–81. Only for one method, the douche, does the proportion of users change by more than 5 per cent between first and last interval of use, among couples practicing contraception three intervals or more.

[4] L. Henry, "La Fécondité Naturelle: Observation-Théorie-Résultats," *Population*, 16 (October–December 1961) p. 31.

ADDITIONAL CLUES

Additional grounds for believing that regularity of contraception is the primary determinant of contraceptive effectiveness during the first two birth intervals is found in a study of the relationships of contraceptive effectiveness to reported coital frequency and knowledge of the ovulatory cycle. The data pertaining to these latter two variables have been described in Chapter III. A crude measure of contraceptive effectiveness will be used, namely the per cent successful in any single pregnancy interval. By "successful" is meant deliberately interrupting contraception in order to conceive and by "failure" is meant experiencing pregnancy either while practicing contraception or omitting it to take a chance. This crude index does not take into account time with contraception preceding success or failure and therefore becomes liable to bias if either coital frequency or knowledge of the ovulatory cycle are appreciably correlated with intended length of pregnancy postponement. However, there is little reason to surmise such links.

Interestingly enough, reported coital frequency fails to correlate with contraceptive effectiveness. Unreliability of measurement is not the whole reason here since the same reports do correlate significantly with conceptive delays occurring in the absence of contraception. This lack of relationship is hard to explain unless one assumes that FGIMA couples are omitting contraception to take a chance often enough during the initial birth intervals so that, for this period at least, regularity of contraceptive practice is the paramount determinant of contraceptive effectiveness. Then if coital frequency was in fact uncorrelated with regularity of contraceptive practice, one would not expect much relationship between reported frequency and contraceptive effectiveness.[5]

[5] To see how these interrelations might work, consider the following hypothetical example. All couples are seeking to postpone pregnancy for 18 months. Couples have fecundabilities of .1, .2, and .3 depending as their coital frequencies are one, two, or three times per week. The regular practicers of contraception omit precautionary measures only once in a hundred times; the irregular practicers omit precautions half the time. Now it is clear that most of the regular practicers will successfully postpone pregnancy 18 months regardless of their coital frequency because their nearly regular contraception is keeping pregnancy risks to a range of .003 to .001. On the other hand, most of the irregular practicers will become accidentally pregnant so that even here differences in contraceptive success rates by coital frequency will not be large. Hence if the frequency of regular and irregular usage is the same for each level of sexual activity, and if the regular users are in large majority, then a very weak relationship between coital frequency and success rates can be expected. Moreover, in the real world, measurement is unreliable and coital frequency is only moderately associated with fecundability, not perfectly correlated with it as assumed above.

What evidence there is does indicate that reported coital frequency is weakly correlated, if at all, with' reported frequency of chance-taking. Of 673 respondents using contraception at the time of second interview, the 211 wives who acknowledge skipping contraception "once in a while" or "quite often" do not differ significantly in their mean coital rate from the 462 wives who claim never to omit contraception. However this result must be accepted with caution since it is suspected that reports about frequency of chance-taking are even less reliable than those relating to coital frequency.

Worth examining next is the relationship between knowledge of the ovulatory cycle and effectiveness of the rhythm method. Use of rhythm alone is distinguished from use of rhythm in combination with another method (Table 20). To increase sample size the experiences of first, second, and third pregnancies preceding second birth have been pooled. Though differences lie in the expected direction they are not statistically significant.[6] This negative result is partly a function of small subsamples since only a minority of the respondents using rhythm lack opinions or hold false notions about the monthly cycle. Another reason why the effectiveness of rhythm is not more strongly conditioned by information about the ovulatory cycle is that chance-taking, acknowledged by roughly one-third of the current users of rhythm, appears to be equally common among possessors of correct, incorrect, and no knowledge about the unsafe period.

TABLE 20

Proportions Successful with Rhythm Used Alone or Used in Combination with Another Method, by Accuracy of Information about the Ovulatory Cycle

Method of Contraception	Knowledge of the Ovulatory Cycle			Total
	Correct	Incorrect	Don't Know	
Rhythm used alone	53% (154)	49% (49)	40% (23)	50% (226)
Rhythm used in combination	52% (54)	22% (18)	28% (7)	43% (79)

When attention is shifted to other methods of contraception besides rhythm used alone or in combination with another method, no association is found between beliefs about the timing of the unsafe period and contraceptive effectiveness. Presumably for the women involved here, a failure to mention rhythm as a supplement to their principal method means that any omissions of contraception are not usually guided by rhythm considerations; and therefore the

[6] A more detailed analysis of these results is given in R. G. Potter, Jr., P. C. Sagi, and C. F. Westoff, "Knowledge of the Ovulatory Cycle and Coital Frequency as Factors Affecting Conception and Contraception," Milbank Memorial Fund *Quarterly*, 50 (January 1962), pp. 51–53.

accuracy of beliefs about the unsafe period becomes largely irrelevant.

A final argument for the primacy of motivation factors as reflected in regularity of usage stems from the very size of the increase in contraceptive effectiveness to be explained. It is difficult to imagine how additional months of contraceptive experience could increase skill to a point where risks of accidental pregnancy would thereby be reduced several fold.[7] On the other hand, it is readily visualized how a large increase in effectiveness could result from a lower incidence of chance-taking. Presumably if practiced correctly and with complete regularity, methods such as the condom or diaphragm and jelly could produce pregnancy rates well under 5 per 100 years of exposure.[8] In contrast, in the absence of contraception, rates of 120 to 200 or over are typically observed.[9] Obviously within this range of 5 to 200, there is ample room in which to postulate a several-fold drop in pregnancy risk for couples shifting from an intermittent to a fairly regular practice of contraception. The L-curve of pregnancy risk, derived in the analysis summarized earlier in this chapter, fits well with the idea that a sizable minority of FGIMA couples practiced contraception irregularly during the first birth interval. Moreover, reduced chance-taking provides a mechanism whereby the couples with high initial risks can improve the most, so that such a large average factor of improvement does not have to be posited in order to account for any specified standard of family limitation.

NEGATIVE EVIDENCE

Taken together, these considerations give multiple reasons for believing in the primacy of motivational factors as reflected in regularity of contraceptive practice. Nevertheless, one piece of neg-

[7] This is not to deny that longer experience with contraception may encourage or facilitate practicing it more regularly and thereby have an important indirect influence on its effectiveness. For example, some couples may have to try several methods before they find one congenial enough to make consistent contraception feasible. Others may require the experience of one or two accidental pregnancies to learn the importance of not taking chances. However such considerations confirm, rather than deny, regularity of practice as a basic determinant of effectiveness.

[8] By definition, this "physiological effectiveness" of a method is greater than any measure of "use effectiveness" recorded for it. Numerous pregnancy rates below 10 and a few below 5 have been observed for particular contraceptive series. Cf. C. Tietze, "The Clinical Effectiveness of Contraceptive Methods," *American Journal of Obstetrics & Gynecology*, 78 (September 1960), pp. 653–654. Elsewhere Tietze has estimated the physiological effectiveness of the condom at roughly 3 pregnancies per 100 years of exposure: "The Condom as a Contraceptive," Publication No. 5, National Committee on Maternal Health, New York, 1960, p. 39.

[9] Westoff, *et al.*, *Family Growth in Metropolitan America*, pp. 52, 97–101.

ative evidence should be noted too. A close relationship between contraceptive effectiveness and reported frequency of chance-taking has failed to materialize. However, since these reported frequencies are suspected of low reliability, this negative finding does not necessarily discredit the hypothesis.[10] Indeed, on hindsight, the authors now consider it to have been a little unrealistic to expect respondents to remember back to the detailed circumstances of an accidental pregnancy, especially when it has been found that these same respondents, asked duplicate questions three years apart, frequently give inconsistent replies concerning the intervals in which they practiced contraception, concerning which methods they used, and concerning whether a particular interval of use was successful or not.[11] In other words, it may be that useful data on regularity of contraceptive practice can be collected only through current written records, as has proved to be the case for length of menstrual cycles and flow.

Summary

This chapter has focused on three questions. (1) How much must the present couples improve their contraception over efficiencies observed in the initial interval of practice in order to realize, by contraception alone, the kind of family limitation claimed by a national sample of wives in their late 30's? (2) How does the improvement observed for FGIMA couples desiring two children at first interview compare with these theoretical requirements? (3) What are the principal mechanisms of this observed improvement?

Fitting a simple waiting time model to the first interval of contraception, one obtains an L-shaped curve of monthly risks of pregnancy. This result indicates that whereas a majority held their pregnancy risks to near-zero values, an appreciable minority, perhaps mainly on account of irregular practice, failed in varying degree to realize the potentialities of their methods. The average reduction in monthly pregnancy risks theoretically required to at-

---

[10] FGIMA wives ascribe one-fifth of their accidental pregnancies to a failure to take precautions. In Chapter IV, attention is called to the fact that the frequency of these reports of "chance-taking and getting caught" vary as hypothesized in relation to distance from desired family size. However, the relationship is quite weak. Another item relates to current frequency of chance-taking at time of second interview, with 211 out of 673 wives acknowledging omission of contraception "once in a while" or "quite often." This variable is suspected of low reliability because none of its correlations prove statistically significant, including even its association with whether or not the last accidental pregnancy occurred while practicing a method or omitting it to take a chance.

[11] C. F. Westoff, R. G. Potter, Jr., and P. C. Sagi, "Some Estimates of the Reliability of Survey Data on Family Planning," *Population Studies*, 15 (July 1961) pp. 52–69.

tain a reasonable standard of family limitation (e.g., 75 per cent avoiding excess fertility) proves sizable even if one assumes that couples of initially high risks improve the most.

FGIMA couples desiring two children at first interview reduced their initial rate of accidental pregnancies from over 30.0 per 100 years of contraceptive exposure to 6.5 following the birth of their last desired child. Whether their current contraception is effective enough to assure an adequate standard of family limitation without recourse to abortion or sterilization remains uncertain because of the sampling error and biases to which the 6.5 rate is subject.

However, there is no question of a sizable increase in contraceptive effectiveness. From several lines of indirect evidence it is argued that the predominant means of this improvement has been through a more regular practice of contraception. Changes in method preference, declines in average fecundability, and increased contraceptive skill are viewed as secondary factors.

Chapter VI. Birth Spacing as Related to Desired Family Size

Couples having large families tend to space their births more closely together than couples bearing few children. This inverse relationship between birth spacing and completed family size, at least as it operates in Great Britain[1] and this country,[2] has several regular features. The greater the completed family size, the shorter are median birth intervals of specified order and the median durations from marriage to births of any given parity. Lengths of consecutive birth intervals are positively correlated. Among couples who have completed their childbearing, last intervals tend to be distinctively long, that is, longer on average than preceding birth intervals and considerably longer than intervals of the same parity but followed by one or more births.

Involuntary factors play a role in these relationships though the size of this role is unknown. Couples who are thwarted from reaching desired family size by subfecundity or early sterility average longer birth intervals in part because of slower conception and repeated pregnancy wastage. Then, too, if upon reaching desired family size, couples practice efficient contraception, this very efficiency ensures a long average gap between last desired birth and first unwanted one among the appreciable minority of couples experiencing such births. The decline in fecundability and increase in fecundity impairments to be expected in the latter portion of the reproductive period also contribute to the relatively greater length of last-birth intervals.

Also involved in the above relationships are more nearly voluntary factors linked with family-size preferences. Desired family size, which presumably is directly correlated with completed family size, is inversely correlated with length of birth intervals. For instance, in the first phase of the present study, the wife's desired family size yields correlations of $-.19$ with the interval between marriage and first birth, $-.32$ with the interval between first and

---

[1] D. V. Glass and E. Grebenik, *The Trend and Pattern of Fertility in Great Britain: A Report on the Family Census of 1946*, H.M.S.O., London, 1954, especially Chapter VII, Part I.

[2] "Marriage, Fertility, and Childspacing: August 1959," *Current Population Reports*, Series P-20, No. 108 (July 1961), Bureau of the Census, Washington. See also "Child Spacing as Measured from Data Enumerated in the Current Population Survey: United States, April 1950 to April 1954," *Vital Statistics—Special Reports*, U.S. Dept. of Health, Education and Welfare, Washington, D.C., Vol. 47, No. 3 (October 1955).

second birth, and $-.36$ with duration of marriage to second birth. Since this association between number of children wanted and birth spacing is so regular, it is worthwhile exploring its bases, and such is the objective of the present chapter. A limited inquiry, based mainly on materials from the first set of interviews, is undertaken with respect to the initial two birth intervals. In addition, the longitudinal design of the present study is exploited by investigating the interval from second birth to next conception as influenced by the number of children desired by the wife near the beginning of this interval.

First Interview Results

Results from the first interviews show that there are at least two tendencies linking family-size preferences to birth spacing. First, wives desiring larger families tend to plan shorter intervals. This tendency is most clearly seen among "successful planners" by which is meant couples who during a particular interval either deliberately interrupt contraception in order to conceive or else forego contraception in order to have another pregnancy as soon as biologically possible. The length of time these successful planners practice contraception may be taken as the length of time they intend to postpone pregnancy. Thus measured, intended postponements of first pregnancy yield a correlation of $-.22$ with wife's desired family size, while intended postponement of the pregnancy following first birth yields a correlation of $-.30$ with her family-size desires.[3]

A second link between fertility desires and birth spacing is the tendency of wives desiring larger families to practice less effective contraception and to delay its use longer for reasons unrelated to spacing objectives. Evidence for this relationship has been given in Chapter IV and needs no elaboration here.

In sum, a preference for more children is accompanied not only by a tendency to plan shorter birth intervals but also a tendency to allow shorter than average intervals to happen through failing to practice regular contraception or any contraception at all. The way in which this second tendency bolsters the correlation between wife's desired family size and length of her first and second birth intervals is seen in Table 21. The associations are as strong, or stronger, in the

[3] The original analysis of these data is given in C. F. Westoff, R. G. Potter, Jr., Philip C. Sagi, and Elliot G. Mishler, *Family Growth in Metropolitan America*, Princeton University Press, Princeton, N.J., 1961, pp. 103–109. See also P. Sagi, "A Component Analysis of Birth Intervals among Two-Child White Couples in Metropolitan America," in *Thirty Years of Research in Human Fertility: Retrospect and Prospect*, Milbank Memorial Fund New York, 1959, pp. 135–150.

total sample, including unsuccessful contraceptors, as among the successful planners taken separately.

TABLE 21

Correlations between Wife's Desired Family Size at First Interview and Length of Her First Two Birth Intervals, By Family-Planning Success[a]

Sample and Birth Interval	Number of Couples	Correlation with Total Interval	Correlation with length of Contraceptive Practice
First birth interval			
Successful planners	596	−.21	−.22
All couples	1,065[b]	−.19	−.21
Second birth interval			
Successful planners	656	−.26	−.30
All couples	1,165	−.32	−.35

[a] SOURCE: Westoff *et al.*, *op.cit.*, p. 108.
[b] Excluded are 100 couples with probable premarital conceptions.

INTERVAL FOLLOWING SECOND BIRTH

Attention now turns to the interval between second birth and next conception. Wife's desired family size at first interview is not directly affected by the number of pregnancies occurring between interviews since it precedes these events in time. This is not true for her desired family size at second interview. At both interviews she was asked for the number of children she wants altogether *including* those already born. Thus, a mother having a third birth between

TABLE 22

Interval between Second Birth and Next Conception, by Number of Children Desired by Wife at First Interview

		PERCENTAGE DISTRIBUTION					
		Interval Second Birth to Next Conception (Months)					
NUMBER OF CHILDREN DESIRED AT FIRST INTERVIEW	NUMBER OF WOMEN	Under 10	11–20	21–30	31–42	NO PREG- NANCY	TOTAL
2	210	5	8	6	7	74	100
2–3	89	3	7	12	7	71	100
3	199	16	12	12	12	49	100
3–4	93	12	29	18	5	35	100
4	201	22	27	14	10	26	100
4–5	51	35	16	14	16	20	101
5 or more	62	47	29	11	5	8	100
Total	905	16	17	12	9	46	100

interviews is constrained to say at the second interview that she wants at least three children.

Forty-five per cent of the respondents report no pregnancies between interviews and therefore their intervals to next pregnancy are open-ended. When completed intervals are grouped into eight classes of length and the open-ended intervals are coded as a ninth class, they yield a correlation of $-.45$ with wife's desired family size at first interview. Details of the relationship are given in Table 22.

In the analysis below, it is convenient to consider first the 112 wives who report no contraception following second birth and then later consider the 793 couples who do report using contraception at this time. In both subsamples, an appreciable correlation is found between the number of children desired by the wife and the interval to her next conception, the correlation being $-.46$ among contraceptors and $-.37$ among the noncontraceptors.

NONCONTRACEPTORS

Eighty-eight per cent of the present couples practiced contraception following their second birth.[4] The proportion of nonusers varies around 10 per cent for women desiring fewer than four children, but climbs to 30 per cent among those wanting five or more (see Table 23).

The reason most frequently given for not using contraception after second birth relates to subfecundity and is followed in order by reasons relating to religion, wanting another pregnancy as soon as possible, indifference about spacing, and dislike of contraception. Many of the respondents give multiple reasons. Moreover, not too much confidence can be placed in the coded separations of such motives as subfecundity, desire for a short interval, or indifference about the timing of the third child. Nevertheless, two trends are evident as one passes from mothers desiring two children to those desiring four or more. The relative frequency of subfecundity as a reason for not practicing contraception declines, while that of religion climbs steeply. No clear trends are found for the other reasons (Table 24).

[4] There are 20 wives who at second interview report not using contraception in order to become pregnant again as soon as possible and who also report no pregnancies since second birth. By an oversight these women were not asked whether they had practiced contraception for a while after second birth. As a stop-gap, this group of 20 respondents has been divided into two classes. First are the 15 who report use of contraception in a previous interval. Presumably most or all of these couples practiced contraception for a time after second birth and for purposes of analysis are so coded. Second are the 5 reporting no use of contraception in any previous interval. Presumably most or all of these did not practice contraception after second birth and for that reason are coded as seeking a minimal interval between second and third births.

TABLE 23

Practice and Nonpractice of Contraception Following Second Birth, by Number of Children Desired by Wife at First Interview

Number of Children Desired at First Interview	Number of Women	Per Cent Practicing Contraception		Total
		Yes	No	
2	210	91	9	100
2–3	89	96	4	100
3	199	89	11	100
3–4	93	94	6	100
4	201	83	17	100
4–5	51	82	18	100
5 or more	62	71	29	100
Total	905	88	12	100

TABLE 24

Reasons for Not Using Contraception in Interval Following Second Birth, by Number of Children Desired by Wife at First Interview

Number of Children Desired at First Interview	Number of Times			Total
	Subfecundity Mentioned	Religion Mentioned	Other Reasons Mentioned	
2 or 2–3	14	1	8	23
3 or 3–4	14	8	6	28
4 or more	14	30	17	61
Total	42	39	31	112

TABLE 25

Number of Pregnancies Since Second Birth, Among Women Not Practicing Contraception Following Second Birth, by Number of Children Desired

Number of Children Desired at First Interview	Number of Women	Percentage Having		Total
		No pregnancy	1 or more pregnancies	
2 or 2–3	23	61	39	100
3 or 3–4	28	46	54	100
4 or 4–5	43	23	77	100
5 or more	18	6	94	100
Total	112	34	66	100

Table 25 provides more decisive evidence that subfecundity is the main reason for not practicing contraception among respondents wanting no additional children, but is not the principal reason among those wanting several more children. Here, proportions failing to conceive during three and a half years of exposure without contraception are compared for the period following second birth.

In a general sample of multiparous women, one would expect 80–90 per cent to become pregnant in this time. Yet among FGIMA wives desiring two, or two or three children, under half become pregnant during an exposure period of 40–42 months. The proportion of conceivers reaches an expected level only among the mothers wanting five children or more.

In sum, most FGIMA mothers unwilling or ambivalent about a third child practice contraception after their second birth and among the few who do not, a majority mention problems of fecundity, and in four cases, a sterilizing operation.[5] In contrast, among respondents wanting four children or more, nearly a quarter do not use contraception in the period following second birth and twice as many explain this nonuse in terms of religion as of subfecundity.

CONTRACEPTORS

As noted earlier, among the 793 couples practicing contraception after second birth, a $-.46$ correlation is found between wife's desired family size at first interview and interval to her next pregnancy. This relationship depends largely on the differential proportion still practicing contraception at second interview. This proportion, three-quarters for respondents desiring two children, declines

TABLE 26
Outcome of Contraception Following Second Birth, by Number of Children Desired by Wife at First Interview

| Number of Children Desired at First Interview | Number of Women | Percentage for Whom Contraception | | | Total |
		Ends in Accidental Pregnancy	Is Deliberately Interrupted	Is Still Being Practiced	
2	191	18	7	75	100
2–3	85	16	13	71	100
3	177	32	23	45	100
3–4	87	40	26	33	99
4	167	44	31	25	100
4–5	42	48	38	14	100
5 or more	44	61	32	7	100
Total	793	33	21	46	100

to less than 10 per cent for wives desiring five or more children (see Table 26). Remove couples practicing contraception continuously since second birth and the correlation drops from $-.46$ to $-.23$.

[5] Nine others, who mentioned a sterilizing operation at first interview, were not reinterviewed on that account.

In turn, this correlation of −.23 depends mainly on the association between desired family size and effectiveness of contraception. Among respondents desiring larger families, the frequency of contraceptive failure is higher (Table 26) and accidental pregnancies tend to occur sooner (Table 27). Of less importance in the −.23

TABLE 27

Mean Interval between Second Birth and Next Conception, by Circumstance of Pregnancy and Number of Children Desired, Among Wives Reporting a Pregnancy and Use of Contraception in the Period Following Second Birth

Number of Children Desired	Mean Interval (Months) from Second Birth to:	
	Accidental Pregnancy	Planned Pregnancy
2 or 2–3	19.8 (48)	27.0 (24)
3 or 3–4	17.9 (91)	19.3 (64)
4 or more	13.6 (121)	19.4 (81)

correlation is a tendency for respondents desiring larger families to have their planned pregnancies sooner (again see Table 27). When the sample is restricted to 169 contraceptors having a planned pregnancy following second birth, the correlation between interval to next pregnancy and size of family preferred drops to −.15.[6]

COMPARATIVE IMPORTANCE OF TWO TENDENCIES

Two tendencies linking desired family size to birth spacing have been distinguished. First is a tendency for wives desiring larger families to plan shorter intervals as evidenced by earlier interruptions of contraception and more nonuse of it for specific purpose of minimizing time to the next pregnancy. Second is a tendency for wives desiring larger families to let shorter than average birth intervals happen as a consequence of ineffective contraception or else nonuse of it for reasons unrelated to spacing objectives. These two tendencies appear to have roughly equal importance in the correlations between desired family size and lengths of first or second birth intervals. However, with respect to the pregnancy interval following second birth, the association of desired family size with contraceptive effectiveness is the important element while the association of desired family size with intended postponements of pregnancy fol-

[6] There are 8 wives coded as not using contraception after second birth in order to have a third birth as soon as physically possible. Adding these 8 to the 169 in order to achieve agreement with the "successful planner" classification used in Table 21 increases the correlation of −.15 to only −.17.

lowing second birth is secondary. Instead of a −.30 correlation between desired family size and intended postponement of the pregnancy following first birth, one finds a −.17 correlation between it and intended postponement of the pregnancy following second birth.

It is doubtful that the truncation of intervals following second birth at 40–42 months wholly accounts for this contrast. It is also plausible that an additional consideration, namely, length of the previous birth interval, influences preferred third intervals in a way that reduces their correlation with desired family size. If the spacing between first and second child is close, then the mother may not want another short interval lest she have three very young children in the house at once. Thus the mother desiring a large family who has her first birth quickly and follows it quickly with another may hesitate to seek still another short interval for the reason just indicated.

Consistent with this thesis are three correlations involving wife's preferred interval between second and third children as reported at first interview. Wife's preferred timing of her third child correlates negatively (−.16) with desired family size, thereby paralleling the negative correlation of −.45 between her desired family size and the actual interval from second birth to next pregnancy. At the same time her preferred spacing of second and third births correlates negatively (−.10) with length of previous interval, even though the latter is positively correlated (.35) with the interval second birth to next conception. In other words, the mother desiring a large family tends to prefer a closer than average spacing of first and second births, and also of second and third births, unless she actually experiences a short interval between first and second children, when she tends to modify her preference in favor of a less close spacing of second and third children.

Preferred Spacing of Third Child

In the original panel of 1,165 wives, 1,118 reported a preferred spacing of second and third children.[7] Roughly three-quarters elected an interval between 24 and 48 months, with only 14 per cent subscribing to an interval longer than four years. Based on this figure, one might predict that among wives desiring three children or

[7] An extended analysis of these preferred third intervals is given in Westoff *et al.*, *Family Growth in Metropolitan America*, pp. 125–133. For the women desiring two children, the preferred spacing between second and third children is a hypothetical affair and most of the 47 nonresponses are found among these women. However, removing wives desiring two or two-three children does not materially alter the few correlations involving wife's preferred third interval, cited in this chapter.

more, roughly 15 per cent would practice continuous contraception between interviews, since the remainder would have to interrupt their contraception if they wanted birth intervals of four years or less. Accordingly it is a little surprising to find in Table 26 that the proportion is not 15 per cent but roughly 33 per cent.

However, this prediction makes no allowance for changes in the number of children desired—a topic which is discussed more fully in the next chapter. To allow for such changes, wives are classified by their desired family size at second interview in Table 28. Of 617

TABLE 28

Still Practicing Contraception and Not Still Practicing Contraception Since Second Birth, by Number of Children Desired at Second Interview

Number of Children Desired by Wife	Number of Couples		Total
	Still Practicing Contraception	Not Still Practicing Contraception	
2 or 2–3	252	36	288
3 or more	113	504	617
Total	365	540	905

respondents desiring three children or more at second interview, only 113, or 18 per cent, are still seeking to postpone that pregnancy. Eighteen per cent is not significantly different from the predicted 15 per cent. However, the figure of 18 per cent is a lower bound since some of the women failing in their contraception or not using it for reasons unrelated to spacing objectives might have preferred a third birth interval longer than four years. Nevertheless, these results indicate that most couples of the present sample prefer to keep their birth intervals to four years or less.

SUMMARY

Contributing to the inverse correlation between length of birth intervals and completed family size is the inverse correlation between length of birth intervals and desired family size. Family-size preferences are linked to birth spacing in two main ways. Wives desiring larger families tend to plan shorter birth intervals as evidenced by less use of contraception for the reason of wanting another pregnancy as soon as biologically possible, and by earlier interruptions of contraception after marriage or a childbirth. At the same time, the closer birth spacing of wives desiring more children reflects less efficient contraception and less use of it for reasons unrelated to spacing objectives. These two tendencies appear to be of fairly equal importance in the correlation of desired family size and length of first and second birth intervals. However, less efficient contraception by wives desiring four children or more proves to be the main source of the association between desired family size and interval from second birth to next conception. An hypothesis is advanced to explain why intended postponement of third birth correlates so much more weakly with desired family size than does intended postponement of second birth.

Chapter VII. Predicting Fertility
Over Three Years

The five preceding chapters have dealt with some of the relationships operating among preferred and actual birth intervals, desired family size, and contraceptive practice. Particular attention has been given to the ways in which desired family size and number of additional children wanted is related to birth-spacing and contraceptive effectiveness. The concern of the present chapter is how highly these variables, as based on information collected a few months after second birth, correlate with measures of desired and attained family size three years later.

Of course all these correlations between predictors and fertility at second interview are affected by the length of the prediction period as well as by the stage of family growth at which the period starts. If a prediction period different from three years, or a starting point other than shortly after second birth had been used, the array of zero-order correlations would have been different. Partly for this reason much of the discussion centers on why particular zero-order correlations are not higher or lower, and for this purpose the previous chapters may be drawn upon to advantage.

Chapter XV also contains a multivariate analysis of factors predictive of fertility at second interview, but with the analysis broadened to include many social and psychological factors, and with the sample divided into three religious groups. To avoid duplication, the analysis of the present chapter is restricted to the total sample without subdivision by religion.

Two Dependent Variables

Two measures will be used as dependent variables: a measure of fertility since second birth and wife's desired family size at second interview. Although the former is most simply measured as the number of pregnancies reported between interviews, this choice has disadvantages. A few women experiencing multiple miscarriages during the three-year period would receive very high fertility scores. More important, a pregnancy that is compensating for a miscarriage has a meaning very different from a pregnancy that follows a live birth.

To avoid these problems, fertility since second birth is defined to mean the number of pregnancies presumably adding to family size. Hence if the first of two pregnancies ends in wastage, so that the two pregnancies cannot contribute more than one live birth, the two pregnancies are counted as one. Under this convention 0 pregnancies are registered for 46 per cent of the sample, 1 pregnancy for 43 per cent, and 2 pregnancies for the remaining 11 per cent.

The number of children desired by the wife at time of second interview is used as the second dependent variable, mainly because it represents the best measure of completed family size available thus far in the present study. As the question about desired family size is worded, the respondent must cite at least the number of children she has already. Accordingly, her stated preference incorporates all births thus far and gives some indication of whether further childbearing is likely or not. Moreover, this indication is made more reliable by eligibility criteria which minimize the incidence of subfecundity.

NUMBER OF CHILDREN DESIRED

The strongest predictor of fertility at second interview is the number of children desired at first interview, whether stated by husband or wife. Wife's desired family size at first interview is measured in the same manner as her desired family size at second interview, which is being used as one of the two dependent variables. Underlying both measures is a pair of questions, one asking about the number of children she wants altogether including those she has already, and a second question asking how sure she is about her stated preference. Allowance is made for hyphenated responses to the first question—such as wants two or three, three or four, and so on—and also for qualifications offered in answer to the second question. For example, the woman who reports wanting four children and who is sure about this preference is placed higher on the scale of fertility desires than a woman who initially reports wanting three or four, or who wants four but might want fewer. Husbands, to whom questionnaires were administered in the first interview, were not asked the second question about degree of certainty and to that extent their family size preferences are less elaborately classified than those of their spouses.

Wife's desired family size at first interview accounts for about one-quarter of the variance of fertility since second birth and nearly half the variance of number of children desired at second interview (Table 30). Husband's desired family size predicts almost as well and the small differential may result in part from measurement differences. Because the number of children wanted by the two spouses is so highly correlated (.64), the multiple correlation based

TABLE 29

Correlation of Number of Children Desired at First Interview with Number of Children
Desired at Second Interview and Fertility Since Second Birth

Independent Variable	Fertility since Second Birth	Number of Children Desired by Wife Second Interview
Number of children desired at first interview by:		
Wife	.48	.69
Husband	.42	.55
Wife and husband	.50	.71
Wife, holding constant average birth interval	.38	.64

TABLE 30

Number of Pregnancies since Second Birth,[a] by Number of Children Desired by Wife
at First Interview

Number of Children Desired	Number of Wives	Per Cent Having			
		No Pregnancy	One Pregnancy	Two Pregnancies	Total (per cent)
2	210	74	23	3	100
2–3	89	71	26	3	100
3	199	49	46	5	100
3–4	93	35	52	13	100
4	201	26	58	16	100
4–5	51	19	63	18	100
5	23	13	39	48	100
5–6 or 6	24	4	54	42	100
6 or more	15	7	33	60	100
Total	905	46	42	12	100

[a] Number of pregnancies since second birth excluding those which follow miscarriages.

on both spouses' preferences is not much higher than the zero-order correlation yielded by wife's preference alone.

The detailed relationship between wife's desired family size at first interview and her fertility since second birth is given in Table 30. Among wives desiring no additional children, 26 per cent have one or more pregnancies, whereas among wives desiring two or more additional children, 79 per cent have at least one additional pregnancy by time of second interview.

It is interesting to compare the predictive value of desired number of children in the present sample with expected number of children collected in a 1955 Detroit Area Study. A selected subsample of the latter wives was recontacted by telephone three years later and their interim fertility ascertained. Those expecting no additional births averaged .22 pregnancies, while those expecting two or more additional births averaged 1.00 pregnancies during the three years.[1] In the present study (Table 31) the 210 wives desiring no more births average .29 pregnancies and the 314 wanting at least two additional children average 1.01 pregnancies during three years. Such a near identity of results is fortuitous but agreement at all suggests that in the present study substituting family-size expectations for family-size preferences might have altered results very little. However, it is still an open question whether earlier in marriage such close agreement between desires and expectations would be met. Goldberg found that in one Detroit Area Study the two sets of attitudes correlated no more than .43.[2]

TABLE 31

Additional Pregnancies Expected or Desired, by Pregnancies Actually Observed During the Next Three Years, in the Present Study and the 1955 Detroit Area Study

Additional Births Desired or Expected	1955 Detroit Area Study[a]		FGIMA Study	
	Number of Couples	Additional Pregnancies Observed	Number of Couples	Additional Pregnancies Observed
0	126	.22	210	.29
1	65	.55	199	.56
2 or more	46	1.00	314	1.01

[a] SOURCE: D. Goldberg, H. Sharp, and R. Freedman, "The Stability and Reliability of Expected Family Size Data," Milbank Memorial Fund *Quarterly*, 37 (October 1959), pp. 375, 378.

Several factors are operating to make family-size preferences a strong predictor of fertility since second birth. Because highly efficient contraception follows attainment of desired family size, most couples wanting two children do not have another pregnancy before second interview unless they change their mind in favor of a third child. Also, as seen in the preceding chapter, most couples prefer birth intervals of four years or less, which means interrupting contraception well in advance of the second interview. Hence most of the couples desiring three or more children can be expected to have at least one pregnancy before second interview except for the slow conceivers and those who change their minds and decide to restrict their families to two children after all. In the present sample the number of such slow conceivers is reduced by eligibility criteria. It is also clear from the last chapter that the respondents who follow a

[1] D. Goldberg, H. Sharp, and R. Freedman, "The Stability and Reliability of Expected Family Size Data," Milbank Memorial Fund *Quarterly*, 37 (October 1959), p. 378.

[2] *Ibid.*, p. 371.

live birth with another pregnancy, all within the three and a half year interval since the second birth, are drawn disproportionately from the wives desiring the largest families and practicing the least effective contraception.

The principal factor limiting the predictive power of family-size preferences is their instability through time. To some extent, of course, this changeability reflects unreliability of reporting rather than genuine change. As indicated by a .69 correlation, wife's desired family size as reported at first interview accounts for about half the variation of her total fertility desires reported three years later.

STABILITY OF FAMILY-SIZE DESIRES

Table 32 portrays the changes in wife's desired family size between first and second interview. At first interview, about one-quarter of the wives offered nonspecific responses such as two or

TABLE 32

Bivariate Distribution of Wife's Desired Size of Family at First and Second Interviews

Size of Family Desired at First Interview	Size of Family Desired at Second Interview									
	2	2–3	3	3–4	4	4–5	5	5–6 or 6	7 or more	Total
2	132	18	43	2	14	—	—	1	—	210
2–3	34	15	25	6	9	—	—	—	—	89
3	44	16	96	14	23	3	2	—	1	199
3–4	3	6	32	18	26	5	2	1	—	93
4	8	7	48	19	84	19	5	7	4	201
4–5	3	—	9	6	21	6	4	2	—	51
5	—	1	—	—	7	2	6	6	1	23
5–6 or 6	—	—	2	—	4	1	2	10	5	24
7 or more	—	1	—	—	2	1	2	3	6	15
Total	224	64	255	65	190	37	23	30	17	905

three children desired, three or four, four or five, and so on. These hyphenated responses complicate estimates of changeability. When it is required that a first interview response—hyphenated or not—be exactly duplicated in the next interview, then only 41 per cent of the family-size preferences prove stable. A more lenient definition raises the frequency of stability to 68 per cent. Here a hyphenated response of three or four which is modified to a specific one of three or a specific one of four is accepted as not changing. Likewise, a specific response of three which is modified to a hyphenated response of either two or three or else three or four is defined as stable. If hyphenated responses had not been allowed, the frequency of stable preferences would doubtless have stood between 41 and 68 per cent and probably nearer the latter. Goldberg *et al.* found that 70 per cent of the wives with two children had stable fertility expectations over a three-year period.[3]

Table 33, bringing into direct comparison the marginals of Table 32, documents two points. First and rather surprisingly, desired family sizes vary as much in the second interview as in the first. It had been expected that failures of contraception would

TABLE 33

Comparison of Wife's Desired Family Size One-Half Year and Three and One-Half Years After Second Birth

Number of Children Desired	Percentage of Wives Having Specified Preference		Percentage Change During the Three Years
	First Interview	Second Interview	
2	23	25	2
2–3	10	7	−3
3	22	28	6
3–4	10	7	−3
4	22	21	−1
4–5	6	4	−2
5	3	3	
5–6 or 6	3	3	
6–7 or more	2	2	
Total	101	100	−1

force many wives to increase their desired number of children to above two, while many who earlier reported desiring 4 children or more would have lowered their family-size objectives. Instead, the few cases of contraceptive failure among wives desiring two children at first interview are more than compensated for by changes of preferences from two or three, or three children desired to only two children desired. Furthermore most wives wanting large families in the first interview still want them.

A second point brought out by Table 33 is the shift away from hyphenated responses to more specific ones, with reported desire for three children showing the largest gain.

AVERAGE BIRTH INTERVAL

Average birth interval refers to the average of the two intervals between marriage and first birth and between first and second births. For purposes of correlation, it does not matter whether this average birth interval is used or the interval between marriage and

[3] Goldberg *et al.*, *op.cit.*, p. 379.

second birth since the latter is simply twice the former. After desired family size at first interview, average birth interval is the best predictor of the two dependent variables under study. It correlates −.41 with fertility since second birth. In part, this predictive power depends on a −.35 correlation with wife's desired family size at first interview. Relevant to this −.35 correlation is the discussion of the previous chapter which explored the dual basis of the association between desired family size and birth spacing. When wife's desired family size at first interview is held constant, the correlation between average birth interval and fertility since second birth declines from −.41 to −.30. Conversely, holding constant average birth interval reduces the correlation between desired family size and fertility since second birth from .48 to .38.

TABLE 34

Correlations of Average Birth Interval with Number of Children Desired at Second Interview and Fertility Since Second Birth

Independent Variable	Fertility Since Second Birth	Number of Children Desired by Wife Second Interview
Average birth interval	−.41	−.40
Average birth interval, holding constant number of children desired by wife	−.30	−.26

Thus, for its predictive value, average birth interval depends partly on its association with desired family size but depends also on other elements. Possibilities here are consistencies of contraceptive behavior independent of desired family size, and differential fecundability. Evidence for the latter is provided by an earlier analysis in which lengths of contraceptive practice (termed "intended components") are subtracted from total birth intervals to leave "residual components," the latter dominated by delays of conception. A .21 correlation was obtained between the residual components of first and second birth intervals.[4]

Preferred Third Birth Interval

Wife's preferred spacing between her second and third children correlates weakly both with fertility since second birth and her desired family size at second interview. These preferences are hypothetical for wives desiring two or two or three children at first interview, but removal of these women increases the associations very little. The correlation with fertility since second birth is raised from

[4] C. F. Westoff, R. G. Potter, Jr., Philip C. Sagi, Elliot G. Mishler, *Family Growth in Metropolitan America*, Princeton University Press, Princeton, N.J., 1961, pp. 112–113.

—.11 to —.13; the correlation with wife's desired family size at second interview is raised from —.13 to —.15.

One likely reason for the low correlations is the vagueness of spacing preferences, especially when respondents are questioned about them so soon after a childbirth. Wife's desired spacing between second and third children correlates only .28 with her husband's in contrast to a correlation of .64 observed between their desired family sizes. Four to seven months after a second birth, many mothers may know only that they do not want another pregnancy yet and have not begun to think seriously about how long they will try to delay that pregnancy. In a prior analysis, this premise was reinforced by the generally low level of correlations found for wife's preferred third intervals.[5]

In addition, rational spacing considerations may conflict with factors of a more impulsive or involuntary character. The woman who has spaced her first two children closely, and who wishes to avoid caring for three infants at once, is being quite rational if she expresses interest in an interval between second and third births long enough so that the eldest child will reach some designated stage, such as prekindergarten, before the third baby arrives. In practice, however, other more powerful factors are operating to produce a positive correlation between consecutive birth intervals— such factors, perhaps, as differential fecundability or differential effectiveness of contraception as linked with desired family size.

Husband's preferred third interval yields a correlation of .36 with the interval between second birth and next conception. However, the wording of the relevant question[6] encouraged husbands who wanted only two children to say they did not expect another child. Actually, 157 of 254 did as encouraged and these husbands were coded, rather arbitrarily, as desiring a third birth interval of maximum length. If one excludes this subgroup, the correlation between desired third interval and actual pregnancy interval following second birth declines from .36 to .27, but still remains, for reasons unknown, a good deal higher than the correlation of .12 obtained with wife's preferred third interval.

Possible reasons why husband's desired third birth interval does not correlate still higher than .27 with the next pregnancy interval are the truncation of next pregnancy intervals at 40–42 months, the concentration of spacing preferences in a fairly narrow range of 24–48 months, and the considerable variation of conceptive delays.

[5] *Ibid.*, pp. 131–133.
[6] This wording is: "If you expect to have another child, how long from now would you like to have it born?" *Ibid.*, p. 129.

These delays materially affect the lengths of the next pregnancy intervals but are largely beyond the capacity of the couples to predict or to control. Failures of contraception play a somewhat similar role.

CONTRACEPTIVE PRACTICE

The last two predictors chosen for consideration relate to contraceptive practice between marriage and second birth. During this period each wife had two or sometimes three pregnancies. To develop an index of family-planning success, an attempt has been made to classify each pregnancy as successfully planned or unsuccessfully planned and then, in a second step of index construction, to rank respondents into four groups according to the proportion of their pregnancies classified as successfully planned.[7]

This index of family-planning success correlates −.18 with fertility since second birth. A higher correlation had been expected. However, as Chapter IV shows, contraceptive effectiveness increases rapidly as desired family size is approached and attained. Because of these rapid changes, the relevance of contraceptive performance before second birth is greatly reduced with respect to events happening after second birth.

With wife's desired family size at second interview the correlation is .20, also lower than anticipated. Appendix C demonstrates that correlations with the family planning index are being lowered by unreliability, but perhaps just as serious are the measurement problems arising from an attempt to reduce multidimensional behavior to a single four-point ranking.

Somewhat higher correlations are obtained with a crude, three-category classification of when contraception is first used: before first pregnancy, between first pregnancy and second birth, and after second birth or not at all. The correlations are .28 with fertility since second birth, and .33 with wife's desired family size at second interview. Couples who practice contraception from marriage are drawn disproportionately from the Jewish group and tend to be relatively more efficient with contraception and to desire smaller families. Those who wait until after the second birth before starting contraception—when it is not for reasons of subfecundity—are disproportionately drawn from the Catholic group who desire larger families on the average.

JOINT PREDICTORS

Of the independent variables considered in this chapter, wife's desired family size at first interview has proved the strongest predic-

[7] See Appendix C.

tor, accounting for about half of the variance of her desired family size at second interview and about one quarter of the variance of fertility since second birth.[8] It is interesting to consider how much these zero-order correlations of .69 and .48 can be increased by combining the single predictor with one or more of the other independent variables.

From Table 35 it is clear that very little predictive power is gained with respect to wife's desired family size at second interview. In particular, husband's desired family size at first interview is too closely correlated with his spouse's to add much information.

TABLE 35
Multiple Correlations with Fertility Since Second Birth and the Number of Children Desired by the Wife at Second Interview

Independent Variables	Fertility Since Second Birth	Number of Children Desired by Wife Second Interview
Number of children desired by:		
Wife	.48	.69
Husband and wife	.50	.71
Wife, plus average birth interval	.54	.71
Wife, plus average birth interval and time		
contraception first used	.56	.72

Moderate increases in correlation with fertility since the second birth are realized by adding into the predictive battery average birth interval and the time contraception is first used. Little extra predictive power is contributed by the index of family-planning success.

SUMMARY

In this chapter several indices relating to birth spacing, desired family size, and contraceptive practice, all based on first interview information, are considered for their ability to predict fertility at second interview, roughly three years later. Discussion focuses on why particular correlations are not weaker or stronger.

The strongest predictor, wife's desired family size at first interview, accounts for about one-quarter of the variance of fertility since second birth and about one-half of the variance of her desired family size at second interview. During the three-year period between interviews, desired family size does not become any less var-

[8] Actually, the maximum correlation possible, given observed marginals, between wife's desired family size at first interview and her fertility since second birth is .85. The observed correlation of .48 might, then, be interpreted as representing $(.48)^2/(.85)^2$, or .32 per cent of the potentially explainable variance.

iable, as originally expected. However there is a trend away from nonspecific preferences—two or three children desired, three or four, and so on—toward specific ones, with three children desired showing the largest gain.

The next strongest predictor is average length of the first two birth intervals. Its .4 correlation with fertility since second birth probably depends on many elements including an appreciable association with desired family size.

Wife's preferred spacing of second and third children yields low correlations and several possible explanations are advanced. Husband's desired third interval does somewhat better.

With respect to contraceptive performance up to second birth, a crude index classifying time of first use of contraception produces stronger relationships with the two dependent variables than a rather elaborate index of fertility-planning success.

When several independent variables are considered, the multiple correlations with wife's desired family size at second interview are very little higher than the zero-order correlation given by wife's desired family size at first interview taken alone. Moderately higher multiple correlations are obtained with fertility since second birth.

PART III

SOCIAL AND PSYCHOLOGICAL FACTORS

Chapter VIII. Religion and Religiousness

The observation that religious preference is the best single predictor of the number of children a couple desires was one of the main conclusions drawn in the first phase of this study. In theory, this finding is much more intriguing than the patterns of association also found between religion and the extent of successful fertility planning and with the length of intervals between births. These latter associations are deducible, at least in part, from knowledge of the Roman Catholic opposition to most techniques of family planning. That Catholics in advance want larger families than either Protestants or Jews is not so immediately obvious. Nor was the extreme success with which the first two pregnancies were planned by Jewish couples, as compared for example with Protestants of comparable socioeconomic status, so clearly anticipated. All of these findings were qualified by uncertainty about their stability over time and validity for predicting subsequent fertility behavior.

Numerous questions were also provoked from analyses of the first interview data. Is the currently evolving doctrine of "responsible parenthood" finding its way into the thinking of individuals? Can the larger family preferences of Catholics, particularly the more religious Catholics, be explained in terms of a popular perception of their church's position on birth control as implying a position in favor of large families? To what extent do Catholic couples tend to distinguish the two ideas? Appropriate questions were included in the second interview in an attempt to disentangle these dimensions.

One of the most promising new leads opened by our first inquiry was the discovery of a relation of our measures of fertility with education in the Catholic school system, particularly higher education. The interpretation of this relationship, however, was clouded by the probability that individuals from more religious backgrounds select Catholic schools. We have attempted to clarify this problem by asking questions about the religiousness of the respondent's home environment when she was a child.

Our multivariate analyses revealed that we had been least successful in accounting for the variations in fertility among Protestants. Although there seemed to be special reasons why the fertility of Catholics and Jews might be more predictable[1] than that of Prot-

[1] See discussion in C. F. Westoff, R. G. Potter, Jr., P. C. Sagi, E. G. Mishler, *Family Growth in Metropolitan America*, Princeton University Press, Princeton, N.J., 1961, pp. 326–327.

estants, it was also felt that the classification "Protestant" might be more heterogeneous than the others. One way of increasing the homogeneity of the classification is to group Protestants according to objective manifestations of a religious or church orientation such as whether they were married by a minister and whether they attend church services regularly. Information on the type of marriage ceremony was collected in the second interview.

CLASSIFICATION OF RELIGION

The ideal classification of the religious factor should accomplish two objectives: (1) it should permit direct comparisons with the original classification used in the first phase of the study, and (2) it should capitalize on any knowledge gained from the first analysis that might improve the classification.

Since the number of Jews in the sample (110 in the second interview) does not permit any further subdivision, modifications are necessarily restricted to Protestants and Catholics. As indicated above, the lack of homogeneity in the Protestant group is considered problematical. In order to avoid the almost meaningless nominal designation of "Protestant," we separated the group into two subgroups called "Active" Protestants and "Other" Protestants. The Active Protestant category was restricted to couples whose religious preference (both husband's and wife's) is classifiable as a Protestant denomination, who were married by a minister, and who currently attend church—the wife at least once a month and the husband at least once a year. The remaining modification was to exclude couples who had changed their religious affiliations,[2] most of which involved former Protestant-Catholic marriages. This Active Protestant category includes 174 of the 372 couples included in the total Protestant group. The 198 Other Protestant[3] category thus includes couples changing their affiliation, all Protestants married in a civil ceremony, all mixed marriages involving a Protestant except those performed by a Catholic priest (included in the Other Catholic classification described below), and all couples whose attendance at church services is less than monthly for the wife and less than yearly for the husband. This is clearly a residual category in many respects but at least the Active Protestant category does achieve a certain homogeneity. If numbers permitted, it would presumably have been advantageous to apply this classification system to each denomina-

[2] A few changes reflect simply unreliability of response or of initial classification.

[3] The term "Nominal" might be a better description of this category than "Other," but it would be grossly inaccurate for many of the Catholics and, since we wished to use the same labels for both groups, the less stringent term was considered preferable.

tion, such as Presbyterians, Methodists, and so forth but this is clearly impracticable and, furthermore, no significant fertility differences were found among the denominations. The combination of Active Protestants and Other Protestants, the total Protestant group, is identical with the Protestant classification used in the first phase of the study.

The 423 couples classified as Catholic have been similarly subdivided into Active Catholics and Other Catholics except that the criteria are somewhat different than for Protestants and are based upon different theoretical objectives. All of our research into the nature of the influence of Catholicism on fertility has indicated that the relationship is largely reducible to the extent of conformity to formal church requirements and exposure to the Catholic value system in the form of education in religious schools. In short, there is a way in which Catholicism can be viewed as a variable ranging from low to high, with fertility as a direct linear function—a model which does not have any analogue in the case of Judaism or Protestantism. It might be argued that the fundamentalist sects of the latter denominations might provide such an analogue, but such groups have little representation in our urban sample. The subclassification of Catholics therefore reflects our attempt to make a sharper distinction than only that of nominal and practicing and to include a background of Catholic education as well.

The Active Catholics comprise couples who in each interview reported both wife and husband Catholic, who were married by a priest, who both attend church at least once a week, and both of whom were educated at least partly in Catholic schools or colleges.

TABLE 36
Distribution of the Sample by the Religious Classification

Religious Classification	Per Cent
Active Protestant	19.2
Other Protestant	21.9
Total Protestant	41.1
Active Catholic	11.8
Other Catholic	34.9
Total Catholic	46.7
Jews	12.2
Total Per Cent	100.0
Total Number	905

This group includes 107 of the total 423 couples.[4] The 316 Other Catholics comprise the residue and include all mixed Catholic marriages which had been performed by a Catholic priest. As in the case of Protestants, the combination of the Active and Other Catholics into the total Catholic group corresponds identically with the usage in the first report except that the total Catholic group now is equal to the sum of what in the first phase were designated Catholics and Mixed Catholics.

The final distribution of the sample by this religious classification is contained in Table 36.

RELIGION AND FERTILITY

The first question to be answered is whether religion has fulfilled its promise as a predictor of actual fertility. The distributions by number of additional pregnancies (see top deck of Table 37)

TABLE 37
Number of Additional Pregnancies by Religion

| Religion | Number of Couples | Number of Pregnancies | | | Total |
| | | 0 | 1 | 2 | |
		(per cent)			
Protestant total	372	49	43	8	100
Catholic total	423	38	46	16	100
Jewish	110	69	27	4	100
All couples	905	46	43	11	100
Active Protestant	174	57	39	4	100
Other Protestant	198	41	47	12	100
Active Catholic	107	28	43	29	100
Other Catholic	316	41	47	12	100

indicate rather sharp differences. Nearly two out of every three Catholic couples reported at least one additional pregnancy during this interval of three and a half years from the birth of the second child, with twice as high a proportion reporting two additional pregnancies as compared with Protestants. As expected, Jewish couples are at the lowest point on the fertility scale with fewer than one-third reporting any additional pregnancy and only 4 per cent reporting two pregnancies. Protestant couples are in the intermediate position with about half reporting one or more subsequent conceptions.

[4] This ratio is in no way intended to imply the actual proportion of Active Catholics in the population since those classified as "Other" include many couples and individuals who fulfill the obligations of their religion.

The striking feature of the comparisons by religiousness (lower deck of Table 37) is the lack of any difference in fertility between Other Protestants and Other Catholics, and the wide gulf between Active Protestants and Active Catholics. The first inference one is tempted to draw is that, since the "Other" designation in both cases implies to some extent[5] only nominal affiliation with the religion or the religious organization, the labels Protestant and Catholic lose any direct significance they may have for fertility. On the other hand, the widely divergent fertility distributions for the couples who report some behavioral evidence of conformity to formal church expectations or doctrine suggest at first glance that the content of Protestantism compared to Catholicism has quite different implications for fertility. In order to explore this possibility as well as to examine the extent of Catholic perceptions of the large-family policy of their church, we tabulated by religious classification the replies to two questions:

"As far as you know, does your religion take any stand on birth control or family planning?"

"As far as you know, does your religion take any stand on size of family? What?"

That the Catholic women in the sample perceive their religion as taking a position on birth control—100 per cent of the Active Catholics answered "Yes"[6]—comes as no surprise, but that 20 per cent of the Protestants and nearly 30 per cent of the Jews replied "Yes" was not particularly expected. The explanation appears to lie mainly in a modern interpretation which includes birth control as an instrument of parental responsibility. This interpretation is also reflected by the replies to the second question about their perception of their religious position on family size.

One woman, for example, who is classified in the Active Protestant category answered the question concerning the stand of her religion on birth control:

"Yes. But just recently. We received a booklet stating the Church (Presbyterian) position. Birth control is legitimate."

And to the question on family size, she replied:

"Not until recently. We received this booklet stating the position of the Church in this matter. Families should limit the number of the total that can be cared for properly."

---

[5] They also include mixed marriages which may or may not imply only nominal affiliation. In the case of marriages conducted by a Catholic priest there certainly is no implication of nominal commitment.

[6] A good proportion of the Other Catholic women who replied "No" to this question are not Catholic themselves but are married to Catholic husbands.

Another woman, classified as Other Protestant replied:

"Yes. The Episcopalians feel that a marriage should include children and the children should be planned."

But with respect to her church's position on family size, she replied:

"No, with reservations. If the minister saw that your family was very poor and had 10 children, he would then give the word that something should be done. Sort of the old family friend or doctor type of advice."

TABLE 38

Perception of Religion's Position on Birth Control

Position on Birth Control	Protestants		Catholics		Jews
	Active	Other	Active	Other	
		(per cent)			
Yes	19	20	100	82	28
No	76	75	—	18	63
Don't know	5	5	—	—	9
Per cent total	100	100	100	100	100
Number of wives	174	197	107	316	110

Although the main secondary response among Protestants is a perception that their religion encourages limiting family size, clearly the main Protestant response (given by 90 per cent or more) is that their religion takes no stand at all on the subject of family size. The Jewish women are somewhat more uncertain about the stand of Judaism on family size. Again the main response (72 per cent) is that their religion takes no stand, but the chief secondary

TABLE 39

Perception of Religion's Position on Family Size

Position on Family Size	Protestants		Catholics		Jews
	Active	Other	Active	Other	
		(per cent)			
Should have large family	—	1	17	28	5
Ambiguous[a]	1	1	8	9	6
No stand	92	90	72	61	72
Should limit size	5	6	3	1	5
Don't know	2	2	—	1	12
Per cent total	100	100	100	100	100
Number of wives	172	192	107	315	109

[a] Includes those who inferred a position on family size from a perceived position on birth control.

response in this group is "don't know" (12 per cent) with the remaining 16 per cent being equally divided among the three categories "should have large family," "should limit size," and responses classed as ambiguous.

One response of this last group, typically following a reply of "don't know" to the question on birth control, is:

"The orthodox may take an official stand against birth control. I am Reformed and I doubt whether they take any stand on size of family—if they do, I am not familiar with it."

Or another Jewish woman who replied "Yes" to the birth control question made the following reply to the question on family size:

"Very religious Jewish people do not believe in birth control, so in other words they also believe in large families and very orthodox people believe in very large families."

Turning to the Catholic responses, again we find that the dominant perception is that their religion takes no position on the matter of family size, thereby largely refuting the theory that rejection of birth control is perceived by the Catholic population to reflect an official encouragement of large families. It is revealing to note in this connection that individuals more closely involved with the Church—the Active Catholics—are even more inclined toward this view than are the Other Catholics.[7]

The fact that the majority Catholic view includes no perception of any church position on family size should not obscure the fact that a sizable minority—17 per cent of the Active Catholics and 28 per cent of the Other Catholics—holds the view that the Roman Catholic Church does encourage large families. The important aspect of the proportions as far as the subject of fertility is concerned is whether this point of view has anything to do with behavior. Do Catholics who hold the view that their church encourages large families actually have more children? It is certainly plausible to speculate that such a belief might reinforce or perhaps affect interpretations of the church's position on family planning in general, such as the philosophy of the rhythm method.

It comes as something of a surprise therefore to discover that the only difference it makes is the opposite from that expected. Among Active Catholics, a comparison of the recent fertility of those who replied that their religion takes no position on family size with those giving some other reply reveals a slightly higher fertility record for

[7] For an interesting account of recent statements of Catholic officials, see "New Trends in Roman Catholic Opinion," *Population Bulletin*, Vol. 17, No. 7 (November 1961).

the former group. A stronger, and also contrary pattern emerges for the Other Catholics—62 per cent of those perceiving no position reported an additional pregnancy compared to 53 per cent of those giving some other answer. Thus, there is clearly no evidenc to support the proposition that higher fertility among Catholics can be attributed to conformity to any direct encouragement of higher fertility. One possible explanation of the apparent reversal of expected results—although it is of dubious statistical reliability—is that this type of response may select those with greater hostility toward their religion or church. It may be for this reason that this inverse relation appears mainly among the Other Catholics, although differences in education may also play a role.

The same pattern appears among Jews as well (Protestants are too concentrated in one category to permit analysis) with 34 per cent of those who reply "no position" reporting a third pregnancy, compared to 20 per cent of those perceiving that Judaism encourages large families or who are uncertain. Unfortunately, insufficient numbers preclude comparing the fertility of those who perceive a small family orientation.

This analysis has elucidated some areas formerly unclear but has not contributed any clarification of the sharp differences in fertility between Active Protestants and Active Catholics. Couples in both of these groups largely denied that their religion took a stand on family size and the Active Catholics who did feel that their church favored large families did not reveal higher fertility. The sharp differences in perception of religious attitudes toward birth control provide the obvious explanation of the difference between Active Protestants and Active Catholics but fall short of providing a complete explanation because Active and Other Protestants are undifferentiated in this regard but they are quire different in fertility. In other words, Active Catholics are differentiated from all other groups by their conformity to a particular doctrine which, if not theoretically at least practically, results in higher fertility. Just how this is translated into desires for larger families is not clear from our data. The indistinguishable recent fertility of Other Catholics and Other Protestants suggests an absence of any religious import to the fertility of these groups. The low fertility of the Active Protestants and Jews thus becomes the more interesting deviation. Although there is some indication of religious overtones to family planning such as the "responsible parenthood" theme, it is not plausible to theorize that the lower fertility of these groups is conformity to religious value systems in the same sense that the higher fertility of the Active Catholics is a response to a different value system. It is more likely that the lower fertility of Active Protestants and Jews, compared, say, with that of Other Protestants and Other Catholics, is due to greater control over fertility perhaps as a consequence of different social class composition.

In order to explore this possibility, let us first examine the extent to which the different religious categories were able to promote the achievement of their fertility goals during the three and a half year period.

Religious Differences in the Control of Fertility

There is a number of different ways by which we can assess variations in the control of fertility. The first of these is to exploit the longitudinal design of the study by comparing the actual recent fertility histories of the sample against the statements of the number of additional children they reported wanting when they were first

TABLE 40
Number of Additional Pregnancies, by the Number of Children Desired by the Wife by Religion

	Protestants					Catholics					Jews				
	Number of Pregnancies			Per Cent	Number of Wives	Number of Pregnancies			Per Cent	Number of Wives	Number of Pregnancies			Per Cent	Number of Wives
Total Number of Children Desired	0	1	2	Total		0	1	2	Total		0	1	2	Total	
	(per cent)					(per cent)					(per cent)				
Two	69	26	5	100	110	77	22	1	100	64	86	14	—	100	36
Two or three	66	32	2	100	47	70	26	4	100	23	84	11	5	100	19
Three	51	42	7	100	83	42	54	4	100	89	67	30	3	100	27
Three or four	35	56	9	100	46	33	45	22	100	36	45	55	—	100	11
Four	17	65	18	100	65	29	55	16	100	122	36	50	14	100	14
More than four	24	57	19	100	21	10	51	39	100	89	(1)	(2)	—	*	3
Total	49	43	8	100	372	38	46	16	100	423	69	27	4	100	110

interviewed. The tabulations in Tables 40 and 41 are not definitive evidence on the subject of fertility control since (a) clearly, genuine changes of mind could have occurred during the three and a half year interval; (b) the reliability of statements about desired family size[8] is not known precisely; (c) only three and a half years have elapsed since the birth of the second child which precludes the achievement of large-family preferences. Despite these limitations, the approach does not suffer from the methodological drawbacks of depending upon the respondent's assessment of whether pregnancies were planned or not.

[8] The correlation of .70 between statements of the number of children desired in the two interviews sets a lower bound on reliability since it is affected by the validity of the measure.

The influence of religion and religiousness on the control of fertility contains a number of interesting facets. In general the *correlations* tend to be rather similar for the different religious categories although a somewhat higher correlation is seen among Catholics, especially the Active Catholics (bottom row, Table 42). This higher correlation results mainly from the fact that these women have been successful in promoting large family goals. This of course emphasizes the multidimensional nature of "planning" or fertility control.

TABLE 41

Number of Additional Pregnancies by Number of Children Desired by the Wife, by Religiousness of Protestants and Catholics

Total Number of Children Desired (I)	Number of Pregnancies			Per Cent Total	Number of Wives	Number of Pregnancies			Per Cent Total	Number of Wives
	0	1	2			0	1	2		
	(per cent)					(per cent)				
	ACTIVE PROTESTANTS					OTHER PROTESTANTS				
Two	80	20	—	100	46	61	31	8	100	64
Two or three	70	30	—	100	20	63	33	4	100	27
Three	70	30	—	100	43	30	55	15	100	40
Three or four	35	57	8	100	26	35	55	10	100	20
Four	23	60	17	100	30	11	69	20	100	35
More than four	22	67	11	100	9	25	50	25	100	12
Total	57	39	4	100	174	41	47	12	100	198
	ACTIVE CATHOLICS					OTHER CATHOLICS				
Two	88	12	—	100	8	75	23	2	100	56
Two or three	(2)	—	—	*	2	67	29	4	100	21
Three	38	54	8	100	13	42	54	4	100	76
Three or four	(2)	(3)	(1)	*	6	33	44	23	100	30
Four	28	47	25	100	32	30	58	12	100	90
More than four	11	43	46	100	46	9	58	33	100	43
Total	28	43	29	100	107	41	47	12	100	316

Couples who want and have larger families are planning size of family just as successfully as those who want smaller families and who practice contraception effectively.

The next highest correlation is found among the Active Protestants whose initial family-size preferences were 40 per cent lower than the Active Catholics. The Jews who wanted the smallest families were even more successful in avoiding conception but paradoxically show a comparatively low correlation of number of children desired with recent fertility. This is due to the comparative failure of those Jewish couples who wanted larger families to have additional pregnancies during this period. In a sense it seems probable that time is on their side since it is easier to become pregnant than to avoid it over the long term.[9]

Our primary interest at the moment lies in the comparative fertility control of the Active Protestants and Other Protestants and, as we hypothesized, the Other Protestants do disclose the poorer record. In fact, the correlation among this group is the lowest of the five categories.

TABLE 42
Summary of Selected Fertility Differences, by Religion

Fertility Measure	Protestant Total	Catholic Total	Jewish	Active Protestant	Other Protestant	Active Catholic	Other Catholic	All Couples
Mean number of children desired, time I	3.0	3.6	2.8	3.0	2.9	4.2	3.4	3.2
Mean number of children desired, time II	3.0	3.6	2.7	3.0	3.0	4.2	3.3	3.2
Per cent planning first and second or second pregnancies	57	52	86	57	57	40	56	58
Mean interval marriage to second birth (months)	59	56	67	61	57	51	57	59
Per cent having a third pregnancy	51	62	31	43	59	72	59	54
Per cent having a third unplanned pregnancy	33	38	13	24	41	46	35	33
Per cent planning a third of those having a third	36	39	59	44	30	36	40	39
Mean interval between second live birth and third conception[a] (months)	20	18	19	21	19	16	18	18
Per cent planning all pregnancies	34	34	61	43	27	27	37	38
Per cent planning no pregnancies	19	24	8	14	24	28	23	20
Correlation of preferences (I) and number of pregnancies since second birth	.38	.50	.39	.47	.35	.51	.45	.48
Number of couples	372	423	110	174	198	107	316	905

[a] Calculated only for those having a third pregnancy.

The differences in fertility control between Active Protestants and Other Protestants are further elucidated by the statistics in Table 42 which summarize many of the fertility differences across all religious groupings. We see that there is virtually no difference between the two Protestant groups in the average number of children desired by the wife as expressed in either interview (rows 1 and 2). We see further that although both groups as well as the Other Catholics experienced the same success in planning either the first two births or the second birth alone—57 per cent (row 3)—the

[9] This is more true of our selectively fecund sample than a general population.

Active Protestants had an average interval of four months longer between marriage and the second birth (row 4). The critical comparison supporting the proposition that different fertility control levels are involved is the difference in the per cent reporting a third unplanned pregnancy (row 6), or for couples having a third pregnancy the proportion successfully planned (row 7). These comparisons clearly indicate that the Other Protestants have been less successful in implementing their family-size preferences than have been the Active Protestants.[10]

The Other Catholic group bears a closer resemblance to the Other Protestant group than to any of the remaining categories. The main differences are that couples in this category express preferences for more children on the average than do the Other Protestants (due primarily to the inclusion of religious mixed marriages) and show a somewhat better control of recent fertility.

The Active Catholics and the Jews represent the extreme opposites in fertility behavior. The Active Catholics expressed desires for an average of more than four children and the Jews for less than three. Partly as a consequence of these different family-size objectives and partly because of differences in attitudes toward birth control, the Active Catholics have appeared least successful in family planning.[11] The Jews in contrast are in a class by themselves when it comes to avoiding unplanned pregnancies.

Lest we conclude this analysis on the misleading note that differences in contraceptive control are the main explanation of all religious differences in fertility, we should reemphasize the interdependence of number of children desired, fertility control, and number of pregnancies. As we have suggested in contrasting the differences in the contraceptive effectiveness of Active Catholics and Jews, it is obvious that the nature of the control problem is quite different when it is a matter of controlling the *spacing* of births as opposed to controlling the *number* of births. Since contraceptive practice therefore responds partly to the level of motivation which in turn is presumably in good part a function of the number of children desired, and since the number of pregnancies actually occur-

[10] There are no appreciable differences in the incidence of contraceptive usage or in methods used between the two groups. The lack of any differences in the extent of birth control practice among Protestants classified by devoutness and very sharp differences among Catholics so classified is reported in a recent study of the British population. See Griselda Rowntree and Rachel M. Pierce, "Birth Control in Britain. Part I. Attitudes and Practices among Persons Married since the First World War," *Population Studies,* 15 (July 1961), p. 23.

[11] This must be interpreted in the light of different family-size objectives. Having an "unplanned" pregnancy when one wants additional children is obviously not the same as when the family is perceived as complete.

ring reflects the number of conceptions deliberately planned as well as those classified as "unsuccessfully planned," one would expect that the number of children desired would be a better predictor of fertility than would prior fertility-planning success. In other words, the number of children desired can be regarded as antecedent to but not unaffected by both contraceptive success and conception and contains more of the relevant predictive ingredients than does planning-success. This expectation is supported by the evidence presented in Chapter IV where the reduction and convergence of contraceptive failure rates as desired family size is approached is described, and in Chapter VII in which the relative predictive validity for fertility of family-size preferences compared to fertility-planning success is examined.

The Fertility of Mixed Marriages

The main type of mixed marriage with some hypothetical relevance for fertility is one involving a Catholic. No differences in family-size preferences were evident in terms of which spouse was Catholic,[12] but couples married by a Catholic priest did express desires for more children (10 per cent more on the average) than did couples in mixed marriages conducted outside the auspices of the Catholic Church. Being married by a priest of course reflects the desire or willingness of the non-Catholic partner to accommodate his or her own religious views to those of the spouse. This concession means that the individual must receive religious instruction prior to marriage and agree to raise children within the Catholic faith. The Catholic individuals in such marriages are undoubtedly better practicing members of the faith than are those who marry outside the church. Viewed in this context, the comparisons of the fertility of mixed marriages conducted within the Catholic religion with the fertility of those couples involving a Catholic individual not married by a priest can be regarded as a particular case of the theory tying membership in the Catholic Church and adherence to its belief systems with higher fertility.

Comparison of the fertility of Catholic-Protestant marriages[13] which had occurred within the Catholic religion with those conducted outside the Church reveals the expected difference of approximately the same magnitude as that initially reflected by the

---

[12] Westoff *et al.*, *Family Growth in Metropolitan America*, p. 180.

[13] Inclusion of the additional 22 Catholics married to individuals who replied other than Protestant (Jewish, None or Other) does not alter the picture at all. The marriages conducted by a priest were classified in the "Other Catholic" category and the remainder in the "Other Protestant" category.

difference in average number of children desired (Table 43). A total of 70 per cent of couples married by a priest had an additional pregnancy compared to 58 per cent of the couples not married within the Catholic religion.[14] The question of which spouse is Catholic, on the other hand, does not exert any apparent influence on fertility. By comparison with the Protestant and Catholic total

TABLE 43
The Fertility of Protestant-Catholic Marriages

| | Number of Pregnancies | | | | Number |
| | 0 | 1 | 2 | Total | of |
		(per cent)			Couples
By Type of marriage:					
Married by a priest	30	58	12	100	60
Not married by a priest	42	46	12	100	33
By religion of spouse:					
Wife Catholic, husband Protestant	37	51	12	100	43
Wife Protestant, husband Catholic	32	56	12	100	50
All Protestant-Catholic couples	34	54	12	100	93

samples (Table 37) the mixed marriages show a higher proportion having had at least one additional pregnancy but they are intermediate in the proportion having two more pregnancies.

RELIGIOUS OBSERVANCE

Although the classifications of religious affiliation contain criteria of church attendance, it is desirable to look separately at the relationship of fertility and observance of religious values both in the form of the regularity of attendance at religious services and at what we have termed "informal religious orientation." This latter variable combines information from two questions, one on the extent to which religion is included in the home activities of the family and the other on the respondent's self-rating on a scale of religious mindedness apart from attendance at religious services.

Identical questions on the regularity of church attendance as well as questions relating to our measure of informal religious orientation were asked in both surveys. The frequency of church attendance increased for women of all religious affiliations over the three-year period, but not for men. This is probably due to the mother's assumption of responsibilities for the early religious training of children.

In the first analysis, we observed a direct correlation between

[14] This difference falls short of reaching statistical significance.

the number of children desired and both formal and informal indices of religiousness (.29 for wife's church attendance in the total sample).[15] The association was mainly produced by the Catholics in the sample; the other religious groups did not reveal any correlations significantly different from zero. When church attendance and the index of informal religious orientation were correlated with success in planning the first two pregnancies, a positive association emerged for Protestants and Jews and a negative correlation for Catholics.[16] In other words, the apparently more religious Protestant and Jewish parents reported greater success in controlling their fertility than less religious members of these two groups while the more religious Catholics tended to report less success than their more indifferent coreligionists. The latter finding is consistent with both the larger family-size preferences of Catholics as well as Catholic religious doctrine on contraception. The positive correlation among Protestants and Jews was attributed speculatively both to the moral theme of responsible parenthood and the general factor of the more socio-economically successful exhibiting greater evidence of religious behavior.

From these findings, the logical inference is that higher rates of subsequent fertility will be found among the more religious Catholics and probably lower rates among the more religious Protestants and Jews. The latter part of this hypothesis derives from the observation that the correlations of religiousness with fertility-planning success were higher than with the number of children desired.

Although the correlations (see Table 44) with number of pregnancies tend to be low, they support this hypothesis for Protestants and Catholics but not for Jews. The correlations involving the indices of religiousness measured in the first interview for Jews do not differ significantly from zero but there is a sharp increase in value with religiousness as measured three years later, and the association is in the opposite direction from that predicted. Evidently, the change in religious behavior for Jews during these three years has some connection with having another child. When Jewish women are cross-classified according to change in their frequency of church attendance there is an appreciable difference in the recent fertility of those who now go more often than they did three years before (31 per cent had another pregnancy) compared to those who now go less frequently (12 per cent reported an additional pregnancy). A similar difference prevails when those who report the same attendance at both times are divided according to frequency.

[15] Westoff *et al.*, *op.cit.*, pp. 195–196.
[16] *Ibid.*, pp. 197–198.

TABLE 44

Correlations of Number of Additional Pregnancies with Frequency of Church
Attendance and Informal Religious Orientation

| | Wife's Church Attendance | | Husband's Church Attendance | | Informal Religious Orientation (Wife) | |
	After Second Child	Three Years Later	After Second Child	Three Years Later	After Second Child	Three Years Later
Protestant total	−.11	−.17	−.11	−.12	−.14	−.10
Catholic total	.12	.09	.13	.16	.13	.15
Jewish total	.06	.31	.12	.28	.01	.18
All couples	.12	.09	.12	.13	.05	.09

Although we have not been able to demonstrate it conclusively, the impression emerges from a number of side analyses that formal religious observance for Jews and higher fertiltiy are both responses to the feelings of security and stability that accompany socio-economic success rather than operating in any causal sequence. A number of mobility measures seem to suggest this interpretation but at best it remains rather speculative.

SOME FURTHER FERTILITY VARIATIONS AMONG CATHOLICS

Catholic Education

As we have seen, there are rather sharp differences in fertility between the two subdivisions of the Catholic sample labeled "Active" and "Other" Catholics. The major factor differentiating these two groups and that presumably responsible for the fertility differences is the factor of religiousness. In the preceding section we looked at the particular effects of religiousness as reflected in measures of church attendance and informal religious orientation. We now direct our attention to the implications for fertility of education in Catholic schools and institutions of higher learning.[17]

In the first phase of our study, the extent of education in the Catholic school system was observed to have a significant influence on both the number of children desired and fertility-planning success. Those Catholics who were educated exclusively within church-related schools expressed preferences for larger families and exhibited less control over fertility than Catholics whose education was in the public schools. This relationship was found to be sharper for

[17] For a general discussion of the role of Catholic education in American life, see John J. O'Brien, "Catholic Schools and American Society," *Social Order* (February 1962), pp. 77–89.

wives than husbands and was primarily of importance among college-educated persons. One disturbing question of interpretation that kept intruding was the selectivity of attendance at Catholic schools. Is the apparent direct effect on fertiltity of education in Catholic schools merely a reflection of the more religious families educating their children in Catholic schools or does the educational program exert an independent effect on values relevant to fertility? As described in the introduction to this chapter, a few questions were included in the second interview in an attempt to answer this question. Our discussion here will present these findings following the primary analysis of whether education in Catholic schools was predictive of fertility over this three-year period.

The distribution of additional pregnancies is related to extent of education in the Catholic school system[18] (see Table 45) but not as

TABLE 45
Extent of Education in Catholic Schools with Number of Children Desired and Number of Additional Pregnancies

Extent of Education in Catholic Schools	Number of Children Desired After Second Child	Number of Additional Pregnancies				Number
		0	1	2	Total	
WIVES						
None	3.3	41	46	13	100	200
Some	3.7	42	46	12	100	120
All	4.0	27	46	27	100	103
Total Catholic	3.6	38	46	16	100	423
HUSBANDS						
None	3.4	41	49	10	100	215
Some	3.8	35	45	20	100	129
All	4.0	33	40	27	100	79
Total Catholic	3.6	38	46	16	100	423

strongly as might have been expected from the relationship with desired family size. The correlations between extent of education in Catholic schools and number of additional pregnancies are .15 for wives and .16 for husbands. However, these values conceal a considerable variation in the relationship visible when amount of education is controlled. As seen in Table 46 and reflected in the correlations in Table 47, the association between education in the Catholic system and fertility is practically nonexistent if the total amount of education received is less than four years of high school. As we move to the high school graduate level, the relationship increases but is

[18] Lenski reports somewhat similar findings. See Gerhard Lenski, *The Religious Factor*, New York, Doubleday, 1961, pp. 252–53.

still irregular. But as we reach the college level, the association becomes sharp and linear.

More refined analyses of these relationships appear in Tables 48 and 49. The main question is the comparative effects on fertility of a Catholic education at the elementary school level, the high school

TABLE 46

Extent of Education in Catholic Schools and Number of Additional Pregnancies, by Amount of Education

EXTENT OF EDUCATION IN CATHOLIC SCHOOLS[a]	WIVES					HUSBANDS				
	Number of Additional Pregnancies				NUMBER	Number of Additional Pregnancies				NUMBER
	0	1	2		OF	0	1	2		OF
	(per cent)			Total	WIVES	(per cent)			Total	HUSBANDS
	LESS THAN FOUR YEARS OF HIGH SCHOOL									
None	44	53	3	100	57	42	51	7	100	82
Some	38	48	14	100	29	36	50	14	100	28
All	56	44	—	100	18	48	44	8	100	25
	HIGH SCHOOL GRADUATES									
None	39	45	16	100	121	43	46	11	100	89
Some	51	40	9	100	63	43	40	17	100	42
All	26	48	26	100	66	33	40	27	100	33
	ATTENDED COLLEGE									
None	41	41	18	100	22	37	52	11	100	44
Some	25	61	14	100	28	29	46	25	100	59
All	5	37	58	100	19	14	38	48	100	21

[a] The terms "none," "some," and "all" relate to all years of education and not any particular level of educational achievement.

TABLE 47

Correlation of Extent of Catholic School Education with Number of Pregnancies, by Amount of Education

Amount of Education	Extent of Catholic School Education and Number of Pregnancies		Number	
	Wives	Husbands	Wives	Husbands
Less than four years of high school	−.04	.01	104	135
High school graduates	.10	.13	250	164
Attended college	.39	.26	69	124
Total Catholic	.14	.15	423	423

level, and the college level. In order to differentiate the influence of the school *per se* from that of present manifestations of Catholic practice it would be desirable to analyze these relationships among Active Catholics only. In this way we hold constant the important variables of regularity of church attendance, the Catholicism of the spouse and the marriage ceremony, and the fact of at least some

Catholic schooling. At the risk of being misled by the instability of small samples we are able to make these comparisons for both husbands and wives for all levels of education except the elementary school. There is simply not a sufficient number of Active Catholics whose education was less than three years of high school[19] to permit comparison. Among All Catholics, the observation recorded above is pertinent—whether Catholics who did not get beyond two years of high school education had their elementary schooling in a parochial or public school appears to exert no influence on their fertility.

TABLE 48

The Association between a Catholic High School Education and Fertility

	WIVES					HUSBANDS				
	Number of Pregnancies			Per	NUMBER	Number of Pregnancies			Per	NUMBER
	0	1	2	Cent	OF	0	1	2	Cent	OF
TYPE OF CATHOLIC EDUCATION	(per cent)			Total	WIVES	(per cent)			Total	HUSBANDS
ALL CATHOLICS WITH EITHER THREE OR FOUR YEARS OF HIGH SCHOOL										
No education in Catholic schools	39	47	14	100	144	41	49	10	100	123
Catholic elementary school, public high school	52	38	10	100	58	31	50	19	100	42
All education in Catholic schools	29	47	24	100	70	38	38	24	100	37
ACTIVE CATHOLICS[a] WITH EITHER THREE OR FOUR YEARS OF HIGH SCHOOL										
Catholic elementary school, public high school	50	32	18	100	22	36	40	24	100	25
All education in Catholic schools	18	42	40	100	33	35	40	25	100	20

[a] All persons classified as Active Catholics received at least some part of their education in Catholic schools and therefore there is no category of "no education in Catholic schools or colleges" as there is for the "All Catholic" group which includes the "Other Catholics" as well.

The effect of a Catholic high school education on fertility is approached indirectly in Table 48. Only a few individuals who received a Catholic high school education did not attend parochial school so only three combinations exist practically: both elementary school and high school Catholic, neither Catholic, and a parochial school and public high school combination.[20] Looking first at the comparisons for "All Catholics" we note the presence of some association between fertility and attendance at a Catholic high school

[19] The educational classification used here differs slightly from that in previous and subsequent usage. In order to increase sample size for our comparison of the importance of a Catholic high school education, we combined those having three years of high school with those who graduated.

[20] This last combination is very similar to the group in Table 46 classified as high school graduates with "some" education in Catholic schools. It differs in that it includes persons with only three years of high school and does not include the few individuals who attended a Catholic high school and a public elementary school.

but it is not unambiguous. The pattern seems clearer if we concentrate on the Active Catholics who had three or four years of high school. It would appear from this comparison that a Catholic high school education does imply higher fertility for women[21] but not at all for men. There is always the problem of selectivity of course—individuals from more religious backgrounds will be more apt to attend a Catholic high school. To some extent, this problem is compounded by an opposite type of selection—individuals who react negatively to parochial schooling undoubtedly drift toward public high schools.

The really sharp influence on fertility exerted by a Catholic education occurs at the college level as we observed earlier. The

TABLE 49

The Association between a Catholic College Education and Fertility

TYPE OF CATHOLIC EDUCATION	WIVES Number of pregnancies 0 1 2 (per cent)			PER CENT TOTAL	NUMBER OF WIVES	HUSBANDS Number of pregnancies 0 1 2 (per cent)			PER CENT TOTAL	NUMBER OF HUSBANDS
ALL CATHOLICS WHO ATTENDED COLLEGE										
No education in Catholic schools or colleges	41	41	18	100	22	37	52	11	100	44
Nonsectarian college, some earlier Catholic schooling	33	62	5	100	21	43	43	14	100	38
Catholic college, some earlier Catholic schooling	4	42	54	100	26	10	45	45	100	42
ACTIVE CATHOLICS WHO ATTENDED COLLEGE										
Attended nonsectarian college	42	58	—	100	12	41	41	18	100	22
Attended Catholic college	5	33	62	100	21	4	41	55	100	27

[a] See footnote to Table 48.

analysis presented in Table 49 elucidates this effect more clearly by comparing the fertility of persons educated in a Catholic college with that of persons whose education was in a nonsectarian college or university. The relationship appears very strong for both women and men[22] and appears both among All Catholics and Active Catholics. The latter comparison is by far the more interesting since it holds constant several indices of associational involvement in the Catholic religion.[23]

[21] This difference is significant between the five and two per cent levels based on the chi square test.

[22] Part of this is probably due to marital selection.

[23] Even with the small frequencies involved for the Active Catholic sample, the relationship is significant around the .001 level.

Why does fertility respond to Catholic school education primarily at the college level? Exactly the same pattern was evident when we examined the association of desired family size with Catholic school education and partial correlation reveals that the association with actual fertility is almost entirely a function of the relation of Catholic school education with desired family size. A number of possible explanations suggest themselves. Students in Catholic colleges receive instruction in the Catholic philosophy of marriage and the family.[24] It may very well be that Catholics who attend non-sectarian institutions are exposed to values which are more antithetical to those espoused in Catholic institutions at the higher level of learning than at lower levels of education. Also the four more years of education in the Catholic system can be viewed as simply that many additional years of exposure to the value system in the same sense that graduates of Catholic high schools have had more exposure than Catholics who do not reach that level of education. And then there is the possibly greater selectivity of the more religious individuals who continue their education in the Catholic school system. And finally, as we observed in our first analyses[25] those attending Catholic schools are weighted with persons of Irish background[26] which probably implies a stricter interpretation of Catholic doctrine than other ethnic backgrounds. It is possible that this type of Catholic may be found disproportionately at the higher educational attainment levels. This possibility was examined and confirmed. Of the 69 Catholic college women, 30 are of Irish descent. However, it is the association of fertility with Catholic education that is critical. To test this aspect, we separated the Irish from the non-Irish college women and compared the correlations of fertility with extent of Catholic school education. The correlations are close, a value of .35 for women of Irish background and a correlation of .28 for women of all other national origins which confirms the fact that the correlation does not operate only among the Irish.[27]

[24] See Roland G. Simonitsch, *Religious Instruction in Catholic Colleges for Men*, The Catholic University of America Press, Washington, D.C., 1952 and Sister M. Gratia Maher, *The Organization of Religious Instruction in Catholic Colleges for Women*, The Catholic University of America Press, Washington, D.C., 1951. Both of these studies report widespread interest in courses in religion on the subject of marriage and the family.

[25] Westoff *et al.*, *Family Growth in Metropolitan America*, pp. 208–209.

[26] Lenski also reports a greater proportion of Catholics of northwestern than of southern and eastern European background who reported having attended Catholic schools. Lenski, *The Religious Factor*, p. 241.

[27] Holding constant Irish and non-Irish (treating it as a dichotomous variable) produces a partial correlation of .31 between fertility and the extent of Catholic school education in the Catholic college sample. This is a reduction from the zero-order correlation of .39.

Some other hypotheses will be elaborated in the next two sections of this chapter as we turn to an examination of the selectivity of the more religious Catholics into the Catholic educational system and the general question of the relation of ethnic origin to fertility.

The Problem of Selectivity

How much of the relationship between education in the Catholic schools and fertility actually reflects the influence of the educational system and the continuous reinforcement of Catholic values resulting from association with persons likely to have similar attitudes and values, and how much merely reflects the initial selection of religiously affiliated schools and colleges by children from more religious backgrounds?[28] In view of this problem which obscured our interpretation of correlations with desired family size in the first analysis, we attempted in the second interview to secure some measure of the religiousness of the respondent's home environment when she was a child. We realize the difficulty of obtaining such information reliably since recall of this nature and duration will undoubtedly be biased by subsequent events and changes in values. Nevertheless, we felt some information was better than none and we asked the following two questions in the second interview:

"When you were a child, to what extent did your parents include religion in the home activities of your family? For example, family prayers, reading the Bible or other religious materials, saying grace at meals, and so forth. Would you say a great deal, more than average, a little, or not at all?"

"In how religious a home were you brought up? Would you say very religious, religious, not too religious, or not religious at all?"

The responses to both items were summed for each individual and the resulting index produced a correlation of .15 with the number of children desired (as reported in the first interview) and a correlation of .33 with extent of education in the Catholic school system. Partial correlation analysis clearly reveals (Table 50) the educational classification to be the more important variable not only in connection with desired family size but with fertility-planning success and number of pregnancies as well.

With the exception of fertility-planning success on which the

[28] The comparative effects of home and school training on religious knowledge and values is the subject of a projected study the plans for which are described in Joseph G. Keegan, "A Study of the Relationship between Religious Atmosphere in the Home and Amount of Catholic Education, on the One Hand, and the Religious Knowledge and Religious Attitudes of Male Catholics Attending College, on the Other," in Stuart Cook, ed. *Research Plans in the Fields of Religion, Values and Morality and their Bearing on Religious and Character Formation*, The Religious Education Association, 1962, pp. 47–55.

TABLE 50

Correlations of Religiousness of Parental Home and Extent of Education in Catholic
Schools with Number of Children Desired, Fertility-Planning Success, and
Number of Additional Pregnancies

Correlation between	Number of Children Desired	Fertility-Planning Success	Number of Additional Pregnancies
Religiousness of parental home and:	.15	−.03	.12
With Catholic education held constant	.07	.01	.08
Extent of Catholic education and:	.26	−.11	.15
With religiousness of parental home held constant	.22	−.11	.12

religiousness of early home environment produces no visible effect,
early home training does seem to enhance slightly the predictive
value of education in the Catholic school system. Thus the highest
proportion of additional pregnancies among the six categories
formed by cross-classifying the two religiousness variables is located
in the group whose parental homes were above average in religiousness and all of whose education was in Catholic schools (see
Table 51). One-sixth of all Catholics were in this category of which
75 per cent reported an additional pregnancy. A total of 32 per cent
had two additional pregnancies. At the opposite extreme, the lowest
fertility appears among couples below average on the index of religiousness of home environment and whose education was all or
mostly nonsectarian. In this group, 55 per cent had an additional
pregnancy among whom the proportion reporting two additional
pregnancies is one-third of that for the highest fertility group. All
other categories are intermediate.

TABLE 51

The Interrelation of Catholic Education and Religiousness of Early Home Environment
with Number of Children Desired and Number of Additional Pregnancies

Extent of Catholic Education	Index of Religiousness of Early Home Environment	Number of Children Desired after Second Child	Number of Additional Pregnancies			
			0	1	2	Total
			(per cent)			
None	Low	3.4	44	43	13	100
	High	3.3	32	54	14	100
Some	Low	3.4	46	47	7	100
	High	4.0	38	46	16	100
All	Low	3.9	32	52	16	100
	High	4.3	25	43	32	100

Before concluding the analysis of this selectivity we should reexamine the validity of our specific inference about the effect of a Catholic college education on fertility. Since our data on family background relate only to women and since the more theoretically interesting comparison is among the Active Catholics, we compared the distributions of scale scores on the religiousness of the wife's early childhood environment for the two groups of Active Catholic college women who attended either a Catholic or non-Catholic institution. The difference, while in the expected direction, is slight and nonsignificant[29]—which supports our main inferences about the more direct consequences of a Catholic college education.

Ethnic Origin

The relation of nationality background to fertility can be approached from numerous viewpoints including social status, economic position, degree of assimilation, and differences in family structure. Although we shall have occasion to return to the subject in some of these contexts later, the primary interest here is in nationality background as it influences the association of religion and religiousness with fertility.

The proportions having at least one additional pregnancy since the second live birth and the proportion with two pregnancies are shown for each religious group by the main nationality background of the wife and husband[30] in Tables 52 and 53 respectively. These statistics should be interpreted very cautiously since the frequencies on which they are based are often quite small. For the most part, the variability in fertility is greater across religious categories within nationalities than it is across nationalities within religious categories. In other words, fertility is more highly associated with religion than with nationality background. Within the two Protestant categories there is greater variation by nationality than among Catholics in the proportions having at least one additional pregnancy, but the variation by nationality is greater among Catholics when the proportion having *two* pregnancies is considered.

In the initial analysis of group differences in number of children desired by the wife, we had been struck with the sharp differences

---

[29] On a seven point scale, the two means differed by less than half a point. The overall distribution comparison produces a chi square value falling between the .50 and .70 probability values.

[30] The question asked in the first interview was: "What do you consider your main nationality background to be?" Although multiple answers were coded, the tabulations reported here include only the first nationality reported in instances where more than one was reported.

TABLE 52

Proportion Reporting at Least One Additional Pregnancy since the Second Birth, by Religion and Main Nationality Background of the Wife

Religion	Irish	Italian	Slavic	German	British	Scandi-navian	Spanish and Latin American
ctive Protestant	50	*	*	50	36	30	*
)ther Protestant	41	*	33	66	64	*	*
ctive Catholic	78	60	62	73	*	*	*
)ther Catholic	68	53	55	49	70	*	65
ewish	*	*	31	37	*	*	*
PROPORTION REPORTING TWO PREGNANCIES SINCE SECOND BIRTH							
ctive Protestant	0	*	*	7	3	0	*
)ther Protestant	14	*	8	9	14	*	*
ctive Catholic	44	7	19	27	*	*	*
)ther Catholic	13	9	9	3	17	*	30
ewish	*	*	3	11	*	*	*

* Proportion not computed for less than 10 cases.

TABLE 53

Proportion Reporting at Least One Additional Pregnancy since the Second Birth, by Religion and Main Nationality Background of the Husband

Religion	Irish	Italian	Slavic	German	British	Scandi-navian	Spanish and Latin-American
ctive Protestant	*	*	*	46	40	42	*
)ther Protestant	65	*	56	66	48	25	*
ctive Catholic	74	67	61	77	*	*	*
)ther Catholic	54	60	55	63	63	*	63
ewish	*	*	28	35	*	*	*
PROPORTION REPORTING TWO PREGNANCIES SINCE SECOND BIRTH							
ctive Protestant	*	*	*	6	4	0	*
)ther Protestant	13	*	0	18	14	8	*
ctive Catholic	37	17	11	32	*	*	*
)ther Catholic	10	11	9	7	13	*	31
ewish	*	*	1	10	*	*	*

* Proportion not computed for less than 10 cases.

between Catholic women of Irish and Italian descent.[31] At that time we pursued an explanation in terms of differences in religiousness based on the well-documented observation that Irish and Italian cultural backgrounds differ radically in interpretation of Catholicism. After a rather extensive analysis, we reached the conclusion that "most of the differences in fertility between the Irish

[31] The mean number of children desired by Catholic wives of Italian background was 25 per cent lower than that for wives of Irish background.

and the Italian can be explained by differences in religiousness, particularly as indexed by church-connected education.[32] However, there is still some variance in fertility associated with ethnic background that cannot be attributed to religiousness."[33]

It is therefore interesting to see what group differences in actual recent fertility prevail. If we think in terms of all Catholic women, 71 per cent of those of Irish nationality reported at least one additional pregnancy compared to 54 per cent of the women of Italian descent. The proportions reporting two pregnancies in the three-year period are 25 per cent for the Irish and 8 per cent for the Italian. Thus the differences hold as expected. The hypothesis that these ethnic differences in fertility are reducible to differences in religiousness (40 per cent of the Catholic women of Irish background are classified as Active Catholic compared to 14 per cent of the Italian group) is again only partially supported. There is still a difference in fertility between Irish and Italian women within the more homogeneous Active Catholic and Other Catholic categories (Table 52). The differences are not as clear when husbands are classified by nationality background (Table 53) but it is clear from both tabulations, including that for the couples in Table 54, that the Active Catholics of Irish background are in a virtually unchallenged position of highest fertility.

The statistics in Tables 52 and 53 relate only to the nationality backgrounds of wives and husbands separately. A clearer picture can be obtained if we confine the analysis to couples with both spouses having the same ethnic origin (see Table 54). Despite the reduction in numbers, several comparisons are possible. Three features of this table are worth comment. The first is the high fertility

[32] For further evidence of the greater tendency of Catholics of Irish background to send their children to church-related schools, see Peter H. and Alice S. Rossi, "Some Effects of Parochial School Education in America," *Daedalus* (Spring 1961), p. 310.

[33] Westoff *et al.*, *Family Growth in Metropolitan America*, p. 209. It has recently come to our attention that there was an error involved in the calculation of the average number of children desired by Catholic women of different ethnic backgrounds cross-classified by extent of Catholic school education. The erroneous figures appear in the first three numerical columns of Table 57, p. 210, where, as the result of a systematic error in converting coded to raw scores, each mean is 0.5 too high. Since the correction involves reducing each average by a constant, the original interpretation remains unaltered. The corrected figures are:

Extent of Catholic School Education	Mean Number of Children Desired		
	Irish	Other	Italian
None	3.2	3.5	3.2
Some	3.8	3.6	3.6
All	4.5	4.1	3.5

of the couples of Irish background discussed above. The second is the comparatively high fertility of the couples with Latin backgrounds who are classified as Other Catholic. This is a group predominantly of Mexican origin currently living on the West Coast. Their high fertility can probably be explained as a straight carry-over of the parental culture.

The third aspect of the table is the high fertility of the Other Protestant couples with a German background which is not only appreciably higher than Other Protestants of British descent but is

TABLE 54

Proportion Reporting at Least One Additional Pregnancy since the Second Birth, by Religion and Main Nationality Background for Couples with the Same Nationality Background

Religion	Irish	Italian	Slavic	German	British	Spanish and Latin-American
Active Protestant	*	*	*	47	40	*
Other Protestant	*	*	*	73	55	*
Active Catholic	77	*	62	*	*	*
Other Catholic	54	57	50	44	*	60
Jewish	*	*	26	*	*	*
PROPORTION REPORTING TWO PREGNANCIES SINCE SECOND BIRTH						
Active Protestant	*	*	*	7	7	*
Other Protestant	*	*	*	13	10	*
Active Catholic	40	*	6	*	*	*
Other Catholic	8	9	8	0	*	27
Jewish	*	*	2	*	*	*

* Proportion not computed for less than 10 cases.

also very much greater than the fertility of Other Catholics of German ancestry. Although these differences based on such small samples are of questionable statistical significance,[34] we explored some presumably relevant characteristics of these groups to see if any clear pattern emerges. By comparison both with the Other Protestants of British background and Other Catholics of German background, as well as Active Protestants of German background, the Other Protestant Germans showed the following characteristics: lowest proportion in the white-collar class; the highest proportion from rural areas or of recent urban origin; the least successful in

[34] The difference in fertility between couples of German origin in the Other Protestant category compared to that of couples in the Other Catholic category is significant at the 2 per cent level while comparison of Other Protestant Germans with Other Protestants of British descent reveals a fertility difference significant between the 10 and 20 per cent level.

planning any pregnancy; the lowest 1959 income; the lowest amount of income change from 1956 to 1959; the lowest rate of intragenerational mobility; the highest proportion of wives not finishing high school; and, on the average, the youngest wives.

SUMMARY

The major objective of this chapter has been to follow up the very promising relationships between religion and different aspects of fertility found in the first phase of the study. In order to minimize the heterogeneity of the classification "Protestant" we divided the group into couples manifesting some evidence of conformity to religious norms—the "Active" Protestants and, for lack of a more appropriate designation, we labeled the remaining group "Other" Protestants. A similar division was employed for Catholic couples except that the criteria for Active Catholics are both more rigid and comprehensive than for the comparable Protestant category. The Jewish group is too small to permit similar subdivision.

Religion appears to exert a very strong influence on the number of pregnancies occurring in the three and one-half year interval since the second birth, with the Active Catholics at the high end of the continuum and the Jews located at the lower end. The fertility of couples classified as Other Protestant and Other Catholic is very similar while that of Active Protestants approximates that of Jews. A considerable amount of this variation reflects differences in the family-size goals of couples in these religious categories although variations in fertility control cannot be ignored. The analysis draws attention to the relationship between number of children desired and fertility-planning success and emphasizes the multidimensionality of the planning continuum which includes planning the spacing as well as the number of children. This topic is explored at length in other chapters.

In an attempt to pursue further the foundations of high fertility among Catholics, particularly the norm of large-family ideals disclosed in the responses of Catholic couples in the first interview, we included questions probing the respondents' perception of their religious position on birth control and family size. We were especially interested to find that only a minority of Catholic couples perceive their religion as taking a stand in favor of large families, apparently indicating a widespread tendency to distinguish the subjects of birth control and family size. We also uncovered some evidence that a substantial minority (about one quarter) of Protestant couples perceive their religion as taking a positive position on birth control with the main impression being that the themes of "responsible parenthood" recently emphasized by Protestant religions has been communicated to some extent.

Analysis of the fertility of mixed Protestant-Catholic marriages reveals a difference of about the same magnitude in the direction of more pregnancies among couples married by a Catholic priest as that predicted from the initial differences in family-size preferences. On the whole, the expectations about the associations between religiousness and fertility derived from our first analyses were also substantiated.

Special interest was attached to the relationship between Catholic education and fertility and an attempt was made to disentangle the selectivity of who goes to Catholic schools from the effects of the schooling. Although this problem could be approached only in a limited way, the impression that emerges is that education in the Catholic school system exerts an influence on fertility over and above that of a religious home environment in childhood. The level of Catholic education that seems to have striking significance for fertility is the college level; the difference between a Catholic or public high school appears to operate only for women and there is no particualr significance for fertility in whether the elementary school was Catholic or public. These are inferences that need further demonstration, however, since our data are severely strained by the subdivisions required to make the comparisons.

One other approach to variations in fertility internal to religion concerned ethnic origin. As expected from our earlier findings, the Catholics of Irish background, in good part because of their greater involvement in the Catholic faith, manifest the highest fertility. Some other ethnic variations among Protestants were also explored.

It is important to reiterate the limitations of our sample which are especially relevant to generalizations about religious differences. Since the sample is restricted to the largest metropolitan areas, the proportion of Catholics and Jews is much greater than it would be if the nation as a whole had been sampled. But more critical is the fact that the Protestants in our sample are probably different in important respects from Protestants that would be included if the study covered rural areas. One implication of this is that the differences in fertility that we have been describing might diminish in a more extended sample. As the study by Freedman, Whelpton, and Campbell suggests, however, clear-cut differences would remain.

Chapter IX. Socio-Economic Status

In the chapter of the same title in our first report we tested a wide variety of hypotheses about the interrelationships of socio-economic status and fertility. Not only the conventional measures of occupation, income, and education but also numerous measures of related attitudes, values, and perceptions were explored for their implications mainly for family-size preferences and fertility-planning success. In the present chapter we will report the more rewarding of the analyses of the socio-economic dimension with actual fertility over the three-year period. We will concentrate primarily on the interconnections of socio-economic status and religion as they relate jointly but in different ways to fertility. Furthermore, our interest will be confined largely to the predictive importance for fertility of socio-economic variables measured just after the birth of the second child. A subsequent chapter, "Social Mobility," will focus on changes in socio-economic status during the three year period.

OCCUPATION

In the first study we analyzed the comparative importance for the number of children desired of the husband's main occupation and the couple's religion and concluded that religion was by far the more important factor. Some slight differences in average number of children desired (mainly among Catholics) were found when couples with the husband in a white-collar class occupation were compared with blue-collar class couples.

Our present analysis also begins with an evaluation of the relative significance of occupation and religion for fertility. As the proportions in Tables 55 and 56 indicate, the highest fertility tends to be identified with the Active Catholic group and the lowest fertility with the Active Protestant and Jewish group regardless of occupation. However, viewing the comparison by occupation within religion reveals some suggestive variations. For example, the lowest fertility among Active Protestants seems to be concentrated in the managerial and sales groups, while among Active Catholics these two occupational classes reveal the highest fertility. Active Protestants and Active Catholics in the clerical and semi-skilled classes tend to have about the same proportions reporting a third pregnancy but for the Active Protestants these are the highest fertility classes and for the Active Catholics they rank lowest in fertility.

Although such apparent occupational differences are intriguing

TABLE 55
Per Cent Having an Additional Pregnancy, by Occupation of Husband

Occupation of Husband	Total	Protestants		Catholics		Jews
		Active	Other	Active	Other	
Professional	54	43	56	77	80	32
Managerial, proprietary and official	46	26	53	90	64	25
Clerical	56	56	*	53	53	*
Sales	52	28	58	85	50	38
Skilled	55	43	52	67	63	30
Semi-skilled	57	60	67	59	54	*
Service	39	*	*	*	29	*
Unskilled	59	*	*	*	53	*
All couples	54	43	59	72	59	31

* Less than 10 cases.

TABLE 56
Per Cent Having Two Additional Pregnancies, by Occupation of Husband

Occupation of Husband	Total	Protestants		Catholics		Jews
		Active	Other	Active	Other	
Professional	8	—	7	32	17	3
Managerial, proprietary and official	7	—	7	40	9	—
Clerical	25	6	*	29	33	*
Sales	16	6	5	50	9	10
Skilled	11	7	18	11	9	—
Semi-skilled	9	10	13	17	6	*
Service	11	*	*	*	12	*
Unskilled	3	*	*	*	—	*
All couples	12	5	12	29	12	4

* Less than 10 cases.

and some particular differences are statistically significant, the general statistical hypothesis that fertility varies significantly by occupation within each religious group for the most part has to be rejected.[1] Even setting the significance level liberally at .05, only among Other Catholics does occupation appear to associate significantly with fertility. On the other hand, fertility does vary significantly by religion in four of the six occupational classes which contain sufficient frequencies to permit such analysis. Only within the clerical and semi-skilled classes is there apparent homogeneous pro-

[1] Freedman, Whelpton, and Campbell observed that: "The occupational differences in expected fertility are much greater for the earlier cohorts than for the more recent cohorts, which suggests that a definite narrowing of the occupational differences in fertility is under way." Ronald Freedman, P. K. Whelpton, and Arthur Campbell, *Family Planning, Sterility and Population Growth*, McGraw-Hill, New York, 1959, pp. 305–306.

portions of additional pregnancies. With the exception of the clerical class the association between religion and fertility declines with the prestige level or social status of the occupational class. This suggests the hypothesis that religion might be freer to operate in its effect on fertility when financial pressures are lower but such a pattern does not appear when this association is examined within income classes.

OCCUPATIONAL PRESTIGE

In the first analyses of the correlates of desired family size and other fertility variables, we observed that occupational prestige[2] associated directly with the number of children desired by the wife slightly among Catholics and moderately among Jews (correlations of .13 and .31 respectively) but not at all for Protestant women (a correlation of .05). Since actual fertility is a product not only of the number of children desired but also success in achieving family-size objectives, the correlations of occupational prestige with the couple's success in planning fertility up to the second child is relevant to the formulation of the hypothesis about the third child. Although the correlations of occupational prestige and fertility-planning success measured in the first phase were low, they suggested opposite patterns of association by religion—positive for Protestants and Jews (.13 and .07) and negative for Catholics (−.08). From these initial findings we infer that occupational prestige should associate positively with number of pregnancies among Jews and Catholics (the latter since it is easier to plan larger families with less planning success) and probably a negative association for Protestants since the correlation with fertility-planning success seems higher than that with number of children desired. The latter prediction is less obvious than that for Catholics and Jews and could plausibly go in the opposite direction. One- and two-step inferences based on such low correlations are risky at best.

The group of relevant correlations in Table 57, however, supports these inferences made from early analyses. Correlations between the prestige rating of the husband's occupation and the number of pregnancies occurring during the three-year interval are negative for Protestants (−.14) and positive for Catholics (.14) and Jews (.10). The hypothesis that the negative relationship among Protestants operates through differences in fertility-planning success rather than family-size desires receives some support from the

---

[2] As measured by the occupational prestige rating scale described in Cecil C. North and Paul K. Hatt, "Jobs and Occupations: A Popular Evaluation," in Logan Wilson and William L. Kolb, *Sociological Analysis*, Harcourt Brace, New York, 1949, pp. 464–474.

fact that the lowest correlation occurs among Protestants who reported successfully planning all pregnancies since marriage. This conclusion is also supported by low but opposite correlations for Protestants and Catholics between occupational prestige and whether the third pregnancy was planned successfully ($-.12$ and $.10$).

TABLE 57

Correlations of Occupational Prestige and Number of Additional Pregnancies by Religion and Fertility-Planning Success since Marriage

| | | | | | | NUMBER OF COUPLES | | |
| | | Pregnancies Planned | | | | Pregnancies Planned | | |
Religion	Total	All	Some	None	Total	All	Some	None
Protestant	$-.14$	$-.04$	$-.13$	$-.14$	372	128	173	71
Catholic	.14	.20	.11	.18	423	145	171	107
Jewish	.10	.15	.06	*	110	67	34	9
All couples	$-.03$	.05	$-.05$	.02	905	340	378	187

* Too few cases.

These findings, although caution about overinterpretation of low correlations is clearly advisable, reinforce a theory of differential fertility that was suggested by some of our earlier findings. The traditional inverse relationship between fertility and socio-economic status may be primarily an association among the Protestant population in which smaller families were characteristic of couples who used contraception effectively. Given the greater availability and utilization of fertility control in the higher socio-economic groups this would of course lead initially to an inverse association between family size and socio-economic status.

The relationship between socio-economic status and fertility appears to work quite differently among Catholics. Superficially it would appear that the higher Catholic socio-economic classes practice contraception less effectively and thus have more children. The fact that the more religious Catholics, particularly those of Irish descent, are concentrated in these classes, is not inconsistent with this description. However, among Catholics who report having planned all pregnancies since marriage there is a positive correlation (.20) at least between occupational prestige and number of additional pregnancies. The explanation lies in the nature of successful fertility planning. Catholics in the higher socio-economic classes tend to desire larger families and being more religious on the average than Catholics in lower socio-economic classes, use either no contraception or only the prescribed rhythm method and thus tend to be classified more as unsuccessful planners than couples using other forms of contraception. In terms of the relation between desiring larger families and controlling fertility, however, they are planning rationally.

If these two generalizations about Protestant and Catholic fertility differentials are valid, then it is plausible to speculate that the frequently observed changes in the national fertility-class differential may reflect the net effect of the following: a) the continuing diffusion of contraceptive knowledge throughout the lower socioeconomic classes of the Protestant and Catholic populations and a continued decline in their average family size; b) the continuing urbanization of the population and its apparent impact on family-size values and contraceptive knowledge; c) the increasing upward social mobility of the Catholic population which is theorized to have

TABLE 58

Correlations of Occupational Prestige with Number of Additional Pregnancies, and Number of Children Desired by the Wife (Time II) by Religion

Religion	Correlation of Occupational Prestige with	
	Number of Additional Pregnancies	Number of Children Desired (II)
Active Protestant	− .20	− .11
Other Protestant	− .06	.05
Active Catholic	.18	.19
Other Catholic	.10	.07
Jewish	.10	.24

a positive effect on fertility as a result of greater involvement with the Catholic value system; and d) some relaxation in the Protestant middle classes of the pressures to restrict fertility.

This is all extremely speculative and our research design is clearly inappropriate to assessing its validity. However, we can at least empirically assess the hypotheses about the differences between Protestant and Catholic fertility.

The general Protestant-Catholic difference in the association between occupational prestige and fertility reveals a negative correlation for Protestants and a positive association for Catholics. Examination of this same relationship by our classification of religiousness indicates that the most widely disparate groups are the Active Protestants and the Active Catholics. For the former, the correlation is −.20, and for the latter, .18. The correlations for the Other Protestants (−.06) and for Other Catholics (.10) are closer as well as lower. Although statistically undependable, these differences suggest that socio-economic status affects fertility differently in the two religious preference groups but especially in those groups which are more than only nominally affiliated with the religion. Additional evidence of these religious differences can be seen from the pattern of correlations of occupational prestige with the number of children desired by the wife as determined most recently (Table 58), that is, at the time of the second interview. Again we see the similarity of the Other Protestants and Other Catholics (virtually no association) and the wide difference between the Active Protestants and the Active Catholics.

ECONOMIC VARIABLES

Thus far we have been concerned exclusively with socio-economic status as represented and measured by occupation. Of perhaps more direct concern for fertility is the economic status of the couple, a dimension measurable both in terms of income and feelings of economic security. Pursuing the same line of analysis followed for occupation, we examined the correlations of income and feelings of economic security with the number of additional pregnancies. The results of the first analysis showed negative correlations with number of children desired by Protestant women and positive but insignificant correlations for Catholics and Jews.[3] The correlations with actual fertility present the same picture (Table 59). For the husband's 1956 and 1959 earnings, and for the wife's feelings of economic security,[4] there is a negative correlation both with number of additional pregnancies and number of children desired most recently among Protestants and mostly positive but lower correlations among Catholics and Jews.[5] And again the values are consistently higher for the "Active" compared to the "Other" categories.

In the first interview each respondent was questioned directly about how relevant finances should be in considerations about having another child. When correlated with number of children desired this single item produced a $-.37$ value for the total sample, that is, women who perceived finances as relevant tended to prefer

---

[3] C. F. Westoff, R. G. Potter, Jr., P. C. Sagi, E. G. Mishler, *Family Growth in Metropolitan America*, Princeton University Press, Princeton, N.J., 1961, pp. 225–228.

[4] A scale measuring the husband's feeling of economic security reveals lower but essentially similar relations with fertility.

[5] Very little association exists between income and fertility (as measured by "most likely expected total births") in data reported by Freedman, Whelpton, and Campbell. There seems to be a slight negative correlation among Protestants and a nonlinear association among Catholics, although the largest families are expected in the lowest income group. The authors observed that: "Even though the Catholic wives in the lower-income groups *expect* more births than those in the higher-income groups, they would *prefer* to have fewer births than those with higher incomes." *op.cit.*, pp. 300–301.

TABLE 59

Correlations of Economic Variables[a] with Number of Pregnancies and Number of Children Desired by the Wife (Time II) by Religion

| | Number of Pregnancies | | | Number of Children Desired (II) | | |
| | Husband's Earnings | | Wife's Feelings of Economic | Husband's Earnings | | Wife's Feelings of Economic |
Religion	1956	1959	Security (I)	1956	1959	Security (II)
Protestant	−.22	−.17	−.18	−.22	−.14	−.10
Catholic	.05	.12	.03	.10	.10	.11
Jewish	.04	.08	.10	.07	.11	−.05
All couples	−.10	−.05	−.06	−.08	.00	−.02
Active Protestant	−.23	−.23	−.21	−.27	−.19	−.12
Other Protestant	−.19	−.09	−.10	−.18	−.10	−.08
Active Catholic	.12	.19	.04	.20	.21	.16
Other Catholic	.01	.07	−.01	.03	.02	.05

[a] The correlation between the husband's 1956 and 1959 earnings is .64 in the total sample, and the correlations of these two income variables with the wife's feelings of economic security are .48 and .45 respectively. The two scales measuring feelings of economic security at the two different time periods show a .50 intercorrelation in the total sample.

fewer children. The correlation with number of additional pregnancies is considerably lower, −.17 for the total sample. However, in both instances the correlations were higher among Catholics (−.25) than Protestants (.02). The Jewish group produced exactly the same correlation with number of children desired as with number of subsequent pregnancies, a value of −.10.

EDUCATION

The number of years an individual spends in acquiring formal schooling is an index of many different variables theoretically connected with fertility. For some it is a reflection of the social class in which the person has been reared, for others it represents social mobility. It also operates to broaden interests and widen knowledge both of which may exert a competitive effect on familial values. This depends of course on the nature of the education. As we have seen both in the first analysis and in Chapter VIII on religion, higher education in Catholic colleges appears to reinforce if not to promote values compatible with high fertility. In brief, amount of education is expected to relate to fertility in opposite directions for the two major religious groups and to affect fertility both through family-size preferences and fertility-planning success.

Study of the relationship between education and the number of children desired after the second birth revealed positive correlations for Catholics and Jews but little in the way of any correlation for Protestants. In connection with family planning, positive correlations with education emerged for Protestants and Jews and negative associations for Catholics. Analysis of the type of education provided the explanation of the reversals in the direction of the association. We concluded then that "Catholics with the highest education *and* the most education in religious schools exhibit the least tendency to plan fertility and express desires for an average of more than five children. When these relationships are examined for Catholics whose education was secular, the same types of associations

TABLE 60

Correlations of Amount of Education with Number of Additional Pregnancies, Fertility-Planning Status of First Conception after Second Birth and since Marriage, and with Number of Children Desired at Time II

Religion	Number of Pregnancies and Education of		Planning of Third Conception and Education of		Fertility-Planning Success since Marriage and Education		Number of Children Desired (II) and Education of
	Wife	Husband	Wife	Husband	Wife	Husband	Wife
Protestant	−.10	−.15	.03	.07	.11	.10	−.03
Catholic	.17	.18	−.15	−.08	−.15	−.11	.23
Jewish	.13	.04	.01	.02	.15	.09	.30
All couples	.00	−.04	−.01	.04	.04	.05	.05
Active Protestant	−.03	−.13	−.08	.02	.04	.06	.02
Other Protestant	−.10	−.12	.06	.06	.13	.08	−.03
Active Catholic	.22	.25	−.20	−.14	−.16	−.18	.27
Other Catholic	.09	.09	−.11	−.03	−.12	−.05	.12

emerge as exist for non-Catholics. This important finding clearly demands a refinement in generalizations about the relation of education to fertility planning."[6]

The relationship between education (as well as a measure of intelligence[7]) and actual fertility (Table 60) is of the type that would be expected from these earlier findings. Negative correlations obtain for Protestants and positive correlations exist for Catholics (especially Active Catholics) and Jews. The same type of finding was reported by Freedman, Whelpton, and Campbell: "In fact,

[6] Westoff *et al.*, *Family Growth in Metropolitan America*, p. 234.

[7] A measure of intelligence based on a standardized twenty item vocabulary test administered to the wife during the first interview produced a correlation with her level of educational attainment of .51. Analysis of the associations of the scores on this test and subsequent fertility yields almost exactly the same results as the level of her education discussed in the text.

among Catholics, the college-educated wives expect to have larger families than do the wives with only a grade-school education. This is the opposite of the educational differences in expected fertility found among the Protestants."[8]

Quite consistent with this as well as with earlier analyses is the opposite type of relationship of fertility-planning success with education for Protestants compared with Catholics. Although the correlations are very low, there is some evidence to support the hypothesis that higher education implies more control of fertility by Protestants and Jews and less control for Catholics.[9] As we have repeatedly remarked, however, this must be interpreted in the light of the quite different family-size goals of Catholics and Protestants. As is quite clear from the correlations between education and number of children currently desired (last column of Table 60) there is no relationship for Protestants but a clear-cut positive association for Catholics, especially Active Catholics. One way of highlighting this difference is by comparing the two groups on the values of the correlations between education (of wife) and number of pregnancies when the initial number of children desired is held constant. The correlation for Protestants *increases* from −.10 to −.12 while that for Catholics decreases from .17 to .04. The Jewish group shares with the Catholics a positive correlation between education and number of children desired but follows the Protestants in the connection between education and fertility-planning success.

In order to clarify this pattern of association we examined the interrelation of education and fertility among couples who reported planning all pregnancies to date. The correlations in Table 61 reveal an interesting reversal of the relationship among Protestants. The correlations for Protestants change from −.10 and −.15 for fertility and education of wife and husband respectively to positive values of .08 and .08. This is consistent with the reduction of the correlations for Protestants between occupational prestige and fertility from −.14 in the total sample to −.04 among successful planners (Table 57). Similar changes occur among Protestants for correlations with income (from −.22 in the total sample to −.02 among planners) and with feelings of economic security (−.18 to

[8] Freedman, Whelpton, and Campbell, *Family Planning, Sterility and Population Growth*, p. 286.

[9] Although Freedman, Whelpton, and Campbell reported greater disapproval of family limitation among Catholic wives who were college-educated than among those of less education (*op.cit.*, p. 166) the relationship between education and fertility-planning success was positive in both religions. However the correlation for Catholics was lower (.14) than that for Protestants (.28) and might reflect either different proportions of Catholic women educated in Catholic colleges or the presence in the sample of some older Catholic cohorts. (These correlations were computed from data kindly supplied to us by Arthur Campbell.)

.04). The positive correlations for Catholics and Jews in the total sample are typically higher among the couples successfully planning all pregnancies.

TABLE 61
Correlation between Education and Number of Additional Pregnancies among Couples Successfully Planning all Pregnancies, by Religion

Religion	Education of	
	Wife	Husband
Protestant	.08	.08
Catholic	.12	.25
Jewish	.22	.10
All couples	.05	.09

Catholic Education

The association between education in Catholic schools and fertility has already been explored in Chapter VIII. Here we will simply approach the question differently, that is, from the point of view of our interest in the association between education and fertility rather than religiousness. Some of the correlations in Table 62 are in this sense the complement of those appearing in Table 47 in Chapter VIII. Here we see that the correlation between education

TABLE 62
Correlation of Amount of Education with Number of Pregnancies, Number of Children Desired by the Wife, and Fertility-planning Success since Marriage, by Extent of Catholic School Education

	CORRELATION BETWEEN EDUCATION AND						
	Number of Pregnancies		Fertility Planning	Number of Children Desired		Number	
EXTENT OF CATHOLIC SCHOOL EDUCATION	Wife's Education	Husband's Education	Success since Marriage	After Second Birth	Three Years Later	Wives	Husbands
None	.10	.06	−.10	.05	.02	200	215
Some	.07	.12	−.21	.31	.24	120	129
All	.44	.34	−.09	.49	.43	103	79

and number of pregnancies is positive but increases sharply among Catholics all of whose education was in Catholic schools and colleges. Concentrated in this group of course are the Active Catholics.[10] The correlations with fertility-planning success and the num-

[10] The possibility that the Irish group alone might be responsible for the association was examined and rejected. Among Catholic women all of whose education was in Catholic schools, the correlation of amount of education and fertility is .44 among those of Irish background and .34 for those of non-Irish background.

ber of children desired further reveal that this relationship between education and fertility operates through preference rather than lack of control.

SUMMARY INDEX OF SOCIO-ECONOMIC STATUS

These reductions of negative correlations or reversals to positive correlations observed when one compares the relationship in the total Protestant sample with that among couples planning fertility successfully was one of the leading findings of the Indianapolis

TABLE 63

Per Cent Reporting at Least One Additional Pregnancy, by Socio-Economic Status,[a] Religion, and Fertility-Planning Success

	PER CENT REPORTING ADDITIONAL PREGNANCY							
	Total Sample		*Protestant*		*Catholic*		*Jewish*	
INDEX OF S.E.S.	All Couples	Completely Successful Planners	All Couples	Completely Successful Planners	All Couples	Completely Successful Planners	All Couples	Completely Successful Planners
0–10 (Low)	66	33						
11–13	57	15	67	27	59	28		
14–16	48	27	49	13	51	36		
17–19	58	36	52	29	64	45	22	0
20–22	47	32	41	21	63	55	33	23
23–26	52	35	42	27	75	58	29	29
27–30	50	37	48	35	81	78	35	37
31–36 (High)	58	48						
	NUMBER OF COUPLES							
0–10 (Low)	101	33						
11–13	120	26	82	15	133	39		
14–16	159	56	55	16	92	36		
17–19	146	50	59	17	78	29	27	13
20–22	116	62	54	29	41	20	21	13
23–26	100	48	47	22	36	12	17	14
27–30	96	38	75	29	43	9	45	27
31–36 (High)	67	27						

[a] The extremes of the socio-economic status scale are collapsed in different ways for the three religious groups in order to provide larger bases for the proportions.

Study.[11] In order to summarize these religious differences in the association between fertility and socio-economic status as well as to provide some continuity with the Indianapolis Study, we constructed a summary index of socio-economic status using the procedure followed by the earlier study.[12] Since we did not have infor-

---

[11] Clyde V. Kiser and P. K. Whelpton, "Fertility Planning and Fertility Rates by Socio-Economic Status," in P. K. Whelpton and Clyde V. Kiser, *Social and Psychological Factors Affecting Fertility*, 5 vols., Milbank Memorial Fund, New York, 1946–58, II, pp. 359–415.

[12] *Ibid.*, p. 415.

mation on some of the components of the Indianapolis index (such as Chapin's social status scale and net worth)[13] we restricted our index to four components: husband's occupational class, husband's 1956 annual earnings, and the education of each spouse. The scale scores were simply added for each couple in the sample. No particular claims are made for this index; it has the virtues only of face validity and simplicity and serves a useful summary function.

The association of socio-economic status and fertility is described in detail in Table 63 and summarized in part by correlations in Table 64. The relationships follow the pattern suggested above. The values change from negative to positive as we move from the total sample of Protestants to those who planned all pregnancies successfully and the positive correlations initially observed among the total samples of Catholics and Jews increase in value among the successful planners.

TABLE 64

Correlations of Socio-Economic Status with Number of Pregnancies, by Religion and Fertility-Planning Success

Religion	Total	Completely Successful Planners	Semi-successful or Unsuccessful Planners
Protestant	−.20	.10	−.23
Catholic	.20	.29	.17
Jewish	.10	.25	−.11
All couples	−.05	.12	−.07

The differences in the correlations for the Protestant and Jewish groups deserve further comment. As developed in our preceding discussion as well as in the Indianapolis Study and the general research literature on this subject, the explanation of the negative correlation between socio-economic status and fertility among the total Protestant group lies in the intervening variable of fertility-planning success and not in the number of children desired. Thus there is a positive correlation between SES and both the number of children desired and fertility-planning success. As the values in Table 65 indicate this is indeed the case for Protestants and Jews. The question thus becomes why is there a negative correlation between SES and fertility among the total Protestant group and a positive (though low) correlation for Jews? The answer lies in the

[13] We also lacked information on the purchase price of the family automobile which is probably of little status significance today anyway. Since some problems of completeness and reliability exist for our data on rental values which was included in the Indianapolis Study index, this item was also excluded from the present index.

fact that the Jewish group contains close to twice as high a proportion of couples who successfully planned all pregnancies (61 per cent) as the Protestants (34 per cent). As we observed in the correlations among the Successful Planners (Table 64) the direction of the relation is positive for both Protestants and Jews. The explanation that the different signs in the two total samples results from this difference in composition is finally corroborated by the appearance of a negative correlation between SES and fertility among Jewish couples who have been less successful in planning fertility. In other words, Protestants and Jews would be much more similar in the type of association between socio-economic status and fertility if they had more similar records of fertility-planning success.[14]

TABLE 65

Correlation of Socio-Economic Status with Number of Children Desired and Fertility-Planning Success since Marriage, by Religion

| Religion | Number of Children Desired by Wife | | Fertility-Planning Success since Marriage |
	After Second Birth	Three Years Later	
Protestant	.00	−.10	.18
Catholic	.22	.23	−.08
Jewish	.28	.21	.10
All couples	.03	−.01	.10

Although the Catholics in our sample exhibit the same rate of fertility-planning success (34 per cent) as the Protestants, the intrinsic relationship of socio-economic status and fertility among Catholics is different in some respects. The main difference lies in a negative association between socio-economic status and fertility-planning success rather than a positive correlation as observed for Protestants and Jews. The reason for this difference is that the more religious Catholics are at the higher socio-economic levels and, as we have seen, these couples tend to want larger families and thus tend to have used family-planning techniques less "successfully." This accounts for the fact that a positive correlation between socio-economic status and fertility remains even among Catholics who have not been completely successful in planning their fertility.

A further analysis of the national survey data in the Freedman,

[14] For a review of recent literature on Jewish fertility, see Erich Rosenthal, "Jewish Fertility in the United States," *Eugenics Quarterly*, Vol. 8, No. 4 (December 1961) pp. 198–217.

Whelpton, and Campbell study has been published recently[15] which bears directly on this subject. Its objectives in effect were to simulate the future socio-economic characteristics of the American population by using the characteristics of the Jewish group as the model toward which the entire population seems to be moving. The theoretical expectation was that as Protestants and Catholics approach this model fertility differences would diminish and all would approximate the highly rational, small-family norm of the Jewish group. By a matching procedure, subsamples of Protestants and Catholics were drawn to approximate as closely as possible the socio-economic characteristic[16] of the Jews. The authors concluded:

"The general results of this analysis appear to be consistent with the hypothesis that Protestant-Jewish differences in the variables of the fertility complex are a function of differences in a few strategic social and economic background variables. When these background differences are controlled, the differences in the fertility complex are greatly diminished, disappear, or are even reversed.

"However, the unique values of the fertility complex of Catholics cannot be explained in this simple way. Not only do their characteristics persist, but the differences are more likely to be increased than decreased when the effect of the specific social and economic characteristics in this analysis is controlled."

Using the Jewish group as the model of course implies a much higher average socio-economic level than that of Protestants and Catholics. In the light of our analyses which show a definite pattern of interrelationships for Catholics among higher socio-economic status, religiousness, Catholic education, and higher fertility and the negative correlations between socio-economic status and fertility observed among Protestants, these findings are understandable. Significantly, the authors concluded that their "present analysis seems to indicate that the persistent differences are unlikely to disappear simply as a result of movement to higher socio-economic status among the Catholic population."[17] Thus it would appear that at least two major fertility models for the future are emerging and crystallizing—the rational small-family norm ordinarily associated with higher socio-economic status, secular values, and urban residence, and the planned large family along the Catholic model

[15] Ronald Freedman, P. K. Whelpton, and John W. Smit, "Socio-Economic Factors in Religious Differentials in Fertility," *American Sociological Review*, Vol. 26, No. 4 (August 1961), pp. 608–614.

[16] They were matched on occupation of husband, education of wife, income of husband, duration of marriage, metropolitan character of present residence, and farm background.

[17] *Ibid.*, p. 614.

also associated with higher socio-economic status and urban residence but coupled with religious values.[18]

THE INFLUENCE OF RURAL BACKGROUND

In the last few years impressive evidence has been accumulating to connect the relationship between socio-economic status and fertility, and the changes over time in that relationship, with the presence in the urban population of people of recent rural origins. These migrants and the next generation of their descendants tend to be concentrated at the lower levels of the occupational, educational, and income hierarchies. The question then became whether the higher fertility of these socio-economic categories was a reflection of *class* differences in family-size orientations and the motivation and skills to use contraception effectively or whether it represented the importation of a rural culture with its implications for fertility. The test of this proposition has taken the form of examining the correlation between socio-economic status and fertility among the indigenous urban population, that is, those whose parents were also residents of urban areas. The results of this work, initiated and carried through mainly by David Goldberg, have been rewarding. There is now evidence from at least three different American studies that the negative correlation between socio-economic status and fertility either changes to a positive correlation or drops to the level of no association when the recent rural segments of the urban population are eliminated. Such a finding was confirmed on population samples in Detroit,[19] Indianapolis,[20] and most recently on a national sample.[21] The general conclusion that Goldberg suggests is that "we have, in effect, been looking at urban-rural differences when we were attempting to examine socio-economic differentials."[22] And as Freedman and Slesinger conclude from their similar results, "the indigenous non-farm couples will form a much larger part of the American population in the next generation" which may lead to the expectation "that the traditional negative correlation of income and education with fertility will be reduced or

---

[18] The hypothesis of convergence in the fertility of Protestants and Catholics is also rejected on the basis of data from Detroit. See Gerhard Lenski, *The Religious Factor*, New York, Doubleday, 1961, pp. 212–218.

[19] David Goldberg, "The Fertility of Two-Generation Urbanites," *Population Studies*, 12 (March 1959), pp. 214–222.

[20] David Goldberg, "Another Look at the Indianapolis Fertility Data," Milbank Memorial Fund *Quarterly*, 38 (1960), pp. 23–36.

[21] Ronald Freedman and Doris P. Slesinger, "Fertility Differentials for the Indigenous Non-farm Population of the United States," *Population Studies*, 15 (1961), pp. 161–173.

[22] Goldberg, "The Fertility of Two-Generation Urbanites," *op.cit.*, p. 218.

will disappear. It is possible that the correlation will become positive, but there is no evidence yet which suggests that this positive correlation will be very large."[23]

Although numerous questions have been provoked by these studies such as the social mechanisms through which transformation of rural to urban fertility patterns proceed (in Chapter XIII some hypotheses about changes in family structure are tested) there are two specific areas that we can advance with our present data. The first is to find out whether the rural "effects" persist until the third generation. All of our respondents were living in the seven most populous areas at the time they were interviewed (six months after the birth of their second child). The great majority (around 75 per cent) of these had been raised in urban areas as well, and a good proportion (nearly half) of their parents had also been raised in an urban environment. Because of the highly urbanized nature of this sample, we can extract three-generation urbanites and thus approach the question of whether the association between socio-economic status and fertility has become more positive for couples who have been exposed to three generations of urban influences compared both with couples whose parents had rural backgrounds, and with couples who themselves were raised in a small town or on a farm. We will label these third, second, and first generation urban.[24]

The second opportunity afforded by the current data is that our sample is such that we are able to extend the analysis to Catholics and provide some replication on a broader sample of Goldberg's early findings in connection with Detroit. His interest then was in the question of whether the Protestant-Catholic difference in fertility was reduced in a pure urban population.[25] The main concern here will be the question of how the relationship between socio-economic status and fertility in the two religious groups is affected

---

[23] Freedman and Slesinger, op.cit., p. 172.

[24] 1) *Rural*—at least three of the four parents of wife and husband lived on a farm or in a small town and both wife and husband had a similar background.

2) *Recent Urban*—at least three of the parents of rural background but the wife and husband have an urban background.

3) *Urban*—At least three of the parents as well as the wife and husband had an urban background.

There is a residual category containing all couples not classified in the above three categories which in order to keep the previous categories pure constitutes the largest category.

These classifications are based upon replies to the question: "Considering the greatest part of your childhood, were you raised in a small rural town, on a farm, or neither of these?" The succeeding questions were phrased identically in reference to the respondent's mother and father, her husband's childhood, and the childhood of her husband's parents.

[25] Goldberg, "The Fertility of Two-Generation Urbanites," op.cit., pp. 217–218.

by the rural-urban dimension. For example, is the positive correlation between socio-economic status among Catholics and the negative correlation among Protestants possibly due to the greater concentration of a population with a rural background within the Protestant group?

The correlations between socio-economic status and number of additional pregnancies as well as number of children currently desired are presented for Protestants and Catholics[26] in Table 66. Among Protestants there seems to be no difference in the correlations for those who have been exposed to urban influences only since they have been adults (the rural migrants) and couples who grew up in the city. In both of these categories, the usual negative

TABLE 66

Correlations of Socio-Economic Status with Number of Additional Pregnancies and Number of Children Desired, by Number of Generations of Urban Background

Religion and Fertility Variable	*Number of Generations of Urban Background*		
	First	Second	Third
Number of pregnancies			
Protestant	−.26	−.29	.10
Catholic	.24	.25	.25
Number of children desired (II)			
Protestant	−.09	−.23	−.01
Catholic	.10	.22	.35
Number of couples			
Protestant	76	56	61
Catholic	40	71	137

correlation prevails. There appears to be a definite reversal of the association, however, when the population is restricted to Protestants who are third generation urbanites—that is, to couples whose parents and grandparents both resided in urban areas. The correlation now changes to a low positive value. The generalization advanced by Goldberg is thus substantiated but not as elegantly as one might wish. It would seem logical to expect a more orderly progression from a negative to a positive correlation as one turns from the couples who moved to urban areas as adults to couples whose parents moved to cities, to the couples whose grandparents[27] were either born in or moved to cities.

[26] Jews have been omitted because their heavy concentration in the urban population prohibits comparisons.

[27] This is an inference from the fact that the respondents reported their parents to have been reared as children in a city. Thus their grandparents presumably lived in the city but the latter were not, of course, necessarily born in cities.

The picture is quite different for Catholics. Briefly, it makes no apparent difference for the association between socio-economic status and fertility whether or not the urban environment is recent. Of course the Catholics are much closer to foreign origins than are the Protestants but restricting the comparisons to couples of native parentage does not alter the picture. In any event there is no evidence to support the notion that the source of the positive correlation among Catholics is their greater urban heritage. There does seem to be some increase among Catholics in the magnitude of the positive correlation between socio-economic status and the number of children desired with increasing length of urban residence, but no particular pattern emerges for Protestants. This increase may be a result of the higher proportion of Active Catholics in the indigenous urban group (35 per cent) compared with the group raised in rural areas (16 per cent of whom are classified as Active Catholic). The intermediate recent urban group reveals an intermediate proportion of Active Catholics (23 per cent). This explanation involves the knowledge of the joint associations among the classification Active Catholic, higher socio-economic status and higher fertility.

One further replication and extension of the research by Goldberg and others is possible with our data. The primary mechanism through which the negative correlation between socio-economic status and fertility becomes converted to a positive correlation is through the increasing ability to have the number of children desired that presumably results from increasing exposure to the urban culture. Thus among the Indianapolis (Protestant) couples Goldberg found a substantial diminution, disappearance, or reversal of the negative correlation among couples of rural origins, comparing all couples with those planning both number and spacing of births. The highest correlations were among the indigenous urbanites in this successful fertility control category.[28]

Our data also support this pattern of relationships (see Table 67) although the samples are small. Among Protestants the highest negative correlations appear in the most recent urban group among couples who were less than completely successful in planning fertility thus far. And within these "planned" categories the magnitude of the negative correlation appears to decline as we move from first, to second, to third generation urban. On the other hand, among Protestants who have so far planned all pregnancies successfully, the correlations between socio-economic status and fertility are positive. Among Catholics, however, none of this seems to matter—a positive correlation between socio-economic status and fertility appears in all categories.

28 Goldberg, "Another Look at the Indianapolis Fertility Data," p. 27.

TABLE 67

Correlations of Socio-Economic Status with Number of Additional Pregnancies, by Number of Generations of Urban Background and Fertility-Planning Success since Marriage

Religion and Number of Pregnancies Planned Successfully	Number of Generations of Urban Background			Number of Generations of Urban Background		
	First	Second (correlations)	Third	First	Second (Number of couples)	Third
All planned						
Protestant	.23	.24	.20	25	18	17
Catholic	.16	.23	.26	14	26	46
Some planned						
Protestant	−.37	−.26	.11	36	29	33
Catholic	.25	.24	.20	14	33	59
None planned						
Protestant	−.34	−.19	−.06	15	9	11
Catholic	.08	.19	.27	12	12	32

ATTITUDES ASSOCIATED WITH SOCIO-ECONOMIC STATUS

The first interview contained many questions asked of both wives and husbands which aimed at complementing objective socio-economic data of the nature presented above with a variety of attitudinal and perceptual variables. Although each one of the variables is derived from somewhat different theoretical considerations we can discuss some of them collectively since they involve the general socio-economic dimension.

Two such variables relate to different aspects of the husband's work. The first, termed Commitment to Work Values, attempted to measure the importance the husband attached to the work life, that is, whether he valued his work as an end in itself rather than simply a means. This variable had produced weak positive correlations with the number of children desired by the husband.[29] Among Protestants and Jews a weak positive correlation with fertility-planning success was seen but among Catholics the correlation was negative. Although all of these initial values were quite low, the differences seem to be reflected in the correlations with the number of additional pregnancies (Table 68). Among Catholics, especially the Active Catholics, a positive commitment to work values by the husband associates directly with number of pregnancies; among Protestants, resulting from the correlation among Active Protestants, and among Jews, the correlation is negative.

The second variable measured the wife's satisfaction with her

[29] Westoff et al., Family Growth in Metropolitan America, p. 223.

husband's job as she perceived its hours, steadiness, income, and opportunities. The correlations with fertility present the same pattern described in connection with the husband's commitment to work values[30]—a negative correlation for Protestants and a positive association among Catholics. Again the larger values appear in the Active rather than the Other groups. No correlation appears for Jews.

Two other variables relate to the couples' degree of satisfaction with their achievements and status in life. A scale labeled Achievement of Life Goals is based on the wife's responses to questions about how life has worked out for her so far and how confidently she can plan ahead for the future. Although other factors are involved, the socio-economic theme predominated in the pretest experience with these questions and the scale also showed strong

TABLE 68

Correlations of Selected Attitudinal Indices and Number of Additional Pregnancies, by Religion

Attitudinal Index	Protestant	Catholic	Jewish	All Couples	Protestant		Catholic	
					Active	Other	Active	Other
Husband's commitment to work values	−.06	.13	−.05	.00	−.16	.01	.24	.09
Wife's satisfaction with husband's job	−.18	.10	−.01	−.03	−.17	−.14	.23	.05
Wife's achievement of life goals	−.03	.10	.04	.03	−.03	.00	.20	.02
Husband's level of status satisfaction	−.08	.20	.00	.03	−.14	.00	.43	.09

correlations with such scales as feelings of economic security. Another scale measured the husband's level of status satisfaction in terms of how satisfied he would feel if his son enjoyed the same standard of living when he reached his age.

When religion is considered, both of these scales again reveal the same type of association with fertility as that described for the previous two scales. A positive correlation occurs for Catholics, especially among Active Catholics, and either a negative or hardly any correlation for Protestants with the sharper value tending to appear for the Active Protestant group.

Most of these correlations individually are unimpressive. Considered together, however, especially in conjunction with the correlations of the socio-economic status variables themselves, they form a rather consistent pattern. Among Protestants the correlations of fertility with these socio-economic attitudes are consistently neg-

[30] The correlation between the two scales is .31.

ative and this pattern appears mainly for those classified as Active. Among Catholics, on the other hand, the correlations are consistently positive, especially among the Active Catholics. It would seem that Catholics, especially those most involved with Catholic values and generally satisfied with their socio-economic status and who are committed to work and career, tend to regard children as quite compatible. No relationships of any magnitude or pattern emerge for Jews. Thus, the different associations tend to cancel each other and to produce no relationship at all in the total sample.

CHANCE-TAKING

One hypothesis advanced in our first analysis was that an increasing income and increasing feelings of economic security might be accompanied by an increasing casual attitude toward fertility control. In other words, under circumstances where the couple's standard of living would not be jeopardized by the advent of an additional child a couple may become less vigilant or more careless about contraceptive precautions. One form of such carelessness is "taking a chance" and occasionally omitting contraception. If such an hypothesis could be substantiated it would provide one theoretical basis for explaining some part of the increase in fertility during the last twenty years which has been presumably accompanied by a steady increase in the availability of contraception. Much of this fertility renaissance undoubtedly reflects a genuine change in concepts of ideal family size but survey research has certainly also revealed a rather high incidence of uncontrolled fertility.

The analyses of chance-taking during the first two birth intervals did not offer any support at all to the hypothesis but we felt at the time that it warranted further testing in the second phase of the study.[31] To be brief, an extensive investigation of this same hypothesis based on experience during the three-year interval between interviews again produces no substantiation whatsoever.[32] Two indices of chance-taking were employed—the proportion of all accidental third pregnancies conceived when contraception had been temporarily omitted, and this same type of exposure expressed as a proportion of all exposure. Although there is some unreliability in the measurement of chance-taking[33] there is probably not enough to obscure the presence of a relationship if any exists. Both of these indices were tabulated by income, changes in income at different

[31] Westoff *et al., op.cit.,* pp. 229–231.

[32] For further analysis of the extent and implication of "chance-taking" see Robert G. Potter, Jr., Philip C. Sagi, and Charles F. Westoff, "Improvement of Contraception During the Course of Marriage," to be published.

[33] See Appendix C on "Reliability of Data on Family Planning."

times during the marriage, the wife's perception of the husband's opportunities to get ahead, occupational mobility, feelings of economic security as measured at both interviews, and change in feelings of security. No evidence of any kind emerges to connect these variables with the tendency to risk pregnancy by omitting contraception. Thus a hypothesis which seems both plausible and theoretically significant continues to be rejected.

SUMMARY AND CONCLUSIONS

One of the leading conclusions of recent American research into socio-economic differences in fertility is that such differences are definitely tending to contract as a result both of the increased fertility of the middle classes and the increasingly greater control over fertility in the working classes. The present study was not designed to make any direct contribution to this subject; our sample does not include a sufficient range of birth or marriage cohorts and is too homogeneous in its initial fertility experience to be particularly useful in this connection. Moreover, the sample was confined to the largest metropolitan areas. However, the nature of the relationship of socio-economic status with religion and religiousness does suggest that possibly the narrowing of socio-economic differences in fertility *may* be occurring in part as a consequence of the widening of religious differences in fertility. This is largely speculative; our findings can in no way be interpreted to bear directly on this point. What does provoke the speculation is the rather consistent differences between Protestants and Catholics in the direction of the association between socio-economic status and fertility. The values are uniformly negative for Protestants and positive for Catholics, regardless of whether education, occupational status or income is considered. Attitudes relevant to the socio-economic dimension also follow the same pattern. For the numerically less important Jewish group the correlations between socio-economic status and fertility are also positive. For both Catholics and Jews these correlations reflect initial positive correlations between socio-economic status and the number of children desired. Successful fertility planning, however, is positively associated with socio-economic status (mainly education) among Jews and negatively for Catholics, a relationship that must be interpreted in the light of the quite different family-size orientations of the two groups.

The picture for Protestants is very different. The association of higher socio-economic status with smaller families is consistent with a tendency toward greater fertility-planning success at the higher socio-economic levels but finds a background in smaller family desires only in the case of income. Education and occupation appear not to be related to family-size desires of Protestants.

One inference that might be drawn from this mosaic is that as the socio-economic status of Protestants improves on the average their fertility will decline. On the other hand, as the level of living of Catholics improves there may be a greater identification with the Catholic value system which could lead to higher fertility. From this point of view, it will be interesting to explore the connections of individual social mobility with fertility within the religious preference groups.

There are some difficulties with this theory however. First we know from the recent national study by Freedman, Whelpton, and Campbell that the "most likely expected total births" of recent birth cohorts of mothers has increased for both Protestants and Catholics.[34] However, it may be important that, despite the overall narrow range of differences, the relative increase in expected family size appears much greater among Catholics than Protestants. Thus, if we compare the increase in expected completed family size of Protestant married women born in 1916–20 with that of Protestant women born in 1931–37[35] we find an increase of 4 per cent on the average (from an average of 2.8 children to 2.9 children). The comparable increase for Catholic women is 23 per cent (from 3.1 to 3.8 children). The Catholic increase, moreover, is entirely due to the expectations among the most religious Catholics. Among Catholic women who attend church regularly the expected completed family size has increased by 40 per cent (3.0 to 4.2 children) from the 1916–20 to the 1931–37 cohort while among those attending church only rarely, there appears to be a 20 per cent *decrease* (from 3.5 to 2.8 children) in the making.[36] The general demographic significance of such changes must of course be qualified by religious group differences in age at marriage, marital stability, and the like. But it would appear that the recent increases in marital fertility were much more sharply manifested among religious Catholics than any other segment of the population.

There is one further consideration relating to these speculations which modifies the hypothesis of increasing divergence—the influence of urban residence on the correlation between socio-eco-

[34] Their 1960 survey indicates a reversal of this trend as evidenced by the expected fertility of the most recent cohort (1936–40) which is lower than the expected fertility of women of comparable age in 1955 as well as that of the next oldest cohort. (From data supplied by Whelpton and Campbell in private correspondence.)

[35] Freedman, Whelpton and Campbell, *Family Planning, Sterility and Population Growth*, p. 276. Calculated from data presented in Table 9-2.

[36] *Ibid.*, p. 283. Calculated from data presented in Table 9-6.

nomic status and the fertility of Protestants. If the correlations are dependable, it would seem that the experience of successive generations of urban living has the effect of making Protestants behave more like Catholics in terms of the relationship between socio-economic status and fertility. This does not imply that the Protestant-Catholic differential in fertility will necessarily diminish—since the religious dimension is much stronger than the socio-economic one—but rather that the fertility of both Protestant and Catholic couples may in the long run respond in similar ways to the socio-economic factor. This convergence will occur for different reasons. Among Protestants it will reflect the increasing control over fertility by couples at the lower socio-economic levels. The basic dynamic in the positive correlation among Catholics, however, seems to be the larger family-size orientations of the more successful and more religious couples.

Chapter X. Social Mobility

There are few areas of research which were so thoroughly explored in the first phase of this study as the connections between fertility and social mobility. At least twenty-five different approaches[1] to its measurement were attempted. Mobility was measured in occupational and financial terms, across and within generations; it was measured from the wife's and the husband's class of origin, and in terms of perceptions, attitudes, and aspirations. The general theme was to test the hypothesis that upward social mobility or higher levels of aspiration would be associated with smaller family orientations on the assumption that "the socio-economic and psychological requirements for upward mobility are inconsistent with expenditures of time, energy, and money for children."[2] This has been the standard, now almost classical, notion connecting fertility with mobility (at the micro socio-economic level) and has been tested in part with varying results in different times and on different samples. Most of the prewar studies and those conducted in the early 1940's confirmed the general hypothesis; more recent studies for the most part[3] suggest a change in this association which is undoubtedly connected with the change in the relation of fertility to socio-economic status.[4]

The analyses contained in the following pages represent a continuation of this line of interest. Although the scope of our inquiry has narrowed, largely as a result of rather unpromising findings in the first phase of the study, we are here concerned essentially with the question whether variations in fertility or changes in the number of children desired over the three-year period between interviews are in any way connected with concomitant change in socio-economic status, or show any evidence of having responded to earlier

[1] For an analysis of the interrelations among 22 of these variables, *see* Charles F. Westoff, Marvin Bressler, and Philip C. Sagi, "The Concept of Social Mobility: An Empirical Inquiry," *American Sociological Review*, Vol. 25, No. 3 (June 1960) pp. 375–385.

[2] C. F. Westoff, R. G. Potter, Jr., P. C. Sagi, E. G. Mishler, *Family Growth in Metropolitan America*, Princeton University Press, Princeton, N.J., p. 237.

[3] In a test of the mobility-fertility hypothesis on Brazilian data collected in 1959–60, Bertram Hutchinson found evidence that the fertility of those moving from a manual parental class of origin to a nonmanual class was intermediate between that of those families remaining in the same classes in both generations. Brazil however is a country in which (according to this same study) fertility is clearly related inversely to socio-economic status. See Bertram Hutchinson, "Fertility, Social Mobility and Urban Migration to Brazil," *Population Studies*, 14 (March 1961) pp. 182–189.

[4] Some of this literature is reviewed in Westoff *et al.*, *Family Growth in Metropolitan America*, pp. 237–240.

patterns of social mobility. The analyses are organized around changes in occupational status, in income, in perception of opportunities, and level of aspirations.

Occupational Mobility

In the first phase of this study we tested the traditional hypothesis that indications of low fertility would characterize couples whose occupational status had improved either by comparison with their own status during the first year of their marriage or with the occupational class of their parents. The hypothesis as a whole was rejected. Only among the Jewish group did movement from a blue-collar class origin in the previous generation to a white-collar status seem to imply lower fertility, and even this association was weak and not unambiguous. Among Protestants, no association appeared at all, and for Catholics the fact of current occupational status had much greater significance for fertility than did the pattern of inter-generational occupational mobility. And even this result was contrary to the spirit of the hypothesis with the indications of highest fertility found in the white-collar class. When by the use of a prestige scale the measure of occupational mobility was expanded to include finer shifts than those implied by the white-collar and blue-collar classification, no correlations with fertility of any significance emerged. This conclusion applied not only to inter-generational mobility but also to changes of occupational status within the husband's own career.

The question which now remains to be answered is whether fertility following the second birth is in any way connected with: (1) movement between white-collar and blue-collar classes across generations; (2) finer changes in occupational prestige achieved across generations; (3) mobility between marriage and the second birth, and (4) changes in occupational status during the three-year period following the birth of the second child. Our first question is answered in Table 69 where the proportions of couples in either the white-collar or blue-collar class (at the time of the second birth) who had additional pregnancies are examined in terms of the occupational class of the husband's father. Among Catholics, the expectations suggested in the first analysis are supported with the highest fertility indicated for couples in the white-collar class, especially in that segment of the class with white-collar class origins. Among Jews also, the same pattern as observed initially appears but among Protestants there is now an appearance of higher fertility among blue-collar couples of blue-collar origin, a difference which in view of the previously observed homogeneity of family-size desires suggests less effective control of fertility. In any event, with the possible exception of the Jews there is still no evidence to support the general hypothesis that upward mobility is associated with lower fertility, at least in terms of the occupational structure crudely dichotomized.[5] The remaining questions posed above are approached in Table 70 where the association of fertility with occupational mobility calculated on scales of social prestige is examined. This form of measurement is intended to permit testing the mobility hypothesis on a more continuous scale than that afforded by the previous analysis, without the disadvantage of limiting the variable of mobility only to changes across the white-collar blue-collar line. The correlations in Table 70 again offer no encouragement to any hypothesis connecting fertility and occupational mobility either across or within generations. The values with a few, probably chance, exceptions are quite low and there is no statistical basis for assuming heterogeneity across religious categories.

TABLE 69

Number of Additional Pregnancies, by Occupational Class of the Husband,[a] Classified by the Longest Occupational Class of His Father

Longest Occupational Class of Husband's Father	Husband's Occupational Class					
	Protestants		Catholics		Jews	
PER CENT WITH AT LEAST ONE ADDITIONAL PREGNANCY						
	White Collar	Blue Collar	White Collar	Blue Collar	White Collar	Blue Collar
White-collar	47	47	73	60	34	*
Blue-collar	47	59	64	57	25	*
PER CENT WITH TWO ADDITIONAL PREGNANCIES[b]						
	White Collar	Blue Collar	White Collar	Blue Collar	White Collar	Blue Collar
White-collar	5	9	26	11	4	*
Blue-collar	5	14	25	8	4	*

* Indicates insufficient numbers.

[a] Occupational class at the time of the birth of the second child.

[b] These pregnancies are included in the preceding percentages of couples with at least one additional pregnancy.

On the chance that the correlations were masking more complex associations, each of the three mobility measures (inter-generational, from marriage to the second birth, and over the last three years) was first divided according to whether the mobility was upward or downward, or showed no change in occupational prestige.

[5] Essentially the same generalizations are appropriate for intergenerational mobility measured from the wife's rather than the husband's father's longest occupation.

Then the patterns produced by this combination were examined for variations in fertility within each religious category separately.[6] However, even capitalizing on chance variations implied by such a procedure produces no theoretically suggestive findings. The conclusion that occupational mobility (as measured) and fertility are unrelated in this sample again seems inescapable. The parenthetical phrase in the preceding sentence is more than merely a standard disclaimer. The measures of occupational mobility employed in this analysis, quite aside from the basic questions of their role in the parent concept of social mobility,[7] are at best crude, superficial, and probably highly unreliable for the nature of the hypotheses being

TABLE 70

Correlation between Occupational Mobility and Number of Additional Pregnancies

Occupational Mobility	Protestant	Catholic	Jewish	All Couples	Protestant Active	Protestant Other	Catholic Active	Catholic Other
*ter*generational mobility[a]								
Total	−.02	.05	.05	.01	−.17	.09	.06	.03
Among successful planners	.00	.12	.10	.07	−.08	.13	.23	.07
*tra*generational mobility[b]								
Total	−.01	.01	.17	.01	.02	−.04	.07	−.02
Among successful planners	.04	.05	−.16	.01	.15	−.11	.36	−.02
*cc*upational mobility, 1957–60[c]								
Total	−.01	.03	−.13	.01	−.05	.02	.01	.03
Among successful planners	.08	.10	−.04	.07	.11	.04	.28	.03

[a] Measured as the difference in the prestige score assigned to the husband's occupation six months *er* the birth of the second child and the prestige score assigned to his father's main occupation.

[b] Measured as the difference in the prestige score assigned to the husband's first full-time occupa-*n* after marriage and his occupation six months after the birth of his second child.

[c] Measured as the difference in the prestige score assigned to the husband's present occupation *60*) and his occupation six months after the birth of his second child (1957).

tested. In addition there are always the questions of whether more homogeneous samples of occupations or stages in the life cycle might be necessary to uncover relationships. In view of these rather serious methodological difficulties it perhaps seems presumptuous to arrive at such a negative conclusion.

CHANGE IN INCOME

The variable of income is fortunately more measurable than the more elusive dimension of occupational prestige. The reliability of its measurement is probably no greater and perhaps even worse

[6] Only 16 of the 27 possible combinations proved large enough to analyze statistically but these accounted for between 85 and 90 per cent of the respondents in the three major religious categories.

[7] See Charles F. Westoff, Marvin Bressler, and Philip C. Sagi, "The Concept of Social Mobility," *op.cit.*

than that of occupation but at least it possesses less difficult scaling problems. The analysis that follows is concerned primarily with the relationship between fertility since the second birth and changes in income during the three-year period under observation. The average earnings of the husbands in this sample during 1959 were $6,270, representing an estimated[8] increase since 1956 of approximately 15 per cent. The largest gains were recorded by the Jewish group, followed by the active members of both Protestant and Catholic denominations, while the lowest increases were experienced by husbands in the nominal Protestant and Catholic categories.

Our previous analysis of the relationship between income change and fertility was complicated by variations in marriage duration. Since income change was measured between marriage and the year (1956) prior to the interview and, since time itself is related to the probability of income change, any connection of income change with future fertility was obscured by their associations with marriage duration. Various techniques of standardization were employed, all of which produced final correlations of negligible magnitude between income change and number of children desired. The present analysis is largely uncomplicated by this factor since the interval of elapsed time (three years) between the points of measurement is a constant for all respondents.[9]

The correlations between the number of pregnancies since the second birth and income change are presented in Table 71 for three different measures of change: (1) change between the husband's earnings in the first year of marriage and his earnings in 1956 (this contains the problems associated with marriage duration); (2) change in the husband's earnings derived by subtracting his 1956 earnings from those of 1959; and (3) a qualitative estimate by the wife of how much she perceived a change in their income over this three year span. The negative correlations between fertility and income change in the interval between marriage and second birth are consistent with earlier findings and involve the interpretive problems described above. Among successful planners, correlations for all groups are negligible except among Active Catholics where the value is .29. The relationship between income change during

---

[8] Lack of more precision is a result of changes made in the scale intervals of income in the second interview.

[9] There is one complication remaining, however. Although we did collect income data for each of the three intervening years, we have not attempted to trace the exact timing of any connection between change in a particular year and the year of the conception because of a lack of information on advance knowledge of such changes. One result of simply analyzing change over a three year period is that some husbands may have taken on extra work as the result of a child and therefore contribute, in a sense deceptively, to a positive correlation between income change and fertility.

1956–59, both quantitatively and qualitatively measured, and number of pregnancies appears to be zero for all intents and purposes. The only importance that should be attached to these values is that they probably constitute a better estimate of the true underlying relationship than does the measure involving marriage duration. Only among Active Catholics does there seem to be some persistent evidence of a correlation between income change and fertility, and this correlation is positive.

The present correlational analysis assumes that the underlying relationship is linear, an assumption that may be particularly inappropriate for the relation of income change and fertility. Income change might be relevant to fertility only at the lower income levels

TABLE 71
Correlations of Changes in Husband's Earnings and Number of Pregnancies

Measure of Income Change	Protes- tant	Catholic	Jewish	All Couples	Protestant Active	Protestant Other	Catholic Active	Catholic Other
Change between marriage and second birth								
Total	−.20	−.11	.02	−.17	−.24	−.17	−.03	−.12
Among successful planners	−.05	.04	.01	−.02	−.08	.00	.29	.00
Change between 1956 and 1959								
Total	.04	.09	.04	.06	−.01	.08	.13	.06
Among successful planners	.04	.04	.04	.02	−.05	.15	.13	−.03
Perceived change[a] between 1956 and 1959								
Total	−.02	.11	.03	.03	−.09	.07	.21	.06
Among successful planners	.04	.13	.02	.06	.01	.07	.36	.04

[a] "Perceived change" is based on the question: "Comparing 1959 income to 1956, has your husband's income gone up a lot, gone up a little, gone down a lot, gone down a little, or remained the same?"

or, as another possibility, the relationship between change in income and fertility might be negative in the lower income classes and positive at the higher income levels. Such possibilities are examined in Table 72 where the full detail is presented for Protestants and Catholics in thousand-dollar income classes ranging from under $4,000 to over $10,000. The number of cases in each income-change category is very small so caution is advisable in interpreting the results. Among Protestants no association of any systematic kind seems to exist. Among Catholics the only sign of any relationship is[10] a tendency for fertility to be somewhat higher among couples who experienced sharp increases in income. This does not occur,

[10] Reorganizing the whole analysis and viewing income change from the vantage of current (1959) income does not offer any further evidence of association.

however, in the lowest income group (where the opposite prevails), but the general pattern is consistent with the low positive correlation observed for Catholics.

TABLE 72

Number of Pregnancies, by Change in Husband's Earnings between 1956 and 1959, for Protestant and Catholics

	Protestants Number Additional Pregnancies				Number of Couples	Catholics Number Additional Pregnancies				Numbe of Couple
Husband's 1956 Earnings and Change by 1959	0	1 (per cent)	2	Total		0	1 (per cent)	2	Total	
Under $4,000										
Same or less	25	56	19	100	16	38	50	12	100	8
Up $1,000	46	39	15	100	13	37	46	17	100	24
Up 2,000	46	27	27	100	11	14	79	7	100	14
Up 3,000 or more	57	43	—	100	14	45	45	10	100	20
$4,000–4,999										
Same or less	27	64	9	100	22	48	44	8	100	25
Up $1,000	36	48	16	100	25	36	39	25	100	36
Up 2,000	29	57	14	100	21	43	40	17	100	30
Up 3,000 or more	27	60	13	100	15	27	55	18	100	11
$5,000–5,999										
Same or less	48	45	7	100	29	45	38	17	100	47
Up $1,000	63	26	11	100	27	73	21	6	100	33
Up 2,000	68	23	9	100	22	28	60	12	100	25
Up 3,000 or more	44	39	17	100	18	24	43	33	100	21
$6,000–6,999										
Same or less	47	47	6	100	21	33	54	13	100	24
Up $1,000	44	56	—	100	9	29	57	14	100	14
Up 2,000 or more	50	50	—	100	12	14	53	33	100	15
$7,000–7,999										
Same or less	53	47	—	100	15	40	40	20	100	15
Up $1,000	79	14	7	100	14	29	57	14	100	14
Up 2,000 or more	54	39	7	100	13	27	55	18	100	11
$8,000–10,000 or more										
Less	67	33	—	100	9	14	72	14	100	7
Same	61	39	—	100	33	40	47	13	100	15
Up	54	46	—	100	13	—	83	17	100	6

THE PATTERN OF INCOME CHANGE

Thus far we have viewed change in income as the difference in annual income at the beginning of a three-year period (1956) and its termination (1959). There are annual variations concealed by this procedure, of course, that might be relevant for our analysis of fertility. Couples whose income goes up every year may have quite different orientations from couples for whom such change is less regular or who may occasionally experience decreases.

Detailing the pattern of income change in each of the three years (in each year it could have gone up or down or remained the same) and holding religion constant simultaneously does not afford sufficient frequencies for analysis. We did examine some of the more common sequences but finally decided in effect to average the reported annual pattern over the three-year period. We assigned a

TABLE 73

Relationship between the Directions of Annual Income Changes during the Three-Year Interval and Number of Pregnancies
(Per Cent Having Additional Pregnancy)

Index of Income Change	Direction of Net Change	Active Protestants	Other Protestants	Active Catholics	Other Catholics	Jews
1–2	Downward	58	54	69	59	23
3	Stable	47	53	64	54	23
4	Slightly up	38	62	62	59	40
5–6	Upward	43	63	83	67	26
Correlation of index with number of pregnancies		−.06	.11	.15	.09	.03

value of zero to a report of a downward change, a "1" to no change, and a "2" to a reported upward change. The resulting index thus ranges from 0 (actually there were no instances reported of three consecutive income declines) to a value of 6 for a couple whose income increased in each of the three years. An increase or decrease from one year to the next was measured only in changes across gross thousand-dollar intervals.[11] The mean score for the total sample on this scale is 3.8.

The proportions in Table 73 are rather mixed and show hardly any discernible association between the average number of changes in income and fertility. There is some slight tendency for the highest

[11] Greater precision would have been possible only had we calibrated the intervals more finely on the cards the interviewers presented to the respondents, or if we had asked income in a direct open-ended question. We did not do this both because we felt that the reliability of such precise estimates is seriously questionable and because we did not wish to risk alienating respondents on this whole subject.

The index we constructed weights any income change equally, regardless of amount of change because we are primarily interested here in the over-all pattern of change. The analysis of amount of income change between 1956 and 1959 provides this other dimension to some extent.

fertility to be located in the groups with the greatest number of upward income changes but this generalization is true only for Catholics and Other Protestants. Among Jews there is no apparent linear relationship and among the Active Protestants there is some slight suggestion of a negative correlation. On the whole, the pattern of association is not sufficiently strong to be convincing.

Change in Income and Change in the Number of Children Desired

Although no strong evidence has emerged to connect income change with fertility over the three-year period, it is possible that shifts in the number of children *desired* are related to income changes. In order to examine this association, we selected women who replied in the first interview that they wanted two, three, or four children, classified them by their family-size preferences expressed three years later and examined the distributions of change in their husbands' earnings over this three-year period. The final tabulation (see Table 74) reveals no consistent pattern of association for either Protestants or Catholics.[12] In fact the pattern is varied enough to suggest a purely random relation. Even restricting the overall comparison to the correlations between the two measures of change among couples planning all pregnancies successfully shows only random values.

Perception of Opportunity

In our first report we developed the hypothesis that wives who perceive their husbands' opportunities for advancement optimistically would be more inclined to favor larger families than wives whose perception of their husbands' future opportunities was less sanguine. This hypothesis was supported in all religious groups but the correlations were uniformly low. In our second interview, we repeated the same two questions on the assumption that changes in perceptions might very easily have occurred in the intervening three years. Thus our interest here is both to test the influence on actual fertility of the perceptions initially measured and to ascertain the significance for fertility of changes in perception.

The index constructed to represent this variable is a summation of the responses to two questions: (1) What do you think your husband's chances are for getting ahead in his present line of work? Would you say very good, good, fair or not so good? (2) How much

[12] The smaller number of Jews in the sample does not permit such detailed cross-classification. The correlation between income change and change in number of children desired ($-.07$) does not promise much however.

TABLE 74

The Relationship between Change in Income and Change in the Number of Children Desired over the Three-Year Period

NUMBER OF CHILDREN DESIRED AFTER THE SECOND BIRTH AND NUMBER DESIRED THREE YEARS LATER

INCOME CHANGE 1956–59	Two				Three					Four				
	Now Desire: Same	More	Per Cent Total	Number	Now Desire: Fewer	Same	More	Per Cent Total	Number	Now Desire: Fewer	Same	More	Per Cent Total	Number
PROTESTANTS														
Down	71	29	100	14	18	45	37	100	11				*	7
No change	66	34	100	35	44	56	—	100	16	65	30	5	100	20
Up $1,000	47	53	100	30	41	41	18	100	29	55	27	18	100	11
Up $2,000 or more	67	33	100	43	30	40	30	100	27	41	52	7	100	27
Total	62	38	100	122	35	45	20	100	83	49	42	9	100	65
CATHOLICS														
Down			*	5	20	60	20	100	15	29	38	33	100	21
No change	64	36	100	14	23	41	36	100	22	27	58	15	100	26
Up $1,000	54	46	100	26	9	65	26	100	23	42	36	22	100	33
Up $2,000 or more	68	32	100	19	28	55	17	100	29	38	42	20	100	40
Total	63	37	100	64	20	55	25	100	89	35	43	22	100	120

* Insufficient number.

is your husband finding it possible to improve his chances for getting ahead? Very much, much, a little, or not at all? The correlations between this index and the number of pregnancies occurring in the following three-year interval are again rather low and appear to differ from zero primarily[13] for Catholics (see Table 75). As for the relationship between the number of children currently desired and current perceptions of opportunity, a similar pattern of positive correlation exists[14] as observed at the time of the second birth.

TABLE 75

Correlations between Wife's Perceptions of Husband's Opportunities and Number of Subsequent Pregnancies

	Protestant	Catholic	Jewish	All Couples	Protestant Active	Other	Catholic Active	Other
Total	−.01	.18	−.01	.06	−.01	.03	.25	.13
Among successful planners	.08	.21	.02	.11	.04	.14	.21	.23

Although there is considerable correlation (.54) between the wife's perception of her husband's opportunities expressed following the second birth and those recorded three years later, there is enough difference to permit analysis of change and its significance for change in the number of children desired. In order to reduce the influence of unplanned pregnancies upon the change in the subsequently recorded number of children desired (as well as its possible effect upon perceptions of opportunity) the tabulation was prepared only for couples who reported no unplanned pregnancies after the second birth. This category of course includes couples who used contraception effectively and had *no* additional pregnancy. The association between change in perception of opportunity and change in the number of children desired (Table 76) is not the same in the different religious groups. There is no association to speak of in either of the two Protestant groups and only a very slight suggestion of the expected positive correlation in the Other Catholic group. The positive association is somewhat stronger among Jews, and among Active Catholics a considerably stronger but negative correlation prevails (the correlation for Jews is .15 and for Active Catholics is −.33). The reason for this negative correla-

[13] The difference in the correlations for Protestants and Catholics is significant at the .01 level.

[14] The correlation for the total sample is .06, for Protestants .10, for Catholics .13 and Jews .01. The values for Active and Other Protestants are .06 and .13 and for Active and Other Catholics the correlations are .23 and .04.

TABLE 76

Change in the Number of Children Desired by the Wife in Relation to Change in Her Perception of Her Husband's Opportunities to Get Ahead, for Couples with No Unplanned Third Pregnancy

	Change in Number of Children Desired									
Change in Perception of Opportunity	Now Desire: More Some Fewer			Per Cent Total	Number of Wives	Now Desire: More Some Fewer			Per Cent Total	Number of Wives
	ACTIVE PROTESTANTS (per cent)					OTHER PROTESTANTS (per cent)				
Improved	24	40	36	100	33	19	57	24	100	37
Remained the same	20	44	36	100	50	23	40	37	100	43
Declined	30	33	37	100	49	16	54	30	100	37
	ACTIVE CATHOLICS (per cent)					OTHER CATHOLICS (per cent)				
Improved	6	47	47	100	17	19	49	32	100	63
Remained the same	35	30	35	100	20	26	46	28	100	57
Declined	29	62	9	100	21	19	40	41	100	84
	JEWS (per cent)									
Improved	27	46	27	100	26					
Remained the same	21	41	38	100	34					
Declined	14	44	42	100	36					

TABLE 77

Number of Additional Pregnancies, by Change in the Wife's Perception of Husband's Opportunities to Get Ahead, for Couples with No Unplanned Third Pregnancy

	Number of Additional Pregnancies									
Change in Perception of Opportunity	0	1	2	Per Cent Total	Number of Couples	0	1	2	Per Cent Total	Number of Couples
	ACTIVE PROTESTANTS (per cent)					OTHER PROTESTANTS (per cent)				
Improved	73	27	—	100	33	68	27	5	100	37
Remained the same	72	22	6	100	50	70	28	2	100	43
Declined	80	20	—	100	49	73	19	8	100	37
	ACTIVE CATHOLICS (per cent)					OTHER CATHOLICS (per cent)				
Improved	47	35	18	100	17	60	37	3	100	63
Remained the same	30	45	25	100	20	72	21	7	100	57
Declined	76	24	—	100	21	60	33	7	100	84
	JEWS (per cent)									
Improved	73	23	4	100	26					
Remained the same	79	18	3	100	34					
Declined	83	17	—	100	36					

tion in the Active Catholic group is not clear, but it does lie in the restriction to those successfully planning the third-birth interval. The corresponding correlation among Active Catholics who did not plan this interval is positive (.09) but very low.

We also examined the relationship between change in perception of opportunity and the fertility of couples who planned this interval on the general assumption that perceived decline in opportunity might relate to lower fertility. For four of the five religious categories (excepting Other Catholics) this hypothesis is correct but the difference in fertility between those who perceived an improvement in opportunity and those who perceived a decline tends only to be on the order of 5 to 10 per cent (see Table 77). Again the association among Active Catholics is much stronger (a correlation of about .30).

DRIVE TO GET AHEAD

A considerable amount of time and energy was invested in the study of mobility aspirations for this research. For reasons enumerated in the earlier volume,[15] the measurement of this variable leaves much to be desired. The indices eventually developed relied upon asking the respondent what values he or she might be willing to sacrifice in order to get ahead. These values included such considerations as leaving friends or relatives, living temporarily in a less desirable neighborhood, sending the children to less desirable schools, and keeping quiet about political or religious views. Although the scales satisfied certain internal criteria,[16] their reliability and validity are uncertain at best.

In the analysis of the relationship between "drive to get ahead" and the number of children desired, the expectation that a high drive would be accompanied by a desire for fewer children was borne out but the association was weak—the correlations for wives and husbands being −.10 and −.13 respectively. The corresponding correlations with the number of pregnancies since the birth of the second child (Table 78) show very little indeed. Only among the Jewish group does the expected association persist.

Whether this absence of association represents the right conclusion or whether it reflects more the primitive level of measurement cannot of course be determined. That measurement in this area is inadequate is obvious but to conclude that there really is a strong association between mobility aspirations and fertility that is being masked seems highly improbable, particularly in view of the failure

---

[15] Westoff et al., *Family Growth in Metropolitan America*, pp. 250–253.
[16] *Ibid.*, pp. 391–398.

of other dimensions of mobility to produce any strong relations to fertility.[17]

TABLE 78

Correlations of "Drive to Get Ahead" with Number of Additional Pregnancies

Religion	Drive to Get Ahead	
	Wives	Husbands
Protestant total	.09	.03
Catholic total	.00	−.04
Jewish total	−.18	−.12
All couples	.00	−.06
Active Protestants	.03	.01
Other Protestants	.14	.02
Active Catholics	.11	−.04
Other Catholics	−.02	−.03

ASPIRATIONS TO SEND CHILDREN TO COLLEGE

In an effort to represent that aspect of mobility aspirations which might involve the parents' ambitions and hopes for their children, we included a series of questions in the first interview designed to measure their aspirations for sending their children to college. We were frankly surprised at the extent to which mothers have apparently given serious thought to this subject and the amount of financial planning reported to have already been undertaken despite the fact that at the time the older child was only three years of age on the average. Our interest in the first analysis was to test the hypothesis that couples who had high levels of aspiration for their children's education would be more likely to desire fewer children than couples whose aspirations were lower. The major findings showed no relationship among Protestant couples, the expected negative correlation among Jews, and a completely unexpected positive correlation among Catholics. Further analysis indicated that the latter relationship was due to the connections between being educated in Catholic schools, greater religiosity, higher education, and desires for larger families.[18]

Our present interest lies in whether these relationships between aspirations for children and family-size desires have been translated into behavior. Do the variations in fertility over the last three years show any association with variations in the level of parents' aspiration for their children's education? Are the differences among reli-

[17] For the details see *Family Growth in Metropolitan America*, pp. 254–256.
[18] *Ibid.*, see pp. 255–259 for this analysis.

gions in the direction of the association maintained? The correlations in Table 79 are consistent with the previous findings. Although

TABLE 79

Correlations between Aspiration to Send Children to College and Number of Additional Pregnancies

Religion	Correlation with Number of Additional Pregnancies
Protestant total	$-.03$
Catholic total	$.12$
Jewish total	$-.10$
All couples	$.01$
Active Protestant	$-.01$
Other Protestant	$-.04$
Active Catholic	$.30$
Other Catholic	$.04$

the values are low, again the correlation is negative for Jews and positive for Catholics, and again there is no association among Protestants. That the source of the positive correlation among Catholics is the Active Catholic group again suggests an explanation in terms of religiousness and Catholic education. To isolate this influence more precisely, we examined the correlation between fertility and aspirations for children's education separately for mothers whose education was or was not in Catholic schools and colleges and who are presently classified as either Active or Other Catholics. The correlations (Table 80) suggest that current religiousness (as indexed

TABLE 80

Correlation between the Mother's Aspiration to Send Her Children to College and Number of Additional Pregnancies for Catholic Women by Extent of Their Catholic Education

Extent of Catholic Education	Active Catholic	Other Catholic	Number of Wives Active Catholic	Other Catholic
All	$.34$	$-.01$	56	47
Some	$.22$	$-.04$	51	69
None	*	$.08$	0	200

* By definition, the Active Catholic group includes only couples with at least some Catholic education.

by being classified as an Active Catholic) is more important in determining the positive correlation than is the extent of Catholic school education.

SUMMARY

Social mobility received probably more attention than any other single dimension in the design of this study. Because of such unpromising findings in the first phase of the study the area was narrowed considerably for purposes of the present analysis. The aim of this chapter has been both to retain the chief variables measured in the first phase in order to test their predictive power for subsequent fertility and to explore the fertility implications of subsequent changes in occupational status and income as well.

Occupational mobility was measured across generations, both in terms of changes in occupational status classified only as white-collar or blue-collar as well as measured on a more detailed social prestige scale. Changes in occupational prestige from marriage to the second birth and since the second birth were also examined for association with fertility in the three and a half years since that birth. Variations in recent fertility as well as change in the number of children desired were examined in relation to changes in income over marriage and since the second birth. Changes in occupational prestige as well as in income were analyzed as changes in pattern and sequence as well as amount. Social mobility was also measured on psychological dimensions, including variables such as perception of opportunity, drive to get ahead, and aspirations for children's college education.

All in all, the results continue to discourage any conclusion other than that social mobility as measured has at best a trivial statistical association with fertility. There are some indications that the relationships, as in the case of socio-economic status, go in one direction (positive) for Catholics and in the other for Protestants, and occasionally the magnitude of the correlation begins to look interesting among Catholics. One is tempted to develop the hypothesis that upward mobility among Catholics, especially the more religious Catholics, signifies the opportunity to "invest" in more children while among Protestants upward movement neither requires restriction of fertility nor has any positive implications for increasing family size. The evidence is far from consistent in support of this inference however.

In conclusion, it should be reiterated that social mobility has been measured with very crude instruments and in a highly specialized sample so that the negative conclusions cannot be considered definitive.

Chapter XI. Reactions to Change in General Economic Conditions

In a recent review of the relationship between business cycles and vital rates, Kirk concludes that the data at least for the United States since the First World War "do not confirm the view that *major* changes in fertility are a function of business cycles."[1] Kirk's view is that "economic fluctuations in themselves should not be regarded as primary causes of fertility trends but as important conditioning influences. . . . Economic costs associated with parenthood presumably bear less heavily in times of prosperity and more heavily in times of depression, but in both cases as a check on motivations and behavior of non-economic origin."[2]

There are numerous statistical as well as interpretive problems arising from the analysis of concomitance of economic and demographic time series which are enumerated both by Kirk and by Dorothy S. Thomas in her discussion of his paper.[3] One of the main unanswered interpretive questions concerns the mechanisms through which economic cycles are supposed to affect fertility. Presumably, bad economic conditions cause anxiety about future personal security. That anxiety is translated into more cautious attitudes toward incurring such added financial responsibilities as either marriage or having additional children. In the aggregate, these decisions to postpone marriage (or to advance marriage in good times) are reflected in the close correspondence of economic time series and marriage rates. In fact Thomas claims that the persistence of correlations ranging between .70 and .90 "over time, and among different areas is, perhaps, one of the most firmly based empirical findings in any of the social sciences."[4]

The relation of economic cycles to the birth rate, as Thomas remarks, is not so simple. The strongest correlations obtain with first births reflecting the primary effect on marriages, and in general only low correlations are found with higher order births.

In view of the unresolved questions about how economic cycles affect the fertility behavior of individuals and about the different relationships that exist with first and with higher order births, the

[1] Dudley Kirk, "The Influence of Business Cycles on Marriage and Birth Rates" in National Bureau of Economic Research, *Demographic and Economic Change in Developed Countries*, Princeton University Press, Princeton, 1960, p. 254.

[2] *Ibid.*

[3] *Ibid.*, pp. 257–260.

[4] *Ibid.*, p. 258.

fact that an economic recession fortuitously intervened between our two rounds of interviews can only be regarded as a windfall research opportunity. Signs of a downturn in business activity appeared in early 1957 when employment in manufacturing industries began slowly to decline.[5] A sharp contraction of economic activity started in the third quarter of 1957 and reached its maximum by April 1958. The recovery already under way by May 1958 was rapid and by the end of that year most of the ground lost during the contraction had been regained. The highest unemployment level nationally (7.6 per cent) was in August 1958. Reduction of unemployment was a slow process, however, and high rates persisted in some cities through early 1959.

Every business fluctuation has unique features, and one cannot be sure that the 1957–58 recession resembled others in its effect on fertility. The recession was short-lived and comparatively mild so that its potential effect on fertility was small. Nevertheless, our interviews after the recession gave us the opportunity to elucidate some of the ways through which general economic conditions are translated into fertility behavior.

To measure the effect of the recession explicitly we asked a direct question:

"A couple of years ago, the country went through an economic recession and some people, through no fault of their own, lost jobs or had lowered incomes. How did the recession affect you?"

The vast majority (82 per cent) reported that they experienced no effects at all which comes as no surprise considering both the nature of the recession as well as our sample. The remaining 18 per cent of the respondents stated[6] that they experienced lower income (6 per cent), unemployment (5 per cent), temporary layoff (4 per cent), reduced working week (2 per cent) and anxiety only (1 per cent). Although residents of all seven Standard Metropolitan Areas in our sample reported such effects, New York, Philadelphia, San Francisco, and Chicago contained the fewest complaints. Cities with heavier industry and a larger proportion of blue-collar workers in the labor force had proportionally more frequent reports of negative effects, especially Detroit and Pittsburgh. The majority of

[5] General descriptive information about the nature and duration of the recession is drawn from the *Economic Report of the President*, U.S. Government Printing Office, Washington, D.C., 1959, pp. 9–10, and *Area Labor Market Trends*, U.S. Department of Labor, Bureau of Employment Security, November 1959, Washington, D.C.

[6] The reliability of such information is certainly open to question. Undoubtedly some respondents were only dimly aware of the existence of a recession; others assume that it simply means unemployment. Unfortunately, we have no way of assessing its reliability.

individuals in our sample who reported that some form of unemployment resulted from the recession were in occupations classified as skilled or semi-skilled. The group reporting lower income or anxiety without any unemployment, however, were concentrated in the professional and clerical classes.

EFFECTS ON FERTILITY

If we group together all couples reporting that the recession had some negative effect on their economic position and compare their recent fertility with that of the 82 per cent who reported no effects at all, we find no differences[7] (see Table 81). In view of the occupational differences involved in suffering loss of income as compared

TABLE 81

Number of Additional Pregnancies, by Effects of the 1957–58 Economic Recession

| | *Number of Additional Pregnancies* | | | | *Number* |
| *Effects of Recession* | 0 | 1 | 2 | Total | *of* |
		(per cent)			*Couples*
No effects at all	46	42	12	100	737
Some negative effect	47	42	11	100	156
No effects: white-collar	47	39	14	100	384
blue-collar	44	46	10	100	342
Some effects: white-collar	49	42	9	100	66
blue-collar	48	43	9	100	87
No effects: Protestant	50	42	8	100	292
Catholic	36	47	17	100	355
Jewish	70	28	2	100	89
Some effects: Protestant	47	44	9	100	73
Catholic	44	45	11	100	66
Jewish	63	25	12	100	16

with various forms of unemployment and the possible fertility implications of such differences, it seems desirable to separate these groups. Comparisons of the recent fertility of those who reported anxiety or some reduction of income but no unemployment with the fertility of those who reported unemployment does reveal some differences (see top of Table 82). Those whose income was reduced or who felt anxiety about the potential economic effects of the recession had lower fertility than either those reporting no effect or those who reported unemployment. The last group, contrary to

[7] The wives reporting some effect had initially desired a slightly smaller-sized family (average of 3.2 children) than those reporting no effects (3.3).

superficial expectations of rational response to reduced financial security actually had slightly *more* pregnancies than couples reporting no effects at all.[8] In view of the differences in occupational composition between those whose income was reduced and those who were unemployed, the same fertility comparisons were made within white-collar and blue-collar classes and the generalization for the difference between these two groups holds (middle of Table 82) but the fertility of the unemployed group is very similar to that of those reporting no effects.

TABLE 82

Number of Additional Pregnancies, by Type of Negative Economic Effect of the 1957–58 Economic Recession

| Effects of Recession | Number of Additional Pregnancies | | | | Number of Couples |
| | 0 | 1 | 2 | Total | |
	(per cent)				
No effects at all	46	42	12	100	737
Some negative effect	47	42	11	100	156
Reduced income or anxiety	57	35	8	100	61
Some type of unemployment	41	47	12	100	95
Reduced income: white-collar	53	35	12	100	43
blue-collar	67	33	—	100	18
Unemployment: white-collar	39	57	4	100	23
Blue-collar	43	45	12	100	69
Reduced income: Protestant	61	39	—	100	28
Catholic	45	37	18	100	22
Unemployment: Protestant	38	47	15	100	45
Catholic	43	50	7	100	44

When differences in religious composition are considered, the picture becomes more complicated. Protestants and Jews were over-represented in the group whose income was reduced (consistent with its occupational composition) while Catholics and Protestants but not Jews shared the brunt of unemployment. Eliminating Jews from the comparisons narrows the fertility differences as expected, but only slightly, because of their overall numerical unimportance. Looking at Protestants and Catholics separately (lower section of Table 81) a reduction of fertility for those experiencing some nega-

[8] This is consistent with slight initial differences in the same direction in number of children desired by the wife. Those whose income was reduced by the recession had initially desired an average of 3.1 children compared to 3.2 desired by those who were subsequently unemployed for some period of time.

tive effect of the recession is apparent for Catholics but not for Protestants. This picture is somewhat clarified by the fertility comparisons by religion for each of the two kinds of recession effects although caution must be exercised because of the small numbers. The Catholic groups, regardless of whether the effect was lowered income or unemployment, experienced lower fertility than Catholics reporting no effects, but the fertility of Protestants seems to have been reduced among those with lowered incomes but appears raised among those who were unemployed. Whether this unexpected variation by religion is genuine is difficult to say. The explanation may lie in the lower socio-economic background of the unemployed group which implies higher fertility for Protestants and lower fertility for Catholics (see Chapter IX).

Further analyses were undertaken which indicate that the higher fertility of the couples where the husband was unemployed compared to that of those whose income was reduced can be attributed mainly to their less effective control over fertility. Among those whose income was reduced, 80 per cent of those expressing an initial preference for only two children were successful in avoiding an additional pregnancy compared to 68 per cent among those who experienced unemployment. Those reporting no recession effects had an intermediate value of 74 per cent. Among couples who had a third pregnancy, half of those occurring to the couples with reduced income were reported as unplanned by comparison with 68 per cent of all third pregnancies conceived by couples reporting unemployment. It seems clear enough therefore that the fertility differences of these two groups can be understood in terms of differences in fertility-planning success. What is not so clear, however, is whether couples who were hit by unemployment are selective in terms of previous fertility-planning success or whether the fact of unemployment simply provided greater exposure to the risk of accidental pregnancy. Examining the proportion of couples in each group who failed to plan successfully their second child or both first and second children reveals a level of 40 per cent among those reporting no effects of the recession, 33 per cent among couples whose income was lowered, and 38 per cent among those who experienced some form of unemployment. These figures do not lend much support to the hypothesis of selectivity. However, if we focus exclusively on the couples who actually lost their jobs as a consequence, presumably, of the recession and ignore those who were just temporarily laid off or who worked fewer days per week, we do find the highest proportion of unsuccessful planners (45 per cent). A case by case investigation also reveals some association between the particular months of unemployment and the month of conception with one out of three of all third pregnancies to this group being conceived during a particular month of reported unemployment. An analysis taking into account the severity of the unemployment does not appear to modify these findings. In all probability both factors are operating—the unemployed group for various reasons connected with their general educational and economic status tend to be less rational or cautious about fertility planning and by virtue of enforced idleness were no doubt exposed more than they would be normally to the risk of unplanned pregnancy. The latter supposition is quite conjectural, however, and it seems more reasonable to place greater emphasis on the selectivity of unsuccessful planners into the group which reported unemployment.

OTHER FACTORS

This analysis has proceeded thus far quite unrealistically on the assumption that an economic recession did or did not affect individuals and that all other relevant factors presumably connected with fertility remained unchanged. One other major economic crisis did occur during this three-year period—the steel strike which began on July 15, 1959, and was terminated by injunction on November 7 of the same year, a total duration of 116 days. As a half-million steelworkers went on strike, related industries were able to sustain production because of inflated inventories. By September, however, as steel shortages began to be felt, the construction, machinery, and durable goods industries—especially the automobile industry—started to lay off workers, an unemployment toll that by the end of the strike also reached the half-million mark. Improvement beginning in mid-November was completed by early 1960.[9]

Approximately 14 per cent of the women interviewed in our study replied to a direct question that their husbands were affected in some way by the steel strike. The main effects were either a temporary layoff due to the strike (5.3 per cent) or loss of income (5.1 per cent). The remaining 3.7 per cent were distributed among: recollections of anxiety (2.3 per cent), reduced work week (0.8 per cent), and loss of job (0.6 per cent). Of the total sample, 75 per cent were affected by neither the recession nor the strike with 6 per cent being hit by both. The remaining 19 per cent reported effects of one but not the other.

The social characteristics of the two main groups affected negatively by the strike are the same as those characterizing couples

[9] This brief description of the steel strike is drawn from *Area Labor Market Trends, op.cit.*

whose income was reduced or who lost their jobs during the recession. Virtually all those who were on strike were in the blue-collar classes (91 per cent) while these classes comprised the minority (39 per cent) of the group reporting reduced income or just anxiety. The two groups affected by the strike were fairly similar in religious composition except that Jews (being mainly in white-collar class occupations) were much more affected by loss of income than direct temporary unemployment.

The main difference is in area of residence with those affected by the strike being heavily concentrated in Pittsburgh and to a lesser extent Chicago.

In general, little relationship at all exists between the effects of the steel strike and the fertility of those people directly involved, at least none that is apparent over the three-year span between interviews. The proportions having a third pregnancy are virtually indistinguishable among the different groups. When the fertility of couples who felt the effects both of the recession and steel strike is examined the sharper differences evidenced by groups differently affected by the recession are reduced somewhat by the added experience of those who were affected by the strike. As suggested above, however, these are rather gross comparisons of fertility behavior over a three-year period for groups categorized by economic experiences of varying intensities and durations. This situation certainly does not encourage unambiguous inferences about cause and effect in spite of the fortuitous before-and-after research design. In order to tie down more securely at least the time sequences of behavior we analyzed certain histories in detail. The records of the thirty-three families in which the husband was idle from his regular job during the steel strike but reported no effects from the recession revealed only four instances of a conception occurring during the actual four month duration of the strike. This low incidence certainly lends no support to the hypothesis suggested above in connection with recession unemployment, namely, that idleness through greater exposure to risk of conception leads to higher fertility.

Lest we somewhat implausibly conclude that the experience of an extended strike is totally inconsequential for fertility, the obvious fact that such an experience varies in its impact depending upon all kinds of factors should be taken into account. Some men were able to find other work almost immediately, others had savings to fall back on, and some wives were able to find employment and cushion the financial shock. Classifying the thirty-three families according to the severity of the economic effect and whether or not a conception occurred produced a strong association. Half were classified as reporting serious effects—none had a conception during the year. In all seven instances of a conception dated in 1959 (including the four mentioned above, which occurred during the actual months of the strike) the women reported the effects as comparatively mild. So it does seem highly probable that there were some genuine consequences depending on the relative severity of the effect.

Summary

This chapter reports the results of an analysis of the effects of an economic recession and an extended strike of steelworkers on the fertility of couples directly involved. The analysis was possible only because of the fortuitous occurrence of both events in the three-year interval between the first (1957) and second (1960) interviews. The chief theoretical interest in such research lies in the connection of traditional demographic research on the effects of business cycles on fertility with an opportunity to explore its ramifications for behavior at the level of the individual. Although this analysis is not relevant to the relationship between cyclical economic trends and fertility over time, it does bear on the question of how macro-economic events are translated into individual reactions and the related question of which groups in the population do react. Is there a fertility reaction which is a negative function of involvement or extent of deprivation?

Most emphasis was placed in this analysis on the recession which is qualitatively different from a strike although there are some similarities in effects on individuals. The main finding is that a recession exerts two types of negative effects which appear to have opposite implications for fertility. One effect is that the family's income is reduced because of a reduction in the volume of business. This effect is perceivable mainly in the white-collar classes such as the professional, proprietary, and sales classes. The fertility of this group over the entire three-year period was 23 per cent lower on the average than that of the bulk of the sample which experienced no adverse effects at all. Even with occupational class and religion held constant this group showed lower fertility.

The other main effect of a recession obviously is unemployment which comes in various forms ranging from fewer days worked to complete enforced idleness. Unemployment, of course, hit blue-collar workers more than white-collar workers. Combining all forms of unemployment, the average fertility of this group was just under 10 per cent *higher* than that of couples reporting no effect and 40 per cent higher on the average than those whose incomes were lowered. Further inquiry confirmed the conjecture that this group is composed disproportionately of couples who have not planned their fertility successfully.

The evidence of a genuine reduction in fertility of the group with lowered incomes is firmer than the evidence of a rise among the unemployed. A more conservative interpretation of the fertility of the unemployed is that it was not affected by the recession at all and almost certainly was not lowered. These findings are of course conditioned by the fact that we are examining the presumed "effects" of a particular economic event on fertility in a longer three-year period when many events could have been influential. Although some effort was made to deal with a more precise and appropriate time period, there is no essentially satisfactory way to define such a period since the duration of psychological reactions is unknown.

As far as can be determined, the steel strike of 1959 exerted little overall effect on fertility over the three-year period. The average number of pregnancies conceived in groups directly affected did not differ significantly from that of couples not involved, but among those affected the rate of conception during 1959 did associate with the severity of the economic effect.

Chapter XII. Residence and Migration

CLYDE V. KISER

Milbank Memorial Fund

The present chapter, like one in the report on the first phase of the study, is concerned with the relation of residence and migration to fertility. Residence and migration are discussed together because of their close interrelation. Residence history is a history of past migrations. Furthermore, the rise of metropolitan areas and the great growth of suburbs in recent years have been due in no small part to the development of the means of transportation which enable people to work in one place and live in another. In addition, frequent migration or change of residence has become a conspicuous part of modern life.

In view of the large proportion of our population living in metropolitan areas and the large amount of migration, it is manifestly of interest to study the relation of residence and migration to the fertility behavior of couples living in metropolitan areas. Metropolitan areas provide the life setting for some two-thirds of our population. Even the ten largest metropolitan areas, those with two million or more population in 1960, contain nearly one-fourth of our total population. It is true that our sample is drawn from seven of the eight areas of this size in 1950 and that one may not expect to find great contrasts in types of residence within such areas. However, our largest metropolitan areas actually contain sharp contrasts in types of residence. There are the possibilities of comparing central cities with outlying districts, residents of residential neighborhoods with those of mixed neighborhoods, and residents of single-family houses with those of multiple-family houses.

With respect to both residence and migration, the present analyses will contain (a) a brief statement of types of past relationships observed from census data; (b) limitations and strengths of study data on the subject—first phase and second phase; (c) results and brief discussion.

RESIDENCE AND FERTILITY

Census Data

Census data and other forms of vital statistics have rather consistently indicated (a) higher fertility rates for rural than for urban areas; (b) an inverse relation of fertility to size of city; (c) higher fertility for outlying areas than for central cities, and (d) higher fertility for residents of single-family houses than for dwellers of apartment houses.[1]

First Phase of Study

Official data on the residence-fertility relationships have generally related to couples of all parities. The analyses based upon the first phase of the present study related to certain aspects of fertility behavior among couples who had recently borne their second child. The chief dependent variables used were those concerning planning status of the two existing children, intervals from marriage to first and second child, total number of children desired, and desired interval between second and third child.

In general, the data from the first phase of the study indicated some differences by religion in the residence-fertility relationships. To some extent these may have been associated with differences by religion in residence-economic status relationships. The relation of residence to fertility planning was more marked for Protestants than for Catholics. Among Protestants the proportion of couples that planned both children or the last child was higher for the suburbanites than for the central city dwellers. It was much higher for people living in single-family houses than for those living in multiple-family dwelling units.

The differentials in birth intervals by residence were in harmony with those by fertility-planning success. Thus among the Protestants (but not among the Catholics) birth intervals preceding the second birth tended to be a little longer for couples living in the suburbs than in central cities, longer for those living in residential neighborhoods than for those in mixed neighborhoods, and longer for those in single-family houses than for those in multiple-dwelling units.

Doubtless the reader has noticed the apparent difference between census data and study data in some of the relationships, particularly those concerning central cities versus outlying areas and single-family houses versus multiple-family houses. The census data indicate that, probably partly through selection and partly through determinative influences, fertility tends to be higher in outlying districts than in central cities of metropolitan areas, and higher in single-family houses than in multiple-dwelling units.

The first phase of the study offered no opportunity to examine fertility differentials in the strict sense because it related to couples who recently had their second child. However, it afforded depend-

[1] Clyde V. Kiser, Fertility Rates by Residence and Migration. *Proceedings, International Population Conference*, Vienna, 1959, pp. 273–286.

ent variables relating to fertility behavior such as intervals and the planning of the first two births. The intervals from marriage to first and second children were relatively long for couples living outside the central cities and for those living in single-family houses. Among these same groups the proportions classified as having planned their first two children were relatively high. It would appear that in data relating to couples of all parities (as in census and official data) selections by size of family play considerable part in the relatively high fertility of inhabitants of suburbs and single-family houses. In a sample restricted to two-child families, the selections of the above-described type are ruled out and selections with respect to high economic status and effective family planning come to the fore.[2]

Second Phase of Study

As indicated in earlier chapters, the chief dependent variables from the second phase of the study are the number of pregnancies occurring during the three years between the first and second sets of interviews, and the planning status of those conceptions. The independent variables on residence are those concerning residence since marriage, residence since the first interview, distance from the central city, and whether husband works in the central city, and characteristics of the dwelling and street of residence. The analyses are carried through by religion.

City Versus Suburban Residence Since First Interview

The classifications regarding city versus suburban residence since the first interview and also those concerning residence since marriage are based upon residential histories collected from the respondents. The record proceeds from that of first residence after marriage (city and state) to the present residence. Space was provided for recording the number of years lived in each place and for indicating whether the residence was in a city, in the suburbs, or in the open country. It should be emphasized that in the histories the "cities" are not restricted to "central cities."

For all religious groups combined there was virtually no difference by residence since first interview in the proportion reporting a pregnancy after the second child. The proportion was approxi-

[2] The fact of higher income among residents of single family houses than among residents of other types of houses was documented. This differential was found for white-collar and blue-collar workers and for each religious group. It was considerably sharper for the Protestant than for the Catholic couples. C. F. Westoff, R. G. Potter, Jr., P. C. Sagi, and Elliot G. Mishler, *Family Growth in Metropolitan America*, Princeton University Press, Princeton, N.J., 1961, p. 275.

TABLE 83

Per Cent of Couples Having One Pregnancy or More after the Second Birth, by Religion, Planning Status of the Conception Following the Second Birth, and Residence Characteristics

RESIDENCE CHARACTERISTICS	All Religions	PER CENT HAVING PREGNANCY AFTER SECOND BIRTH							NUMBER OF COUPLES		
		Protestant			Catholic			Jewish			
		Total	Planned	Not Planned	Total	Planned	Not Planned	Total	Protestant	Catholic	Jewish
Residence since marriage											
All in city	53	55	18	36	60	26	34	24	121	187	54
Most in city	58	55	20	35	70	29	41	41	75	63	32
All in suburbs	53	42	11	30	65	20	45	22	53	71	9
Most in suburbs and "other"	54	50	20	30	60	22	38	40	123	102	15
Residence since first interview											
All or most in city	54	57	20	37	61	26	35	23	160	211	57
Other	54	47	17	30	64	23	41	40	212	212	53
Distance from central city											
Lives in central city	50	57	13	43	57	25	32	24	76	167	66
Outside (total)	56	50	20	30	66	24	42	42	292	251	43
1–9 miles	56	40	14	26	69	25	44	55	72	81	20
10–19 miles	50	47	20	27	57	22	35	} 30	81	83	7
20–29 miles	60	52	20	32	73	29	44		50	45	10
30+ miles	62	60	25	35	69	19	50		89	42	6
Husband works in central city											
Yes	52	52	16	36	61	24	36	30	139	237	84
No	56	51	19	31	63	23	41	38	226	178	21

mately 54 per cent for those classified as having spent "all or most of the time in cities" and also for the "others"—those who had resided all or most of the time in the suburbs or open country (Table 83).

When the analysis is done separately by religious group some relationships emerge. Among the Protestants the proportion having one or more pregnancies after the second was higher for those living in cities "all or most of the time" since the first interview than for others. For the Catholics the difference was in the other direction. For the Jewish group the proportion having one or more pregnancies after the first interview was lower for those living most or all of the time in cities than for the others. Few of the differences by residence in the proportion of couples having one or more pregnancies after the second child stand up as statistically significant.

The differences by religion in the fertility-residence relationships described above appear to be due to differences in extent of fertility planning. In some of the analyses below, the couples that had no pregnancy are combined with those that had a planned pregnancy and are labeled "planned families" in that they had no unplanned pregnancies, but the inexactness of this is emphasized. The resulting proportions of family planners were as follows:

Residence Since First Interview	Protestant	Catholic	Jewish
All or most of the time in cities	63	65	88
"Other"	70	59	87

City Versus Suburban Residence Since Marriage

The range in proportion having one or more pregnancies within three years after the second child is also quite narrow by residence for both Protestants and Catholics. Among the Protestants the proportions having one or more pregnancies after the second child ranged from 42 per cent for the "all suburb" group to 55 per cent for both the "all city" and "most city" groups. Among the Catholics the range was from 60 per cent for the "all city" group to 70 per cent for the "most city" group (Table 83).

Although the data are not precise on the point, they indicate that among Protestants the percentage of couples practicing family planning since the first interview was higher for those who lived in suburbs since marriage than for those who lived in cities. More specifically, for Protestants the per cent of couples having either no pregnancy or a planned pregnancy since the first interview was 70 per cent for those living all or most of the time in suburbs, and 63 per cent for those living all or most of the time in cities.

Among the Catholics the proportion of planners was somewhat higher (65 per cent) for those reporting residence in a city all or most of the time since marriage than for those reporting that all or most of their married lives were spent in the suburbs (59 per cent). Although none of these differences is statistically significant, the relation of family planning to residence is consistent with patterns of fertility by residence for each religious group.

Although not shown in the tables, it is of interest to note that the total number of children desired according to statements of wives *at the first interview* was lowest for those who had spent all of their married lives in suburbs according to information on residence supplied at the second interview.

Distance from Residence to Central City

In the effort to improve the data on residence in the second interview a question was asked regarding distance from the person's home to the nearest boundary of the central city of the given metropolitan area. The precise question was "Approximately how far is it from your house to the nearest point of _____?" In asking the question the interviewer inserted the name of the pertinent city (New York, Newark, or Jersey City; Chicago, Los Angeles, Philadelphia, Detroit, San Francisco or Oakland; Pittsburgh, or central city of other metropolitan areas for distant migrants). Actually the question was not asked for persons interviewed *within* one of the above central cities. The question was asked only of those living outside the central cities of the given metropolitan areas. Answers were recorded in miles.

As expected, the proportion of respondents living in central cities of the metropolitan areas considered was lowest for the Protestants (20 per cent), intermediate for the Catholics (40 per cent), and highest for the Jews (60 per cent). The proportion living 30 miles or more from the nearest point of the central city was 24 per cent for the Protestants, 10 per cent for the Catholics, and 6 per cent for the Jews.

No significant difference was found between those living in central cities and those living in outlying areas combined with respect to proportions having one or more pregnancies after the second child. The distance of the residence from the central city was found to be somewhat more systematically related to fertility among the Protestants than among the Catholics. Thus among the Protestants the percentage of couples having one or more pregnancies since the first interview was lowest (40 per cent) for those living outside the central city but within 10 miles of it (Table 83). The percentage increased slightly, but consistently, with increasing distance and it was highest for couples living 30 miles or more from the central city

(60 per cent). Interestingly, this was but little above the proportion (57 per cent) observed for those living in the central cities. The high proportion for the central cities reflects the greater prevalence of unplanned births; the high proportion for the areas 30 or more miles from central cities reflects a relatively high proportion of planned births. Among the Catholics, the percentage having a pregnancy after the second child was relatively low for those in the central cities and for those living 10–19 miles away (57 per cent). In the remaining areas 69–73 per cent had pregnancies after the first interview. For the Jews the percentage was lower in central cities than in outlying areas.[3]

The prevalence of family planning according to distance from central city helped to account for the differences in percentages having one or more pregnancies after the second birth. Thus among the Protestants the percentage classified as planners after the second birth as described above was lowest (57 per cent) for those living in the central cities, highest (73–74 per cent) for those living 1–19 miles from the boundary of the central cities and in intermediate position (66–68 per cent) for those living 20 miles or more from the central city.

Among the Catholics, the proportion classified as successful family planners after the second birth was highest (67 per cent) for those living in central cities and in areas 10–19 miles from the central city. These were the areas with lowest proportions having a conception after the first interview. In other areas the percentages of planners extended from 50 to 56 per cent.

Among the Jews the percentage of family planners defined as

---

[3] Again, attention is called to the fact that the less consistent tendency in the present data than in the census materials for fertility rates to be lower in central cities than in outlying areas probably is due to the restriction of the present study to couples who had their second children three years before the second interviews.

The subdivision of the pregnancies by planning status yields interesting results. Thus the percentage of the Protestant women in the second interviews that had pregnancies that were planned after the first interview is lowest (13.2) for those in central cities and it increases consistently with distance from the central city. However, the percentage of *planned pregnancies* among Protestants classified as family planners in the sense described above, follows the pattern described above for all pregnancies, i.e., among the family planners the percentage having a pregnancy after the second birth was higher for those living in central cities than for those living outside but within ten miles of the nearest boundary. Otherwise there was a sharp direct relation of planned fertility to distance from the city; the per cent having a pregnancy ranged from 19 for those living within 10 miles of the city boundary to 38 for those living 30 miles or more from the central city. The percentage of Protestant women having unplanned pregnancies after the second birth followed the same pattern but the range of variation was narrow. The existence of a pattern of *unplanned* pregnancies by distance from the city probably arises from the fact that unplanned pregnancies may have been accidents or results of unsuccessful efforts at control as well as results of no effort at control.

above was virtually the same for those living in central cities as for those living outside, 85–86 per cent.

That the proportion classified as family planners within central cities was actually higher for Catholics than for Protestants probably reflects a greater tendency for middle-class Protestants than for middle-class Catholics to shun central cities. Probably it also reflects Protestant-Catholic differences as to what constitutes family planning and planned pregnancies.

Finally, attention may be given to a few characteristics of couples according to distance from central cities. As pointed out previously, in the total samples the median annual incomes of husbands in both 1956 and 1959 (the twelve-month periods preceding the two interviews) were highest for the Jews and lowest for the Catholics. The medians were slightly higher for Protestants than for Catholics in each category considered.

Among the Protestants the highest median income in 1959 according to distance from city was that for people living outside the central cities but within ten miles of them. This area was generally characterized as one with relatively high proportion of family planners and relatively low proportion of families reporting a pregnancy after the second child. The lowest median income was that for families living thirty or more miles distant from the central cities.

There was no marked or systematic difference by distance from city with respect to educational attainment of the wife or of age or age at marriage of the wife or husband.

Husband's Place of Work and Commutation

Information was collected regarding place of work as well as place of residence of the husband. The simple dichotomy based upon whether or not the husband works in the city yields virtually no relationship with fertility. Among the Protestants, the proportion reporting one conception or more since the second birth was 52 per cent for husbands working in central cities and 51 per cent for those not working in central cities. Among the Catholics the respective percentages were 61 and 63. However, commutation to work was a discriminating factor. Among those living outside the central city but commuting daily for work, the proportions reporting one or more pregnancies after the second birth were 46 for the Protestants and 70 for the Catholics. Among those *living and working* outside the central city the proportions having one or more pregnancies after the second birth was 51 per cent for the Protestants and 64 per cent for the Catholics. Among those residing in the central cities and assumed to be working there, the respective proportions were 52 for the Protestants and 61 for the Catholics. Thus whereas the Protestant commuters are characterized by *lower* fertility after the second birth than either the residents of central cities or the noncommuting residents of outlying areas, the Catholic commuters are characterized by *higher* fertility than either of the two reference groups. Correspondingly, the Protestant commuters are characterized by relatively high proportion (73 per cent) of family planners and the Catholic commuters by relatively low proportion (55 per cent) of family planners.

Type of Home and Neighborhood

The statement on this topic in the report on the first phase of the study was as follows:

"Some of the sharpest relations observed in the present analysis were those between fertility-planning status and characteristics of the home and neighborhood of residence of Protestants in the study. In general, the proportion of successful planners was relatively high for home owners, for occupants of single-family houses, for residents of streets that are predominantly residential in character, and for residents of streets that were graded by interviewers as being of high or upper-middle economic status. In short, high economic status of the individual families appears to be a common factor . . ."[4]

In general, the statement made above also applies to the experience after the second child. First of all it may be noted that among the Protestant couples the proportion classified as family planners between the first and second interviews, determined as previously described, was highest (66 per cent) for occupants of single unattached houses, intermediate (63 per cent) for occupants of "attached" and "row" houses, and lowest (54 per cent) for occupants of apartments or flats. A similar situation is found in the classification by number of families in the house. The category single-unattached house mentioned above is virtually the same as that for one-family houses. Among the Protestants, the proportion of planners after the second child was 70 per cent for occupants of one-family houses and 50 per cent for occupants of multi-family houses (Table 84).

Among the Catholics the percentage classified as family planners for the period following the first interview was lower for occupants of unattached-single houses (59 per cent) than for those in "attached" or "row" houses (64 per cent) or apartments (74 per cent). On the basis of number of families in the house the proportions classified as planners in the above sense were: 1-family house, 59 per cent; 2–4 family house, 69 per cent; and 5+ family house, 70

---

[4] C. V. Kiser, "Residence and Migration," in Westoff *et al.*, *Family Growth in Metropolitan America*, p. 272.

TABLE 84

Per Cent of Couples Having One Pregnancy or More after the Second Birth, by Religion, Planning Status of the Conception Following the Second Birth, and Dwelling and Street Characteristics

DWELLING AND STREET CHARACTERISTICS	ALL RELIGIONS	PER CENT HAVING PREGNANCY AFTER SECOND BIRTH							NUMBER OF COUPLES		
		Protestant			Catholic			Jews			
		Total	Planned	Not Planned	Total	Planned	Not Planned	Total	Protestant	Catholic	Jews
Type of dwelling											
Single-unattached	57	51	19	32	66	25	41	42	310	283	50
Attached-row	52	53	16	37	56	20	36	25	38	98	16
Apartment	41	58	13	46	52	26	26	20	24	42	44
Number of families in house											
1	56	50	19	30	65	24	41	41	319	290	58
2-4	52	61	11	50	53	22	31	17	36	100	12
5 or More	46	65	18	47	67	36	30	20	17	33	40
Type of street											
Residential	53	50	18	32	61	23	38	31	343	363	97
Mixed	63	62	17	45	70	30	40	31	29	60	13
Street traffic											
Local	52	48	18	30	60	22	38	37	226	245	62
Light	56	53	15	38	67	28	39	21	94	111	29
Heavy	58	63	27	37	63	25	37	22	52	67	18

per cent. The foregoing differences by religion are consistent with the previously mentioned higher proportion of "planners" among Catholics than among Protestants within *central cities* considered.

Among the Protestants, the proportion of couples having one or more conceptions after the first interview was 51 per cent for those in single-unattached houses, 53 per cent for those living in "attached or row-type" houses and 58 per cent for those in apartments. However, the incidence of unplanned pregnancies accounted for this direction of the relationship. The proportion of couples having planned pregnancies and also the proportion of family planners having pregnancies were highest for residents of single-unattached houses and lowest for the apartment houses.

Among the Catholics the proportion of couples having one or more conceptions after the second child was higher for occupants of single-unattached houses than for occupants of attached row houses and apartment buildings. This pattern was even sharper for the unplanned pregnancies than for the planned pregnancies (Table 84).

As pointed out in the previous report, "In view of the more effective use of contraception in the suburbs than in central cities it is perhaps not surprising that among Protestants the median interval between marriage and first birth was longer for couples in single-family houses than for the others . . ." and that "these same differentials were found among Protestants with respect to interval between first and second births. . . ."[5]

Type of Street

In general the statements made above regarding type of house also apply to the classification by predominant *type of house on the street*. Among the Protestants, the percentage having one or more conceptions after the second birth differs little by predominant type of house on the street. The percentage of pregnancies among couples classified as having planned their families after the second child was higher for residents of streets in which single-unattached houses were predominant than for residents of other types of streets. Among Catholics the highest proportion having one or more conceptions after the first interview was that for those couples living on streets where single-unattached houses predominated. The lowest percentage was for those living on streets where apartment houses were predominant.

A two-fold classification of streets (residential and mixed) suffered from the same limitations as those mentioned above—i.e., there were not enough Protestants in "mixed" neighborhoods to

[5] *Ibid.*, p. 272.

afford valid comparisons. This was especially true of interval data. In general, however, data suggest that among Protestants and Catholics the percentages having one or more pregnancies after the second child were lower for the people in "residential" than in "mixed" neighborhoods (Table 84).

Another variable regarding residential character of the street and neighborhood is that of type of traffic on the street. Among the Protestants, the proportion having one conception or more since the second child was highest for those living on streets of heavy traffic, intermediate for those on streets of light traffic, and lowest for those on streets with local traffic. The percentage of the couples that might be classified as family planners after the second child was higher (70 per cent) for those on streets with only "local" traffic than for the others (62–63 per cent). The median interval from second child to next conception was longest for those on streets characterized by "local traffic" but the small numbers of pregnancies to Protestants in *other* types of streets prevent reliable comparisons of intervals. Among the Catholics neither the eventuation or the timing of conceptions after the second child appeared to be significantly related to traffic conditions in the neighborhood (Table 84).[6]

MIGRATION

The relation of migration to fertility is a complex one. Much depends upon the type of population, migration, and index of fertility considered. Different types of selection accompany different types of data. This fact was emphasized in the writer's previous articles on this subject, based upon census data and the materials from the first phase of the present study.

Census Data

Two types of census data were analyzed and these yielded somewhat different results. One type was that of the 1940 census data concerning fertility ratios (children under 5) in relation to migration status (as determined by place of residence five years prior to the census date).[7]

As indicated in the writer's analysis of census materials, "When the simple two-fold division 'migrants and nonmigrants' is utilized, there is a marked tendency for the fertility ratios of ever-married

[6] See opposite page for footnote.

[7] The 1940 Census contained a question "Where did this person live April 1, 1935?" In the tabulation of those materials, the census considered as a "migrant" any person whose reported 1935 residence was in a county other than the one in which he resided at the time of the 1940 Census.

[6] The significances of difference between given residence classes with respect to proportions of couples having one pregnancy or more after the second birth and with respect to proportions classified as planned families are given below, by religion. The symbols may be interpreted as follows: VS, significant at 1 per cent level; S, significant at 5 per cent level; N, not significant.

Residence Classes Compared	Per Cent Having Pregnancies After First Interview				Per Cent Classified as Planned Families			
	All Religions	Protestants	Catholics	Jews	All Religions	Protestants	Catholics	Jews
Residence Since First Interview								
All or Most in City–Other	N	N	N	N	N	N	N	N
Residence in Central City								
In Central City–Outside Central City	N	N	N	N	N	S	S	N
Type of Dwelling								
Single Family–Attached or Row	N	N	N	N	N	N	N	N
Apartment House–Attached or Row	N	N	N	N	N	N	N	N
Single Family–Apartment House	VS	N	N	S	S	N	N	N
Number of Families in House								
1–2 to 4	N	N	S	N	N	S	N	N
2 to 4–5 or more	N	N	N	N	N	N	N	N
1–5 or more	N	N	N	S	N	N	N	N
Type of Street								
Residence–Mixed	N	N	N	N	N	N	N	N
Traffic on Street								
Heavy–Light	N	N	N	N	N	N	N	N
Light–Local	N	N	N	N	N	N	N	N
Heavy–Local	N	S	N	N	N	N	N	N

women to be lower for migrants than nonmigrants. Among the native-white women the differences were largest at ages 20–29, when fertility ratios themselves were generally highest. The differences at those ages were larger for urban and rural-nonfarm women than for rural-farm women.

"For native-white women 30 years old and over, however, the fertility ratio was virtually the same for migrants and nonmigrants within each type of residence. . . . The subdivisions of both the migrant and nonmigrant groups necessitate some qualifications but also help to clarify some of the relationships. [Among the migrants,] the lowest fertility ratios were those for migrant women who lived in urban areas in 1935 and the highest were those for migrant women who lived in rural-farm areas in 1935 . . . [As for nonmigrants,] higher fertility ratios [were found] for the nonmigrant wives moving from one house to another than for those living in the same house . . ."[8]

The other type of census data mentioned above concerned total number of children ever born to ever-married women in relation to migration status as determined by comparison of geographic region of birth and region of residence. From these data three categories were established for each geographic region considered: born and living here (nonmigrants); born elsewhere and living here (in-migrants); and born here and living elsewhere (out-migrants). These related to native-white ever-married women in the 1940 census and the comparisons were made specific by age and urban-rural type of residence in 1940.

In most cases the age-specific fertility rates (children ever born) were lower for the migrants, either in-migrants or out-migrants, than for the nonmigrants. However, the combined urban areas of the north central states provided an interesting exception in that the in-migrants exhibited *higher* fertility than the nonmigrants. The probable explanation is that native-white in-migrants residing in the north central cities are composed largely of former farm tenant and hillbilly whites from Kentucky and the states bordering the Mississippi River to the south.[9]

First Phase of Study

As for data from the first phase of the present study, a finding of central importance was that among the Protestants (but not among

---

[8] Clyde V. Kiser, "Fertility Rates by Residence and Migration," *Proceedings, International Population Conference*, Vienna, 1959, pp. 278–280.

[9] *Ibid.*, pp. 280–281.

the Catholics or Jews) the proportion of planners (couples having planned both births) was significantly lower for migrants than for nonmigrants. Among the Protestants, the proportion planning both births was 61 per cent for those who *never* moved from marriage to first interview. It was 39–43 per cent for those who moved varying numbers of times.

The data from the first phase of the study yielded little indication of a wide or systematic variation in birth intervals by number of moves since marriage. "There was some tendency among the Protestants for the interval between marriage and first birth to be relatively long at the two ends of the migration scale—i.e., for those who did not move at all and for those who moved four or more times. As already indicated the nonmovers had a relatively high proportion of highly successful planners. Probably many of them did not move because they had had satisfactory homes and jobs since marriage. As for those moving four times or more, the longer interval may be in part a bias inherent in the nature of the data."[10]

Since the first phase of the study relates to couples who recently had their second birth, the interval from marriage to second birth was equivalent to duration of marriage. This bias inherent in the design of the study marred the data on *number* of migrations in relation to length of interval from marriage to second birth. Thus the long average intervals for couples reporting several migrations was partially selective in that couples with long intervals had a greater time period in which to migrate.

Second Phase of Study

The above-mentioned bias does not obtain in the second phase of the study because the time period from first interview to second interview is the same (three years) for all couples. To put the situation cryptically, in the first interview the number of births was held constant at two and the intervals varied; in the second interview the interval from first to second interview was held constant (three years) and the advent of the third birth within the three-year span was a dependent variable for study.

Although the bias described above was avoided in the second phase of the study a potential bias especially relevent to study of the interrelation of migration and fertility was the factor of cases lost because of migration to an unknown address. Its special relevance to the present analysis is considered at the end of the present chapter.

---

[10] C. V. Kiser, "Residence and Migration," in Westoff, Potter, Sagi, and Mishler, *op.cit.*, p. 277.

Pregnancies Since First Interview

For each religious group the proportion of couples having one or more pregnancies within three years after the first interview was higher for those that moved than for couples that did not move between the first and second interviews. The difference between the movers and nonmovers was significant ($P < .01$) for all religions combined and for the Protestants considered separately. (As in the first phase of the study the category of movers included those moving from one house to another as well as more distant migrations.) Among the Protestants about 61 per cent of the migrants and 43 per cent of the nonmigrants had one or more pregnancies between the first and second interview. The percentages were, respectively, 69 and 59 among the Catholics, and 41 and 27 among the Jews (Table 85). For neither the Catholics nor Jews was the difference significant.

Family Planning

The fact that among Protestants in particular the migrants were characterized by relatively high fertility after the second birth is due in part to the lower proportion of family planners among the migrants. Thus among Protestants about 57 per cent of the movers as compared with 76 per cent of the nonmovers had avoided an unplanned pregnancy after the first interview, i.e., they had either a planned pregnancy or none at all. For the Catholics the respective percentages were 58 and 64. For the Jews they were 78 and 91 (Table 85). The difference was significant for all religions combined and for Protestants but not for the Catholics and Jews.

Characteristics of Migrants

In view of the fact that a larger proportion of migrants than of nonmigrants had one or more pregnancies after the second birth, it is of interest to ascertain whether the higher fertility is associated with lower economic status of the migrants. Among both Protestants and Catholics, the husband's earnings for both 1956 and 1959 were lower for the migrants than for the nonmigrants. However, the differential was wider for 1956 than for the 1959 earnings. This suggests that the migration itself was to some extent prompted by opportunities for economic advancement and that to some extent the goal was realized. However, the percentage increase in median income from 1956 to 1959 tended to be almost as high among nonmigrants as among migrants despite the fact that the initial levels were higher among the nonmigrants.

Indices of Fertility after Second Birth, according to whether the Family Moved after First Interview[a]

MIGRATION AND FERTILITY BEHAVIOR AFTER SECOND BIRTH	ALL RELIGIONS	PROTESTANTS				CATHOLICS				JEWS			
		Total	None	Pregnancy Planned	Not Planned	Total	None	Pregnancy Planned	Not Planned	Total	None	Pregnancy Planned	Not Planned
Per cent having pregnancy after second birth													
Moved	62.3	61.1		17.7	43.4	68.5		26.7	41.8	40.6		18.8	21.9
Did not move	48.7	42.6		18.8	23.9	59.2		23.1	36.1	26.9		17.9	9.0
Pregnancies per 100 couples after second birth													
Moved	77.6	74.9				88.4				43.8		—	
Did not move	58.5	47.2				74.4				30.8		22.5	
Number children desired by wife (first int.)													
Moved	3.4	3.1	2.7	3.3	3.4	3.8	3.1	4.1	4.0	3.0	2.8	—	—
Did not move	3.2	2.9	2.6	3.3	3.1	3.6	3.0	3.9	4.1	2.7	2.5	3.4	—
Number children desired by husband (first int.)													
Moved	3.3	3.0	2.6	3.3	3.2	3.7	3.2	3.9	4.0	3.0	2.6	—	—
Did not move	3.2	2.7	2.5	3.2	3.0	3.5	2.9	4.0	3.9	2.8	2.7	3.4	—
Median earnings husband 1956													
Moved	4,731	4,550	4,833	4,750	4,318	4,625	4,500	4,719	4,656	5,200	6,250	—	—
Did not move	5,125	5,302	5,574	5,083	4,719	4,915	4,863	5,143	4,818	3,708	5,725	6,333	—
Median earnings husband 1959													
Moved	6,633	6,229	7,200	6,750	6,188	6,310	5,833	6,688	6,786	3,400	8,500	—	—
Did not move	6,733	6,908	7,132	6,900	6,313	6,418	6,372	6,385	6,524	7,778	7,625	10,000+	—
Number of couples													
Moved	353	175	68	31	76	146	46	39	61	32	19	6	7
Did not move	552	197	113	37	47	277	113	64	100	78	57	14	7

[a] Index not shown if based on fewer than 10 cases.

There was virtually no difference between migrant and non-migrant groups with respect to educational attainment. As for age, the wives and husbands were a little younger in the migrant than in the nonmigrant group.

Character of Change in Residence

Persons reporting a change of family residence since the first interview were classified according to type of residence (city, suburbs, and open country) at the time of the first and second interviews. Thus the "city-city" group consists of persons making a move but still living in a city environment. It includes persons moving from one city to another and those moving within the same city (mainly the latter in the present sample). The "city-suburbs or open country" group consists of persons moving from a city to either suburban or open country environment. The suburbs-suburbs group consists of people moving from one house to another within a given suburban area or from one suburban area to another. Since "migrants" include those moving to another house in the same area, the higher fertility of migrants is partly selective. The advent of another child may prompt the need for a larger house.

The relation of character of migration to economic status differs somewhat by religion. Among both Protestants and Catholics those reporting no migration were of higher economic standing (as determined by husband's earnings in 1956 and 1959) than the migrants (Table 86). Among the Jews the husband's income in both 1956 and 1959 was somewhat higher for those that moved than for those that did not move after the first interview in 1957. Among the Protestant migrants, the highest incomes of husbands were for those reporting suburban residence in both interviews. Among the Catholic migrants the highest incomes of husbands were found for those that moved from a city to the suburbs. The Jewish group was too small to permit close analysis in this detail.

Among no religious group of migrants did "character of change of residence" bear any sharp relation to fertility since the first interview. The percentage of Protestant migrant wives reporting one or more pregnancies after the first interview ranged from 56 for the suburb-suburb group to 63 for the city-city group. The proportion of family planners having pregnancies (women having planned pregnancies divided by women having planned pregnancies plus those having no pregnancies) ranges from 27 to 34 for the same two groups.

Among the Catholics, the percentage of women having one or more pregnancies after the first extended from 65 per cent for the

TABLE 86

Indices of Fertility after Second Birth, according to Character of Change of Residence after First Interview*

CHARACTER OF CHANGE IN RESIDENCE AND FERTILITY BEHAVIOR AFTER SECOND BIRTH	ALL RELIGIONS	PROTESTANT				CATHOLIC				JEWS			
		Total	None	Pregnancy Planned	Pregnancy Not Planned	Total	None	Pregnancy Planned	Pregnancy Not Planned	Total	None	Pregnancy Planned	Pregnancy Not Planned
Per cent having pregnancy after second birth													
No move	48.7	42.6		18.8	23.9	59.2		23.1	36.1	26.9		17.9	9.0
City–city	64.0	63.2		19.3	43.9	69.1		32.4	36.8	36.4		9.1	27.3
City–sub/open country	60.0	60.0		20.0	40.0	67.6		17.6	50.0	43.8		25.0	18.8
Sub.–sub.	57.6	56.4		16.4	40.0	64.7		26.5	38.2	—		—	—
Other	74.3	69.6		13.0	56.5	80.0		20.0	60.0	—		—	—
Number children desired by wife (first int.)													
No move	3.2	2.9	2.6	3.3	3.1	3.6	3.0	3.9	4.1	2.7	2.5	3.4	
City–city	3.4	3.1	2.8	3.3	3.4	3.7	3.1	4.2	3.8	2.7	—	—	
City–sub./open country	3.4	3.2	2.7	—	3.6	3.9	3.3	—	4.1	3.2	—	—	
Sub.–sub.	3.3	2.9	2.6	—	3.1	3.8	3.0	—	4.4	—	—	—	
Other	3.5	3.3	—	—	3.6	3.9	—	—	—	—	—	—	
Median earnings husband 1956													
No move	$5,125	5,302	5,574	5,083	4,719	4,915	4,863	5,143	4,818	5,708	5,725	6,333	
City–city	4,278	4,306	4,188	4,750	4,125	4,000	4,125	3,750	4,083	5,750			
City–sub./open country	5,000	4,438	4,500	—	4,167	5,000	5,125	—	4,625	6,500			
Sub.–sub.	5,083	5,179	5,375	—	4,750	5,000	4,500	—	5,583				
Other	4,850	4,750	—	—	4,375	4,750	—	—	—				
Median earnings husband 1959													
No move	$6,733	6,908	7,132	6,900	6,313	6,418	6,372	6,385	6,524	7,778	7,625	10,000+	
City–city	6,040	6,050	5,700	6,250	6,250	5,850	5,357	6,667	5,722	7,500			
City–sub./open country	7,000	6,556	6,667	—	6,500	6,778	6,700	—	6,750	10,000+			
Sub.–sub.	6,944	7,313	8,286	—	6,167	6,500	5,667	—	7,250				
Other	7,214	6,500	—	—	4,833	7,250	—	—	—				
Number of couples													
No move	552	197	113	37	47	277	113	64	100	78	57	14	7
City–city	136	57	21	11	25	68	21	22	25	11	7	1	3
City–sub./open country	90	40	16	8	16	34	11	6	17	16	9	4	3
Sub.–sub.	92	55	24	9	22	34	12	9	13	3	3	—	—
Other	35	23	7	3	13	10	2	2	6	2	—	1	1

* Index not shown if based on fewer than 10 cases.

migrants from one suburban area to another to 69 per cent for those moving from one city address to another.

RELEVANCE OF LOST CASES TO THE ANALYSIS OF RELATIONSHIP OF MIGRATION TO FERTILITY

A well-known limitation of longitudinal studies is the attenuation of the sample and the possibility that the lost cases are a select group and hence force a bias on the sample that is maintained. The extent and implications of the reduction in size of the sample for the second (1960) as compared with the first (1957) round of interviews has been discussed in detail in Appendix B.

The matter is introduced again here because it has special relevance to the question of the relation of migration to fertility. More specifically, some of the reduction from 1,165 to 905 in number of couples interviewed was due to the fact that couples moved during the three-year period to an unknown address. One might suppose that people who move to *unknown* addresses tend to be those who move long distances. Thus in an attempted analysis of the relation

TABLE 87

Distribution of Couples in First Phase of Study, according to Status in Second Phase

Study Status	Total	Protestants	Catholics	Jews
		(per cent)		
In first phase	100	100	100	100
In second phase	78	79	75	88
Not in second phase	22	21	25	12
Refused	8	6	11	3
Not located	3	4	2	2
Moved—no address	8	7	10	4
Other	3	5	2	3
Number of couples	1,165	473	567	125

of migration to fertility during the three years since the first interview, one would be faced with the possibility of biased results because of the absence of data for an extreme group of migrants.

First of all the couples classified as "moved-no address" may be viewed in the context of the total loss of cases. As indicated in Table 87, a total of 22 per cent of the couples in the first interview, were absent in the second stage of the analysis. There were 8 per cent that refused, 8 per cent that moved to an unknown address, 3 per cent that could not be located after several revisits, and 3 per cent that had been classified as ineligible because of death, divorce, separation, widowhood, the advent of sterility, etc.

As indicated, the percentage loss in sample size was somewhat higher for the Catholics (25 per cent) than for the Protestants (21 per cent) and it was lowest for the Jews (12 per cent).[11]

The higher proportionate loss of Catholics from the initial sample was especially marked for the two major categories of losses in the sample, refusal and moving to an unknown address.[12] For the other two classes, "not located" and "other," the percentages were somewhat higher for Protestants than for Catholics. Because of the religious differentials the tests for bias inherent in sample attenuation will be carried out separately for the two major religious groups.

It should be emphasized, however, that in all cases there may not be a clear-cut distinction between the "refused" and the "not located" groups, or between the "not located" and the "moved-no address" categories. Absence or reported absence possibly sometimes was simply an indirect form of refusal.

It would be well to have data regarding the eventuation and timing of third births not only for the 905 who cooperated in the second study (movers and nonmovers) but also for several classes of couples who were absent from the second study.[13] For present purposes it would be particularly desirable to compare the data for the migrants in the second study with those for the 95 not in the second study because they were in the category "moved-no address." The comparison of the two migrant groups is not possible in the nature of the case.

However, it is possible to compare these and other classes with respect to certain indices of fertility *relating to the first phase of the study*, i.e. intervals (from marriage to first birth and from first to second birth), number of children desired, and extent to which the first two children were planned. This is available for Protestants and Catholics separately.

Thus fertility indices from the first phase are available for comparisons between two classes of persons who moved after 1957: those in and those not in the second phase of the study. Also, for the cou-

[11] In this classification the Protestant-Catholic mixed marriages were combined with the Catholics if the marriage ceremony was performed by a priest. They were added with the Protestants if the ceremony was not performed by a priest. As of the time of the first interviews there were 54 mixed marriages added to the Protestant group and 86 to the Catholic group.

[12] In neither of these cases can the higher rates be laid at the door of the 86 Protestant-Catholic mixed marriages. A side analysis indicated a total sample loss of 16 per cent for the mixed marriages as compared with 27 per cent for strictly Catholic unions.

[13] In the nature of the case a relatively low proportion of couples having third births can be presumed for the 40 couples classified as absent for "other" reasons. This group contains those declared ineligible for reasons of sterilizing operations, dissolution of marriage, illness, etc.

TABLE 88

Indices of Fertility and Family-Planning Status in the First Phase of the Study, according to Religion and Status in Second Phase

Religion and Indices of Fertility from First Phase	First Phase Total	In Second Phase			Not in Second Phase				
		Total	Moved	Did Not Move	Total	Refused	Not Located	Moved—No Address	Other
PROTESTANT									
MEDIAN INTERVAL									
Marriage to first birth	18.2	18.0	14.8	23.9	19.1	21.0	14.0	17.3	28.5
First to second birth	28.7	29.5	24.9	33.6	26.5	29.7	20.5	26.5	26.2
Marriage to second birth	52.0	52.5	42.3	65.1	50.5	61.5	36.0	46.5	56.0
Preferred second to third	29.1	29.3	30.8	28.6	28.5	28.6	28.7	30.0	28.0
Ave. no. children wanted by wife	3.0	3.0	3.1	2.9	3.1	3.1	3.0	3.4	2.6
Fertility-planning status:									
Per cent highly successful	42.7	43.5			39.6	40.7	44.4	37.5	37.5
" " semi-successful	17.5	18.8			22.8	11.1	5.6	21.9	8.3
" " semi-unsuccessful	15.0	15.1			14.9	7.4	22.2	9.4	25.0
" " highly unsuccessful	24.7	22.6			22.8	40.7	27.8	31.3	29.2
Number of couples	473	372	175	197	101	27	18	32	24
CATHOLIC									
MEDIAN INTERVAL									
Marriage to first birth	15.7	16.7	14.9	17.8	13.4	15.6	9.7	12.4	14.0
First to second birth	27.2	27.7	24.8	29.1	25.6	31.4	22.0	21.2	23.0
Marriage to second birth	47.0	48.5	45.4	51.9	43.2	54.0	34.5	37.3	40.0
Preferred second to third	27.3	27.4	28.1	27.0	27.0	27.5	23.5	27.0	27.6
Ave. no. children wanted by wife	3.6	3.7	3.8	3.6	3.6	3.5	3.5	3.8	3.5
Fertility-planning status:									
Per cent highly successful	34.6	35.0			33.3	36.0	23.1	34.5	25.0
" " semi-successful	17.5	17.3			18.1	19.7	15.4	15.5	25.0
" " semi-unsuccessful	15.9	17.0			12.5	9.8	23.1	13.8	8.3
" " highly unsuccessful	32.1	30.7			36.1	34.4	38.5	36.2	41.7
Number of couples	567	423	146	277	144	61	13	58	12

ples in the study, it will be possible to ascertain the extent to which migration differentials in fertility indices measured in the first phase are consistent with migration differentials in percentages having a third child. Whereas we are still left in ignorance as to whether the lost cases had a third birth, we shall be able to form a fairly good

judgment on whether they were a select group with respect to fertility and whether their absence tends to bias the remaining group
very much or very little.

In the first place it will be noted in Table 88 that on the basis of
the several indices available, fertility behavior during the first phase
of the study was much the same for the 905 couples present in the
second phase of the study as for the total 1,165 in the first phase. In
other words, the loss of the 260 couples did not appreciably alter the
median intervals from marriage to first birth, from first to second
birth, or from marriage to second birth. The average length of the
"preferred interval" from second to third birth, the average number
of children desired, and the fertility-planning status with respect to
the first two children were much the same for couples cooperating
in the second phase as for the original universe of couples in the first
phase. The above holds true for Protestants and Catholics considered separately.

Although the above comparisons indicate that the sample was
not affected appreciably by the loss of the 260 couples insofar as
available indices of fertility behavior prior to the first interview are
concerned, it is of interest to make the comparisons between those
cooperating and those not cooperating in the second phase.

As may be seen in Table 88 the fertility indices for the cooperating and non-cooperating couples are much the same for both
Protestant and Catholic couples. The differences between the cooperating and non-cooperating couples (Cols. 3 and 6) are only a little
larger than those observed between the cooperating couples and all
couples (Cols. 3 and 2).

To come more specifically to the 95 couples who moved and left
no address we may note first of all that prior to the first interview
the fertility behavior of this group differed little from that of the
total group in the second phase (cf. Col. 3 and 9) of the study, but
resembled very closely that of *migrants* included in the second study
(cf. Col. 4 and 9).

As compared with the total group of couples in the second phase
of the study, the 95 that were absent because they moved to unknown addresses were characterized by somewhat shorter intervals
between marriage and first and second births; by somewhat larger
numbers of children wanted at the time of the first interview, and
by somewhat lower proportions that had planned the first two
births. However, these differences are relatively small and in most
cases not significant. Furthermore, similarity of fertility behavior of
the two groups of migrants (those absent from and those included
in the second study) indicates that the 95 couples were not *a select*

TABLE 89

Relation of Number of Pregnancies Experienced in Second Phase of Study to Fertility Behavior During First Phase of Study, by Religion and Planning Status of Pregnancies

RELIGION AND INDICES OF FERTILITY FROM FIRST PHASE	*None*	NUMBER OF PREGNANCIES IN SECOND PHASE OF STUDY					
		One			*Two or More*		
		Total	Planned	Not Planned	Total	Planned	Not Planned
		PROTESTANTS MEDIAN INTERVAL					
Marriage to first birth	22.3	16.2	19.4	15.0	14.0		15.0
First to second birth	35.6	25.1	27.5	23.7	21.6		21.5
Marriage to second birth	68.3	43.7	47.1	41.0	37.0		36.8
Preferred second to third birth	28.8	31.0	27.9	36.0	28.2		29.0
Ave. no. children wanted by wife	2.6	3.2	3.3	3.2	3.5		3.5
Number of couples	181	159	59	100	32	9	23
		CATHOLICS MEDIAN INTERVAL					
Marriage to first birth	23.1	15.1	14.9	15.2	12.4	14.4	11.8
First to second birth	38.4	25.8	28.4	23.9	19.7	23.5	18.6
Marriage to second birth	68.7	46.8	49.7	43.2	33.0	38.4	31.7
Preferred second to third birth	28.1	27.7	27.0	28.2	24.9	24.0	25.4
Ave. no. children wanted by wife	3.0	3.8	3.8	3.8	4.7	4.8	4.6
Number of couples	159	196	83	113	68	20	48
		JEWS MEDIAN INTERVAL					
Marriage to first birth	29.3	25.0	28.8	14.4			
First to second birth	37.7	26.7	26.2	28.0			
Marriage to second birth	69.3	54.0	60.0	42.0			
Preferred second to third birth	34.0	32.3	31.5	33.0			
Ave. no. children wanted by wife	2.6	3.3	3.4	3.1			
Number of couples	76	30	18	12	4	2	2

group of migrants insofar as fertility behavior during the first phase of the study is concerned.

The question still remains as to whether fertility behavior during the first phase of the study is pertinent to fertility behavior during the second phase.

In Table 89 the indices of fertility from the first interview are presented for couples in the second study classified according to number of pregnancies between first and second interviews and planning status of those pregnancies. More specifically the categories relating to experience after the first interview (i.e., after the second child) are: 0 pregnancy, 1 pregnancy (planned and not planned), and 2 or more pregnancies (planned and unplanned). Within each religious group the birth intervals during the first phase of the study were longest for those that had no pregnancy after the first interview and shortest for those that had two or more pregnancies after the first interview. They were longer for those who had a planned pregnancy after the first interview than for those having an unplanned pregnancy after the first interview. Among the Protestants, for instance, the median interval from marriage to second birth was longest (68.3 months) for those that did not have a pregnancy after the first interview (i.e. after the birth of the second child). The interval decreased sharply with number of pregnancies after the first interview. It was 47 for those having 1 planned pregnancy, 41 for those having 1 unplanned pregnancy, and 37 for those having 2 or more unplanned pregnancies after the first interview. Correspondingly, there is a direct relation between the number of children desired as expressed by the wife at the first interview and the actual fertility after the first interview. The preferred length of a third interval, as stated at the first interview on the assumption that there would be a third child, also tended to decrease with number of pregnancies after the first interview.

The above statements relate to Protestants but they hold in general for the Catholics and Jews (within the limits of the data).

In general, therefore, the attenuation of the sample effected by the group "moved-no address" does not appear to result in any material biassing of the remaining group with respect to fertility. A slight selection probably was involved in that migrants were of somewhat higher fertility. However, the migrants *not in the study* did not appear to differ from migrants *in the study* with respect to fertility.

SUMMARY

Census and official data generally indicate fertility rates to be lower in urban than in rural areas, lower in central cities than in other parts of metropolitan areas, lower in residential than in "mixed" neighborhoods, and lower in apartment and multiple-dwelling houses than in single-family houses. Although exceptions have been found, they also tend to indicate lower fertility rates for migrants than for nonmigrants. They suggest that children, like baggage, may be "impedimenta" insofar as migration is concerned.

The data from the present study, relating as they do to couples having second births in September 1956 are virtually unaffected by selections regarding size of family. Analysis of the first phase of the study suggested that among Protestants higher economic status, higher proportions that planned both births, and longer intervals between marriage and second birth characterized the residents of outlying areas as compared with those of central cities. These attributes also characterized occupants of single-family houses as compared with those of apartments and multiple-family houses, and nonmigrants as compared with migrants.

Likewise, data from the second phase of the study suggested that among the Protestants the proportion of couples having a conception within three years after the first interview was lower among those living in suburbs than in cities, lower among those living in residential than in "mixed" neighborhoods, lower among occupants of single-family houses than among apartment dwellers, and lower among the nonmovers than among those that moved during the preceding three years. The Protestant groups characterized by relatively low fertility were also characterized by relatively high economic status and by higher proportions classified as family planners.

The relationships mentioned above apply mainly to Protestants, and it was only for Protestants that any difference stood up as statistically significant. The economic selections involved in type of residence appeared to differ by religion. There was a greater tendency for suburbs to be selective of higher economic status among Protestants than among Catholics. The number of Jews in the study living outside central cities was too small to yield reliable comparisons.

Since 95 of the couples present in the first phase of the study were absent in the second phase because they had moved to unknown addresses, there was the possibility of a bias inherent in the absence of these migrants. Tests indicated that the fertility behavior of this group *during the first phase* was much like that of migrants who had moved to a known address and were interviewed. Furthermore, tests indicated a close relation of fertility during the first phase to fertility during the second phase among couples interviewed a second time. Therefore, there is rather strong circumstantial evidence that no serious bias was engendered by the loss of the 95 couples insofar as relation of fertility to migration is concerned. This conclusion is in harmony with the results of other types of tests described elsewhere in this volume.

Some of the results obtained from the study differ from expected results from census type data because of the sample design. Thus selections with respect to children ever born are ruled out in a sample initially recruited on the basis of a specific order of birth. It is by comparing results of samples of varying designs that we may hope to learn more about the causal nexus of fertility differentials.

Chapter XIII. Some Family Relationships

In the first phase of this study, weak associations were found between various aspects of fertility and measures of specific intrafamilial relations. Despite these disappointing results, the more promising measures were retained for further analyses with the additional fertility information gained in the second phase of this longitudinal study. It was the hope that intrafamilial relations measured soon after the birth of the second child would differentiate from among all couples those who increased their family size in the period of three years between interviews. Also, the *post factum* nature of prior analyses was not a sound basis upon which to make final judgments.

One further reason may be cited in favor of retaining measures of familial relations. The inclusion of marital adjustment and adjustment to mother role in the second interview as well as the first permits the view of a new dimension of familial relations and its presumed correlates. If, for example, marital adjustment or adjustment to mother role change appreciably from time to time then there is further evidence for evaluating and explaining the findings obtained in the first phase of this study. With a dynamic picture of the family in mind, familial relations at a given moment represent, so to speak, one observation from a sample space of relationships for a given family. How this sample of one observation in time is related to fertility rests, it seems first, on the intrafamilial variability[1] and, second, on whether the particular sample coincides in time with the fertility behavior measured. Thus if there is within-family variability over time, simple cross-sectional analyses ought to yield weak relationships between the two adjustment variables and fertility behavior.

The analysis of second phase materials parallels the work done before with four exceptions. The first exception has to do with the addition of fertility as a dependent variable. The second phase is different in that couples now vary in the number of their children. In addition, recent fertility, birth intervals, and contraceptive information complement and bring up to date desired size of family, contraceptive histories, and birth interval information gained at the first interview.

---

[1] Unreliability of measurement gives the appearance of change and, unfortunately; in this study, we cannot assess the comparative magnitudes of error variance and true change.

The second exception is the introduction of a few new independent variables. Among these are the wife's participation in community organizations, the immediacy of her plans to seek employment, and visiting patterns. These variables have been included to facilitate the further exploration of the hypothesis that fertility as a value is incompatible with values supporting extrafamilial identifications such as employment, friends, and community activities.[2]

The third exception is the opportunity to study changes in the wife's evaluation of her own adjustments to marriage and motherhood, her employment expectations, and her self-appraisal of her own childhood as they may associate with economic change, and fertility history. In the first analyses, an *ad hoc* hypothesis was advanced that marital adjustment and adjustment to mother role are affected by a couple's ability to control fertility. And further, the hypothesis stated that the direction of the association between the adjustment variables and fertility was determined by the ability of couples to avoid undesired and excess fertility.

The final exception is the introduction of four new variables that represent new hypotheses stimulated from the first analyses. These variables are: recency of urban migration, patterns of visiting, problems with children, and husband-wife agreement. Since these are new to the study, their treatment is reserved for a later part of this chapter.

More detailed elaborations of these hypotheses and rationales behind the second phase analyses do not seem justified given the many weak or ambiguous correlations among the variables under scrutiny. The hoped-for evidence did not materialize in sufficient strength for any one or more of reasons such as poor measurement, invalid hypotheses, or the complexity of the phenomena. The remainder of this chapter is devoted therefore to the reporting of what are essentially negative results.

ADJUSTMENT TO MARRIAGE AND MOTHER ROLE

Correlations between measures of adjustment variables (adjustment to marriage and mother role) and dependent variables are not close. A glance at Table 90 is sufficient to verify this. Two hypotheses carried over from Phase I analyses—that marital adjustment and adjustment to mother role are each correlated positively with desired size of family and the ability to plan fertility successfully—are rewarded by statistically significant coefficients. However, the meaning of these coefficients remains unclear.

[2] C. F. Westoff, R. G. Potter, Jr., P. C. Sagi, E. G. Mishler, *Family Growth in Metropolitan America*, Princeton University Press, Princeton, N.J., 1961, pp. 302–304.

If the causal sequence relating marital adjustment to fertility proceeds from marital adjustment to number of children desired ($r = .10$) and the latter in turn manifests its causal link to number of pregnancies with the observed correlation of .48, then the expectation is that marital adjustment will correlate with the number of additional pregnancies. That correlation turns out to be zero. A similar argument produces similar results for the variable of adjustment to mother role.

TABLE 90

Correlations between Adjustment Variables and Dependent Variables, Phase I and Phase II

Selected Measures of *Fertility and Related Variables*	*Marital Adjustment*		*Adjustment to Mother Role*	
	I	II	I	II
Number of pregnancies since 2nd birth	.00	.05	.00	− .02
Interval 2nd birth to next conception	− .01	− .06	− .02	− .04
" marriage to second birth	.03	− .04	.04	.01
" first to second birth	.02	− .07	.05	.01
" marriage to first birth	.03	.04	− .01	− .01
Number of children desired by wife I	.10	.12	.09	.09
" " " " " " II	.05	.09	.05	.04
Changes in children desired by wife	− .06	− .05	− .05	− .07
Number of children desired by husband I	.07	.07	.07	.06
Fertility planning success I	.07	.05	.06	.00
" " " since marriage	.08	.07	.07	.06
" " " first conception after 2nd birth	.04	.00	.04	.05
Knowledge of ovulatory cycle	.00	.05	− .05	− .05
Coital frequency	− .02	.02	.06	− .04
Routinization of sex	− .02	− .02	− .07	− .06

The absence of any correlation between the adjustment variables as measured at the first interview and sebscquent pregnancies does not rule out the possibility that the causal sequence begins with desired size of family and affects adjustment only if desired fertility is exceeded by actual fertility.

According to this notion, the .10 correlation just mentioned is due to wives who have exceeded desired fertility at the birth of their second child.[3] The rationale here is one that was advanced earlier as a possibility.[4] Adjustment to marriage and mother role were viewed as expressions of reactions to the stresses placed on a wife and mother and excess fertility is considered one such stress.

[3] This possibility arises since desired fertility is measured from the birth of the second child—the questions were in terms of the number of additional children desired. Thus of the nearly 300 wives wanting no more than two children, an unknown number may have wanted fewer than two.

[4] Westoff *et al.*, *Family Growth in Metropolitan America*, p. 302.

A test of this hypothesis, Table 91, reveals that marital adjustment does respond to excess fertility but in a direction contrary to the hypothesis. The greatest improvements in marital adjustment occur with unplanned and excess fertility. For this reason and because the pattern is not repeated with adjustment to mother role, this line of investigation is terminated. Instead, and no validity is claimed for these last observations, two hypotheses suggested by simple scanning of correlation matrices are advanced.

TABLE 91

Changes in Marital Adjustment, by Fertility-Planning Success following Second Birth, and by Wife's Fertility Desires following the Second Live Birth

Number of Children Desired	Average Change in Marital Adjustment		
	Pregnancy Planned	No Pregnancy	Pregnancy Not Planned
2	.12	.06	.49
3 or more	.23	.21	.28

The first is that adjustment improves with real or perceived improvements in the economic condition of the family. Since husbands in this sample are in an age group on a rising earnings curve, economic problems as a source of marital discord are diminishing at this point in time. This inference follows from a consistent pattern of positive correlations between adjustments and income, income change, feelings of economic security, and estimates of husband's chances for getting ahead. Change in income correlates .13 with change in marital adjustment while in the interim of the change there has been a general improvement in both income and marital adjustment.[5]

The second hypothesis is that under favorable conditions of an upward movement of income, increased sense of economic security, and the desire on the part of at least one spouse for an additional child, efficient contraception becomes less of an imperative. Unplanned pregnancies occur, therefore, with the reduction of contraceptive vigilance. Here the supporting facts are the greater upward change (about $500 dollars) in income between those initially desiring two children and going on to have unplanned pregnancies and those holding their fertility at the desired two. In a similar manner, the number of children desired by the husband discriminates between these two groups of wives.

These hypotheses do not by themselves explain the lack of relationship between adjustment and number of pregnancies. Nor do

[5] Sample attrition between interviews was selective to an unknown degree for couples with serious marital and/or economic problems.

they explain the lack of relationship between the adjustment scores and such variables (Table 90) as coital frequency and birth intervals. They do suggest another avenue of approach and indicate that a final judgment regarding these variables is still premature.

Attitudes toward Children and Extrafamilial Activities

The premise that fertility as a value is incompatible with values supporting extrafamilial identifications such as employment, friends, and community, implies the existence of an inverse correlation between desired size of family and wife's employment as well as the wife's social participation in both formal and informal groups. Data collected in the first interview were examined with these hypotheses in mind and, here too, the results are inconclusive. The opinion stated at that time was "that a desire for a small family leads to long birth intervals which in turn permit long duration of employment as well as non-employment between marriage and second birth."[6] Thus opportunity for employment and not conflict between values supporting fertility on the one hand and employment on the other, accounts for the correlation between employment and desired size of family.

The homogeneous and special nature of the sample (all women having a second child 6 months prior to the interview) first excludes the intensively career-oriented since they are presumed to want fewer than two children and, second, depresses the correlation of desired fertility with employment duration while exaggerating the importance of the correlation of employment duration with birth intervals because employment is primarily terminated by the first pregnancy.

To some extent, the homogeneous nature of the sample has been altered by the additional pregnancies of the wives. Presumably, if the opportunity argument is valid, subsequent employment histories of wives should show little variation by desired fertility once time lost due to pregnancies is considered. Since a correction for time lost due to pregnancies is impossible with these data, only a partial test of this hypothesis is supplied by data in Table 92. Employment since September 1956, for those having no additional pregnancies, bears little relationship to desired size of family. Even the direction of association is unclear. However, those wives having one or more unplanned pregnancies in the interim of three years between interviews regardless of number of children desired report the highest rates of employment. The suspicion arises here that wives who worked are selected from among poor planners.

[6] Westoff et al., op.cit. p. 304.

TABLE 92
Per Cent of Wives Who Have Worked since September 1956 within Categories Defined
by Number of Children Desired and by Fertility Planning Success of First
Pregnancy Following Second Live Birth

Number of Additional Children Desired	Pregnancy Planned	Pregnancy Not Planned	No Additional Pregnancy	Total
None	12	30	23	23
One	12	25	26	23
Two or more	18	28	18	27
Total	16	27	22	25

Associations with timing of future employment, that is when wives expect to go to work, follow an analogous pattern. Among wives having no additional pregnancies, the association between fertility desires and immediacy of work intentions, though *not* significant shows the more children desired the greater the incidence of current employment and plans for employment in the future.

It appears from these comparisons that the correlation between the timing of future employment and number of pregnancies since the second live birth is due partly to the effect that pregnancies have in forcing women to delay or interrupt employment. Secondly, the correlation is as low as .19 because wives planning to have no additional pregnancies after the second live birth tend also to have no future work intentions.

TABLE 93
Correlations among Wife's Employment Variables

Employment Variable	1	2	3	4
1 Duration of employment from marriage to second birth		.24	.18	.25
2 Future work intentions as expressed in 1957			.47	.40
3 Future work intentions as expressed in 1960				.78
4 Timing of future work				

Going beyond these meager data still further and placing stress on the intercorrelations among the four measures of wife's employment history and intentions, some evidence is found to support the probability that women who worked in the past are likely to work in the future. Duration of employment from marriage to second birth is correlated .25 with the immediacy of future employment. The other measures show similar intercorrelations (Table 94). To an extent seemingly beyond chance, women who in the past made use of time between pregnancies to work appear to persist in the pattern. The relationship, however, is sufficiently weak to suggest the overriding importance of contingencies. Among these contingencies, pregnancies and very young children in the household have already been suggested. The necessity to work as a means of supplementing family income may well be another. Data collected in this survey are consistent with national patterns. The lower the husband's income the more likely the wife is to work.[7] Correlations, (Table 94) indicate that the intent to work is also related to income. Some improvement (Table 95) is seen when additional pregnancies do not intervene.

TABLE 94

Correlations of Employment Variables with Husband's Income and Wife's Feeling of Economic Security

	Duration of Employment from Marriage to Second Birth	Future Work Intentions as Expressed in 1957	Future Work Intentions as Expressed in 1960	Timing of Future Work
Husband's income, 1956	.05	−.13	−.12	−.10
Wife's feeling of economic security, 1957	.03	−.12	−.12	−.12
Husband's income, 1959	.00	−.17	−.16	−.15
Wife's feeling of economic security, 1960	.00	−.12	−.15	−.13

TABLE 95

Correlations of Employment Variables with Husband's Income and Wife's Feeling of Economic Security among Wives with No Additional Pregnancies

	Duration of Employment from Marriage to Second Birth	Future Work Intentions as Expressed in 1957	Future Work Intentions as Expressed in 1960	Timing of Future Work
Husband's income, 1956	.00	−.15	−.19	−.14
Wife's feeling of economic security, 1957	.04	−.13	−.17	−.15
Husband's income, 1959	.06	−.13	−.19	−.19
Wife's feeling of economic security, 1960	.06	−.07	−.18	−.16

Provided there is the opportunity in terms of time, employment tends to be associated with low income whereas social participation tends to be associated with high income, high prestige occupations and education. The original hypothesis asserted that extrafamilial activities functioned in lieu of childbearing as a consequence of

[7] Gertrude Bancroft, *The American Labor Force: Its Growth and Changing Composition*, John Wiley and Sons, Inc., New York, 1958, p. 125, Table 83.

values in competition with fertility. Such extrafamilial activities, as far as these data indicate, take one of two forms neither of which represent alternative choices to fertility. The hypothesis is not sustained. Social participation, like employment has no special priority. Briefly, the correlations with social participation supporting this contention are −.18 with number of additional pregnancies, magnitudes of approximately .2 with income variables, and approximately .3 with education and occupational prestige variables. Neither of these latter two correlations is altered meaningfully if number of pregnancies is held constant. In Table 96, social participation is seen as the analogue and complement of work intentions. Comparisons with Table 92 show that where social participation is greatest, employment since 1956 is low and where employment is greatest, social participation tends to be lowest.

TABLE 96

Average Number of Organizations Participated in, by Wives by Planning Status of Pregnancy Following Second Live Birth and by Number of Children Desired

Number of Additional Children Desired	Pregnancy Planned	Pregnancy Not Planned	No Additional Pregnancy	Total
None	.8	.8	1.2	1.1
One	.9	.7	1.3	1.1
Two or more	1.1	.9	1.4	1.1
Total	1.0	.8	1.3	1.1

Before the conflict of values hypothesis is abandoned entirely, it is well to mention that neither liking for children nor visiting patterns as variables behave in a manner lending credence to the original notion. Liking for children is unrelated to number of additional pregnancies,[8] employment, or social participations, while visiting patterns appear related more to socio-economic variables than to fertility. Rather than a conflict of interests hypothesis, data suggest socio-economic class and time available to the wife affect the choice of and intensity of extrafamilial activity.[9]

Patterns of Dominance and Help Available to the Wife

Patterns of dominance and help available to the wife proved to be as poor indicators of fertility performance as they were indicators of fertility intentions. Number of pregnancies since the birth of the

[8] Perhaps it is naïve to assume that liking for children is translated solely into additional pregnancies. No less plausible is the notion that liking for children becomes expressed in a concern for quality rather than quantity.

[9] The reader must bear in mind that the definition of the population in this study may have eliminated career oriented wives from inclusion in this sample.

second child as well as the ability to control fertility show no association with any of the three dominance variables, or the extent to
which the wife receives help in household chores from others. The
three dominance variables are: dominance in running the house,
dominance in social affairs, and dominance in nonsocial areas. Presumably, families which are husband-dominated or in which the male
separates himself from the family and is not involved with domestic
affairs are the more prolific families and those with poorest
contraception.[10]

Statistical tests of these hypotheses as well as a series of *ad hoc*
cross-tabulations yield no supporting evidence or encouraging leads.
The results are negative in these respects.

Patterns of Visiting

The interest in the variable of visiting patterns stems from two
sources. The first is the attempt to explain the correlation of family
size in successive generations. Supposedly, this correlation is due to
the perpetuation from one generation to the next of similar attitudes
and behavior affecting fertility. It appears reasonable to argue that
the closer the family connections as opposed to contacts with
friends, the higher the association between family size in successive
generations. The second reason for the inclusion of visiting patterns
is statistical evidence from another study that it is related to fertility
desires. The frequency of family gatherings and the proportion of
all visits with relatives were found to be associated directly with
expected number of children for zero and one parity couples and,
inversely, for three and higher parity couples, given certain controls.[11] With these correlations in mind, three questions were framed
in an attempt to measure visiting patterns.

"With whose friends, your husband's or your own, do you as a
couple visit or entertain the most?"

"Whose relatives, your own or your husband's, do you as a couple visit or entertain the most?"

"Whom do you as a couple visit or entertain the most, friends or
relatives?"

The sample of responses to these items discloses no outstanding
associations[12] between visiting patterns and fertility to date or de-

---

[10] See Westoff, *et al.*, *Family Growth in Metropolitan America*, pp. 305–306, for an
elaboration on this theme.

[11] David Goldberg, "Some Recent Developments in American Fertility Research,"
in *Demographic and Economic Change in Developed Countries*, Princeton University Press,
1960, p. 147.

[12] Pearsonian correlation coefficients were computed despite the qualitative and
trichotomous response categories.

sired size of family. The relationships as seen in Table 97 are not high nor are they, with exceptions, in hypothesized directions. Religious Catholics provide the largest coefficients but the significance of the coefficients, in a statistical sense, is in doubt, given the variety of comparisons and the lack of independence between tests.

TABLE 97

Correlations[a] of Visiting Patterns with Number of Additional Pregnancies and Number of Children Desired by Religion

	Number of Additional Pregnancies and Visiting Patterns			Number of Children Desired and Visiting Patterns			
	Wife's Friends	Wife's Relatives	Relatives More than Friends	Wife's Friends	Wife's Relatives	Relatives More than Friends	N
Active Protestant	− .09	.02	− .06	− .07	− .05	.01	174
Other Protestant	− .06	.00	.06	− .06	− .05	.14	198
Active Catholic	− .13	− .07	− .19	− .11	.02	− .24	107
Other Catholic	.00	− .06	.04	.00	− .06	− .01	316
Jews	− .11	− .06	− .11	− .04	− .03	− .08	110
Total	− .06	− .04	.01	− .05	− .04	.02	905

[a] Hypothesis of heterogeneity of correlation coefficients is not supported by statistical test at the nominal level of 5%.

Along the lines of analysis indicated in prior paragraphs, data are at variance with the hypothesis. In Table 98 materials are presented analogous to data published elsewhere.[13] In the Detroit

TABLE 98

Partial Correlations[a] between Visiting Relatives in Preference to Friends and Number of Children Desired Measured Currently with Age Constant

	No Additional Pregnancies		With Additional Pregnancies	
	Correlation	N	Correlation	N
Active Protestant	.04	99	.08	75
Other Protestant	.15	82	.20	116
Active Catholic	− .18	30	− .27	77
Other Catholic	.05	129	− .10	187
Jews	− .13	76	.21	34

[a] Some evidence of heterogeneity of correlation coefficients at the nominal level of 5%.

Area when age and parity were held constant, visiting patterns correlated inversely with the number of children expected for those couples having three or more children. In our data the negative association is found among Catholics only, and a heterogeneity of

[13] David Goldberg, op.cit. p. 147.

associations exists among religious groups. Further, this table indicates that the difference in direction of association between low and high parity couples reported by Goldberg can be due to selection. The higher parity groups have a greater representation of Catholics. But even this explanation begs the question.

One possibility is that friends more than relatives, among Catholics, support high fertility orientations. Missing in our data is corroborative evidence such as the religious composition of friendship groups among Catholic couples. Among Active Catholics the correlation between number of children desired and visiting friends or relatives is −.24 (Table 97). If it is assumed here, without ancillary evidence, that the friends of Catholics tend to be Catholic and of roughly the same educational background, then the correlation −.24 appears to measure the effect of the peer group in determining high fertility desires among Catholics. Similarly suggestive are, first, the .02 and −.11 correlations (Table 97) with visiting wife's relatives and wife's friends among Active Catholics. The implication here, assuming these coefficients to be reliable, is that relatives on both sides have little effect whereas wife's friends have a greater effect.

Problems with Children

During the analysis of first phase materials, it was noted that birth intervals following the birth of the first child were longer by more than three months if the first child was a male. An hypothesis that a male first birth compared to a female first child presents greater and more discouraging problems to the neophyte parent[14] was advanced as the explanation of difference in length of birth interval. For this reason as well as for the more general concern that fertility, since it is subject to control, would be curtailed if the parents experience undue difficulties with their first two children, measures of problems with children were included in the second interview schedule. Wives were asked to rate on a six-point interval scale from serious problem to no problem at all, each child's health, sleeping habits, eating habits, sociability, personality and behavior. Items were then combined to form a cumulative scale for each child as well as for both children considered together.

Resulting data fail to meet the criterion of statistical significance for indicated comparisons. Some differences and associations are in the directions specified but not in any convincing manner. To conclude that problems with children have little bearing on future fertility behavior seems in order except for plausibility. In view of

[14] Westoff, et al., Family Growth in Metropolitan America, p. 295.

the paucity of correlations of variable with problems with children, measurement and not hypothesis may well be at fault.

Recency of Urban Migration

In a provocative study of the relationship between socio-economic status and fertility, recency of rural to urban migration was posed as the connecting variable.[15] The notion entertained is that the recent migrant whose socio-economic status is low also carries with him, to the urban center, a form of family structure different from the established urban pattern. In turn, family structure is said to affect fertility.

This latter assertion is also of concern here. Data permit classification of couples by recency of migration to urban centers. This classification, to support the thesis, should be associated both with family structure and with aspects of fertility. The relationship of recency of urban migration and socio-economic status is examined in Chapter IX.

TABLE 99

Average Number of Pregnancies since the Birth of the Second Child, by Religion and Urban Background

| | Generations Urban | | | |
	1st	2nd	3rd	Mixed
Active Protestant	.52	.59	.46	.43
Other Protestant	.70	.65	.72	.72
Active Catholic	1.33	1.06	1.12	.79
Other Catholic	.71	.64	.73	.72
Protestant	.62	.62	.61	.58
Catholic	.80	.73	.87	.74
Jewish	—	.16	.46	.29
Total	.68	.60	.71	.63

Religion as a control is justified by large differences in background since Jewish couples are, for the most part, at least three generations urban and Catholics are generally at least two generations urban, whereas Protestants show greater variability.

Where religion is held constant the average number of pregnancies since the birth of second child by urban and religious background (Table 99), varies not at all for Protestants and only little for Catholics. Catholic variation is at least partially explained by

[15] David Goldberg, "The Fertility of Two-Generation Urbanites" *Population Studies*, 12 (March 1959). See also "Another Look at the Indianapolis Fertility Data," Milbank Memorial Fund *Quarterly*, 38 (January 1960).

the concentration of high-fertility Active Catholics in the third generation migrant category. Sample size does not permit a closer scrutiny of this explanation or the explanation that ethnic background, which affects fertility as well as urban history, causes or obscures the association.

Because this study utilizes number of children desired as an index of completed family size, the data in Table 99 constitute a weak attempt to document further the hypothesized relationship between fertility and urban migration. The hypothesized relationship between family organization and recency of urban migration can be tested directly.

As before, most measures of family organization fail to exhibit the wanted associations. When religion is controlled, recency of urban migration appears to have little bearing on the dominance variables, patterns of help available to wife, or the wife's employment history. At least, all associations are weak. Religion is the dominant factor determining contraceptive behavior, employment, and number of pregnancies. The fact that religion and urban background are associated leads to the supposition that urban background differences in part, reflect religious composition.

Husband-Wife Accommodations

The subject of communication between husband and wife as it is related to family planning has been investigated at some length. Communication (as well as empathy) appears related to the use of birth control.[16] However, it seems reasonable to suppose that this relationship does not operate without an intervening variable. Only when communication leads to accommodation, compromise, or agreement between spouses can it be viewed as adding to the unity of the marital relationship. Communication, if it exposes the existence of differences, may actually be divisive in its consequence.

Communication between husband and wife on matters related to family size, family planning, spending, child care, household duties, religious matters and the like, is presumed to exist to some degree in each on-going family. Obviously however, spouses may not always agree or perhaps may never agree on certain issues. In order to maintain dependable familial patterns and minimize friction, compromise or accommodation by one or the other of the spouses at times becomes essential. The notion here is that the stability of the marital relationship and the ability to plan depend to a

[16] Reuben Hill, J. Mayone Stycos, and Kurt W. Back, *The Family and Population Control*, The University of North Carolina Press, Chapel Hill, 1959, pp. 147–152, 311–321.

measurable extent on a lack of conflict between spouses through agreement or the delegation of areas of responsibility.

Two measures, a general accommodation score covering sixteen areas of possible conflict and a two-item score on birth control

TABLE 100

Total Husband-Wife Accommodation Scores Correlated with Selected Dependent Variables

	Number of Pregnancies	Fertility Planning Success since Marriage	Fertility Planning Success since 2nd Birth	Interval since 2nd Birth	Interval Marriage to First Birth	Number of Children Desired by Wife		Number of Couples
						Six Months after Second Birth	Cur- rently	
Active Protestants	−.10	−.18	−.09	.16	−.02	.04	−.14	174
Other Protestants	−.18	−.12	−.13	.18	.21	−.10	−.11	75
Active Catholics	.07	.04	−.01	−.08	.19	.15	.18	107
Other Catholics	−.07	−.17	−.17	.08	.02	.01	.02	316
Protestants	−.17	−.15	−.17	.20	.12	−.03	−.13	372
Catholics	−.01	−.12	−.12	.02	.04	.08	.09	423
Jews	.21	−.07	−.10	−.12	.06	−.08	−.06	110
All couples	−.08[a]	−.14	−.13	.09[a]	.08	.01	−.02	905

[a] Heterogeneity of correlations among religious categories at the nominal level of 5%.

TABLE 101

Husband-Wife Accommodation on Matters of Birth Control and Number of Children Desired Correlated with Selected Dependent Variables

	Number of Pregnancies	Fertility Planning Success since Marriage	Fertility Planning Success since 2nd Birth	Interval since 2nd Birth	Interval Marriage to First Birth	Number of Children Desired by Wife		Number of Couples
						Six Months after Second Birth	Cur- rently	
Active Protestants	−.12	−.11	−.12	.17	−.01	−.08	−.17	174
Other Protestants	−.31	−.23	−.27	.28	.15	−.13	−.31	75
Active Catholics	.15	.11	.20	−.19	.01	.27	.27	107
Other Catholics	−.05	−.20	−.14	−.01	.13	−.11	−.10	316
Protestants	−.23	−.18	−.21	.24	.08	−.10	−.25	372
Catholics	.01	−.12	−.05	−.06	.10	.01	.02	423
Jews	−.02	−.21	−.17	.02	.16	−.14	−.22	110
Total	−.11[a]	−.17[a]	−.14[a]	.09	.11	−.09[a]	−.14[a]	905

[a] Heterogeneity of correlations among religious categories at the nominal level of 5%.

and family size, were developed in keeping with the theme just presented.

The correlations in Tables 100 and 101 support the gross inference that husband-wife accommodations have a bearing on number of pregnancies, birth intervals and the number of children desired. These associations, for the sample as a whole, are each statistically significant. Active Catholics appear to differ the most in these associations from other religious categories. Perhaps accommodation— or consensus among Catholics, implies a sharing of values consistent with church doctrines, a policy close to Church-connected precepts. Similar consensus and accommodation among other religious categories implies effective fertility control, fewer children, and longer birth intervals. In summary, this reasoning supposes that among Active Catholics accommodation and agreement are more easily achieved in keeping with Church doctrine, whereas for Other Catholics and non-Catholics accommodation is achieved at the expense of the partner oriented toward large family size.

Further data on this point are lacking and in light of weak associations presented in Tables 100 and 101, it would be presumptuous to go much further in our interpretation.

Summary and Conclusions

This chapter has investigated the relationship of fertility and numerous aspects of family relationships and has uncovered only weak associations. The results are nevertheless instructive. For example, unless some fundamentally new way of specifying what is meant by patterns of dominance is developed, this hypothesis deserves no further attention. In the same category as dominance patterns, we may well consider patterns of help, liking for children, adjustment to marriage, and adjustment to mother role. These latter variables have not yet distinguished themselves in fertility research though in one or more studies each has yielded a statistically significant association with some fertility variable. The less researched areas of problems with children, husband-wife accommodation, and visiting patterns may constitute more promising leads. However, the case against strong associations between single dimensions of family relationships and fertility appears sustained by the evidence presented in this analysis.

Until nagging questions pertaining to the validity of measures are answered or until some radical departure is introduced, there seems to be little point to further investigations in these areas of family relationships and fertility.

Chapter XIV. Age, Family Composition, and Sex Preference

The relationships of age, size of parental family and sex preference with the fertility of couples are well documented.[1] In specific and capsule form: age at marriage is inversely associated with size of completed family; family size between two successive generations is correlated and family size and sex composition are also associated. Though documented, none of these associations is impressively strong nor are the reasons for all of the associations entirely clear.

This study, so far as its design permits, confirms the existence of these relationships. Obviously we are in no position to say anything definite about the correlation between age at marriage or size of parental family and completed family size of the couples in this sample. All that can be said is that results obtained so far are not inconsistent with the previously demonstrated relationships. The main task of this chapter is to explicate the mechanisms that underlie and generate these relationships.

Current Age and Age at Marriage

The relationship between age at marriage and size of completed family is well known to demographers—the younger the age at marriage, the larger the completed size of family.

This relationship is assured in a noncontracepting population by loss of fecundity with age—the younger the age at marriage, the more years of reproduction. However, this relationship is less than perfect in such a population because of varying sexual activity and fecundity among individuals of the same age. To the extent that couples have a notion of a desired family size and practice contraception to achieve the size of family desired, the relationship between age at marriage and completed family size becomes more complex and may become altered in magnitude. It is within the realm of the possible, in the presence of perfect contraception to reverse this relationship if for some reason the smallest families are sought by couples marrying the earliest. In other words, given variation in desired size of family and the capacity to control fertility,

[1] P. K. Whelpton and Clyde V. Kiser, "Differential Fertility among 41,498 Native White Couples in Indianapolis," in *Social and Psychological Factors Affecting Fertility*, Milbank Memorial Fund, New York, 5 vols., 1946–58, I, pp. 12–13. For additional documentation see C. F. Westoff, R. G. Potter, Jr., P. C. Sagi, E. G. Mishler, *Family Growth in Metropolitan America*, Princeton University Press, Princeton, N.J., 1961, pp. 282–283.

the form and magnitude of the tie between age at marriage and completed size of family is no longer determined solely by biological factors.

How number of children desired and contraceptive effectiveness co-vary with age and fertility are crucial questions. Their answers provide some appreciation of factors bearing on an otherwise inverse relationship between age at marriage and completed size of family.

DATA

To judge by data, if the association between age at marriage and number of children desired exists at all, it is weak. In fact, a reading of Table 102 suggests that age at marriage is of minor consequence for fertility variables in general. For all couples, age at marriage correlates −.07 with desired number of children, −.10 with number of pregnancies since the second live birth, .08 with fertility-planning success after the second live birth and .07 with length of the next birth interval after the second live birth. Similar values with fertility-planning success and birth intervals obtain for the period up to the second live birth.[2]

The meaning of the −.07 correlation between age at marriage and number of children desired is ambiguous because these desires were measured *after* the birth of the second child and therefore do not exactly correspond to the variable we want. However, materials collected by Kelly[3] also show a small but positive, though not statistically significant, correlation of .06 between age at marriage and number of children desired at marriage. The lack of a decisive association between number of children desired and age at marriage indicates that this relationship is truly weak, if it exists at all, at least for the population studied.

On the other hand, age at marriage and fertility-planning success in both these samples are related in the same direction. The Kelly data yield a correlation of .19, a somewhat larger value than the .08 reported here. It appears then that age at marriage affects the ability to control fertility to a slightly greater extent than it relates to the number of children desired.

In contrast to age at marriage, current age (see Table 102 again) has an appreciable inverse association to the number of children

[2] Westoff *et al.*, *op.cit.*, p. 285, Table 83. The magnitudes of these correlations are undoubtedly affected by the eligibility criteria defining the population. There is little variation on age at marriage. All have demonstrated fecundity and all are first marriages.

[3] Charles F. Westoff, Philip C. Sagi and E. Lowell Kelly, "Fertility Through Twenty Years of Marriage: A Study in Predictive Possibilities," *American Sociological Review*, Vol. 23, No. 5 (October 1958), pp. 549–556.

desired. The closer relationship can be attributed to factors determining the length of the interval between marriage and the birth of the second child. The interval between marriage and the birth of the second child (marriage duration) correlates −.35 with the number of children desired, and thus reflects the more rapid pattern of pregnancies by wives seeking the largest families. This has the effect of producing a correlation of −.29 among all couples between number of children desired and current age simply because a part of current age is marriage duration (the correlation between the two is .63).

Some Speculations

A plausible causal sequence consistent with our data and linking these observations starts with the assumption that age at marriage is unrelated or at best only weakly related to the number of children desired. However, because of three facts: first, variation in number of children desired; second, the relationship between contraceptive effectiveness and fertility, and third, the direct relationship, though weak, between age at marriage and fertility-planning success, the youngest wives at marriage and wives desiring the most children acquire their first, second, and third births in the shortest period of time. Hence, the age of the wife after the birth of the second child reflects the dispatch with which the family is being acquired. The result is that by the second live birth, the youngest wives are those that either married early and had the poorest records of fertility-planning success or those wives that want the most children. The latter would also tend to have high contraceptive failure rates.[4]

This selective effect on age can be seen by comparing wives having a pregnancy after the second birth with the remaining wives. At marriage, the mean ages differ by half a year. By the second birth the difference in mean age is 2.1 years. Also at the second birth, the two subsamples differ in the number of children desired. Those having a third pregnancy on the average desire one or two more children than the remaining wives.

While our sample is still some years and children away from completing its fertility we can, on the basis of the foregoing, guess as to the determinants of the association between completed family size and age at marriage. Because we have reason to assume little or no relationship between age at marriage and number of children desired, such association as will be found between age at marriage and completed size of family is attributable to relationships of con-

---

[4] Since failure rates are a function of the differences between number of children desired and number acquired, these wives would have a high failure rate.

traceptive effectiveness, changes in number of children desired and changes in fecundity with age. Fecundity is now perhaps the least important for its effect is decreased by the material improvement in contraceptive effectiveness as the number of children desired is realized.[5]

This improvement in contraceptive effectiveness alone would be an attenuating influence. An opposing tendency is for younger wives to be poorer planners. As children are acquired faster by young wives, there is a greater opportunity for them to have additional planning failures before the terminating effect of menopause. In short, the correlation between age at marriage and size of completed family is not one of design, but one of neglected or poor planning.

Size and Composition of Parental Family

The typical interpretation of the association of family size in successive generations is appealing. In effect, the association is attributed to parental influence supporting, by persuasion or example, particular family-size desires or attitudes toward family planning.

Findings consistent with this explanation were reported in the previous volume.[6] To summarize, parental family size appeared to affect both the number of children desired and the planning success of the first two births. Whether or not these desires were to be translated into actual fertility remained to be answered until some couples had gone on to have additional children. Also sought was an explanation of the apparent nonlinearity of the relationship between family size in successive generations. An hypothesis advanced earlier was that nonlinearity of association was due to an overreaction to parental family size without stipulating the reasons for overreaction.

Data subsequently collected include the number of live births in the interim between interviews, and the sex composition of the parental family. This latter information affords the opportunity to test whether overreaction to family size—if this exists at all—can be linked in any way to birth order and sex composition in the parental family.

Size of Parental Family

Unfortunately, nonresponse to the second interview is sufficiently correlated with parental family size so that our data in this area cannot be considered entirely valid. Losses progress from an

---

[5] See Chapters III and IV of this volume.
[6] Westoff, *et al.*, *Family Growth in Metropolitan America*, pp. 290–292.

approximate 15 per cent among wives with no brothers or sisters to over 30 per cent among wives with five or more siblings. This selective bias had the interesting effect of eliminating the suggestion of nonlinearity of association between size of parental family and number of children desired.

TABLE 102
Correlation between Age of Wife, Current and at Marriage, with Selected Dependent Variables by Religion

	Number of Children Desired Six Months after Second Birth	Number of Pregnancies since Second Birth	Fertility-Planning Success after Second Birth	Length of Birth Interval after Second Birth
Active Protestant				
Age, current	− .27	− .40	.26	.37
Age at marriage	− .22	− .23	.11	.24
Other Protestant				
Age, current	− .35	− .40	.33	.34
Age at marriage	− .15	− .18	.09	.09
Active Catholic				
Age, current	− .33	− .36	.28	.37
Age at marriage	.02	− .02	.09	.03
Other Catholic				
Age, current	− .35	− .29	.26	.26
Age at marriage	− .13	− .05	.05	.02
Protestant				
Age, current	− .31	− .41	.30	.32
Age at marriage	− .17	− .22	.11	.17
Catholic				
Age, current	− .31	− .29	.26	.28
Age at marriage	− .04	− .01	.04	.00
Jewish				
Age, current	− .30	− .19	.09	.20
Age at marriage	− .16	− .05	− .01	.01
All couples				
Age, current	− .29	− .33	.27	.30
Age at marriage	− .07	− .10	.08	.07

The irregularities in the Catholic rows of Table 103 are in all likelihood accentuated by these losses. The appearance of association between the number of wife's siblings and mean number of children desired among all couples in Table 103 is exaggerated somewhat by rounding, though it is in any case not much weaker than the association reported in the prior volume.[7] Perhaps for the same reason, namely the selective nature of the attrition on parental family size, the association between number of wife's siblings and number of additional pregnancies (see Table 104) is weak.

TABLE 103

Number of Children Desired by Wife after the Birth of Second Child, by Religion and by Number of Wife's Siblings

| | Number of Wife's Siblings | | | | | |
	0	1	2	3	4	5+
Protestants						
Active	2.8	2.9	3.0	3.2	3.1	3.3
Other	2.8	2.9	3.0	2.8	3.7	3.2
Catholics						
Active	4.4	4.4	4.1	3.7	3.9	4.5
Other	3.5	3.4	3.2	3.5	3.5	3.4
Protestants	2.8	2.9	3.0	3.0	3.5	3.2
Catholics	3.7	3.7	3.4	3.6	3.6	3.7
Jews	2.3	2.4	2.4	2.0	2.1	2.4
All couples	3.1	3.2	3.2	3.3	3.5	3.5

TABLE 104

Average Number of Additional Pregnancies since Second Live Birth, by Number of Wife's Siblings and by Religion

| | Number of Wife's Siblings | | | | | |
	0	1	2	3	4	5+
Protestants						
Active	.29	.38	.31	.46	.64	.44
Other	.34	.52	.65	.68	.46	.54
Catholics						
Active	1.33	.78	.75	1.00	.80	.73
Other	.79	.47	.58	.52	.69	.54
Protestants	.32	.45	.49	.56	.51	.50
Catholics	.92	.57	.61	.66	.71	.58
Jews	.20	.26	.23	.42	.20	.20
All couples	.52	.45	.51	.60	.60	.55

Except for Protestants, Table 104 does not provide any convincing association. However, when data from Tables 103 and 104 are presented in the form of correlation coefficients the results are seen to be at least consistent with data reported elsewhere for Prot-

[7] *Ibid.*, p. 291, Table 90.

TABLE 105

Correlations between Number of Wife's Siblings, Number of Husband's Siblings, and
Selected Dependent Variables, by Religion

	Number of Children Desired Six Months after Second Birth		Number of Pregnancies Since Second Birth		Fertility- Planning- Success after Second Birth		Length of Birth Interval after Second Birth	
	Husband	Wife	Husband	Wife	Husband	Wife	Husband	Wife
Protestants								
Active	.01	.18	−.02	.16	.06	−.06	−.02	−.13
Other	.07	.10	.11	.06	−.07	−.02	−.08	−.06
Catholics								
Active	−.02	.00	−.09	−.15	−.13	.11	.09	.16
Other	.06	−.01	−.05	.02	.10	.00	.04	−.01
Protestants	.05	.13	.07	.11	−.03	−.05	−.07	−.10
Catholics	.01	−.02	−.07	−.03	.05	.03	.06	.03
Jews	.01	−.05	.02	.00	−.12	−.04	−.09	−.05
All couples	.04	.11	.04	.08	−.03	−.04	−.04	−.07

estants.[8] In Table 105 the correlations for Protestants most closely
conform to expectations. The correlations for all couples are seen to
be determined primarily by the pattern for Protestants, though not
as a simple average of coefficients. There is a more complex sort of
relationship here. The conclusions based on these data and those
reported in the prior volume are mainly two. First, what appears to
be a genuine pattern of association between the size of successive
generations among Protestants is strongest among the White-collar[9]
and the Active Protestants. Secondly, and more tentatively, because
of the heterogeneity of family size as well as desired family size
among religions, associations for the total sample are greater than
weighted averages of within-religion correlations.

BIRTH ORDER AND SEX COMPOSITION IN THE PARENTAL FAMILY

In the effort to trace down factors that weaken the association
between size of family in successive generations, two, not unrelated,
themes were pursued. The first approach is based on the suggestion
that couples with recollections of a happy childhood are moved

[8] *Ibid.*, p. 290, Table 88, and John F. Kantner and Robert G. Potter, Jr., "The
Relationship of Family Size in Two Successive Generations," C. V. Kiser and P. K.
Whelpton, eds. *Social and Psychological Factors Affecting Fertility*, 5 Vols., Milbank Memo-
rial Fund, New York, 1946–58, IV, pp. 1069–1086.

[9] Westoff *et al.*, *Family Growth in Metropolitan America*, p. 290, Table 88. Among
white-collar Protestants the correlation between number of wife's siblings and number
of children desired is .18.

toward reproducing the physical characteristics of the parental family so far as size of family is concerned. This approach yielded results—at least for the association between number of children desired and size of parental family—that are opposed to expectations.[10]

The second approach represents an innovation of sorts. The main idea is that birth order of the wife (or husband) and the sex composition of the parental family affect the wife's (or husband's) outlook on fertility. An oldest daughter in a large family may resent, as an example of one hypothesis, the child-caring duties thrust upon her or the preferential treatment accorded her brothers or younger sisters. For her, marriage means an opportunity to escape from family chores and responsibilities of child care with the consequence that she restricts her own fertility.

This view is more stimulating in thought than compelling in logic. With equal authority we could assert that such a set of experiences ideally socializes the eldest daughter to the traditional wifely role of mother.

As is common to much research, data prove to be stubbornly unyielding to the plausible. Tests fail to detect any relationship between sex composition or birth order in the parental family and either number of children desired or the fertility of couples. For example, holding size of parental family constant, sex composition and birth order appear to have little or no influence on age at marriage, desired family size or fertility. About the only effect noted is that the oldest daughter in a parental family of all daughters is likely to receive the greatest amount of formal education when compared to wives of different birth order or wives born to families having different sex compositions. In turn, there is the hint that oldest daughters of all-girl families marry better educated husbands. However, the transitivity of this relationship to fertility is lost in further comparisons. Nor is the socializing argument supported by data. Birth order and sex composition do not affect the wife's adjustment to marriage or the role of mother. The results—barring poor measurement—are negative.

SEX PREFERENCE

In the preceding volume evidence of a preference for both sexes among offspring was presented. Variation in number of children desired was found between couples having children all of the same sex and couples having both a boy and a girl. On the average, those having two boys or two girls as their first two children, desired the largest number of additional children (see Table 106). Left to the

[10] *Ibid.*, p. 292.

future was the question of whether this difference in number desired was to be translated into actual performance.

The pattern of largest average values among MM and FF families in Table 106 is partially reproduced in Table 107 by the number of pregnancies experienced among the 905 couples since the

TABLE 106

Mean Number of Children Desired Following the Birth of the Second Child, by Sex of First Two Births and by Religion

| | Sex Composition | | | |
	MM	MF	FM	FF
Protestants				
Active	3.2	2.8	2.6	3.3
Other	3.0	2.7	2.8	3.2
Catholics				
Active	4.2	4.1	4.0	4.6
Other	3.4	3.2	3.3	3.6
Protestants	3.1	2.7	2.7	3.3
Catholics	3.6	3.5	3.5	3.9
Jews	2.8	2.7	3.0	2.8
All couples	3.3	3.1	3.1	3.5

TABLE 107

Average Number of Additional Pregnancies since the Birth of the Second Child, by Sex of First Two Children and by Religion

| | Sex Composition | | | |
	MM	MF	FM	FF
Protestants				
Active	.38	.32	.13	.61
Other	.55	.47	.50	.61
Catholics				
Active	.97	.83	.89	.65
Other	.60	.53	.47	.62
Protestants	.46	.40	.34	.61
Catholics	.70	.61	.58	.62
Jews	.31	.37	.19	.13
All couples	.56	.50	.43	.56

birth of the second child. Some Catholics, and again the small sample of Jewish couples behave atypically and for this we have no ready explanation except the ever available one of a sampling quirk. Otherwise, Table 107 conforms adequately to expectations. In view of the fact that most couples indicated a desire for additional children regardless of the sex of the first two children, additional pregnancies were to be expected in all categories. The differentials in mean number of pregnancies are therefore actually stronger evidence of a preference for both sexes than the magnitudes of differences indicate.

Among those couples going on to a third live birth, differentials in the number of children desired persist. Among families with three children all of the same sex at the time of the second interview (111 couples), the average number of children they desire counting the three they already have is 4.1. Among those that achieved both sexes with the third birth (104 couples), the average number desired is 3.8 children.

It seems safe to conclude that sex preference operates to affect family size if the desired sex composition is not readily achieved. Implicit to this is the couple's model of an ideal family size and composition. If they fail to achieve desired composition within the number they want, there is pressure to raise the number originally wanted in order to achieve the desired composition.

Conclusions

This chapter explored some mechanisms that underlie and generate well-known relationships between age, size of parental family, and sex preference with the fertility of couples. Because of limitations in the nature of the population studied—principally couples with at least two children each and with still some years to go before menopause—only modest claims for findings seem appropriate.

First, among the wives studied, age at marriage has little bearing on the number of children desired. However, based on prior studies, age at marriage will be correlated with completed size of family. The slightly poorer planning success of younger wives with their longer interval between marriage and menopause assures the ultimate correlation between age at marriage and size of completed family. The immediate reason for this latter relationship is, therefore, poor or neglected fertility control over a longer period of time and not a relationship brought about through a calculated design on the part of wives.[11]

---

[11] At this point we can only guess the reasons for the poorer planning success of younger wives. A weaker sense of responsibility, a narrow education and experience in sexual matters, or a less calculating, more spontaneous approach toward family life are some reasonable conjectures. An answer would be of considerable value not only in the context of the age at marriage-family-size relationship but more importantly as a means of accounting for fertility in excess of the number of children desired when the means of controlling such fertility is common knowledge.

The association of family size in two successive generations is due in part to a genuine association among Protestants and in part to the heterogeneity of average fertility among religions and class groupings.

Finally, the number of children desired by a couple is often contingent upon the realization of both boys and girls in the same family. The failure to achieve this preferred sex composition results, among some couples, in an increase in the number of children originally desired.

Chapter XV. Multivariate Analyses

It is difficult to form a comprehensible picture of a multidimensional relationship, particularly with the complexity introduced by varying intercorrelations among the independent variables. We have chosen to summarize by using the statistical technique of multiple factor analysis, which like multiple correlation, permits an assessment of the amount of variation of fertility explained. In addition, it offers the possibility of providing some insights into any social-psychological vectors that may be important in influencing fertility.

The main objectives of this multivariate analysis are as follow:

1. To achieve a reduction in the number of dimensions necessary to "explain" the variation of fertility. This is the objective of parsimony common to most applications of factor analysis.

2. To show how much of the variation of fertility is explained by the factors extracted. Does this differ by religion?

3. To examine the factor structure underlying different aspects of fertility. To what extent does a common factor underlie the number of pregnancies since the second birth, the number of children desired, length of birth intervals, and fertility-planning success?

4. To compare the structure of the factors affecting fertility for the religious groups. How similar are they? What are the chief differences?

To answer these questions requires different factor analytic procedures which will be described in the appropriate sections that follow.

SELECTION OF VARIABLES

In the first phase of the study we retained for multivariate analysis only those variables showing significant zero-order relationships with the dependent variables.[1] Manifestly redundant variables were also eliminated with a total of 25 variables being ultimately retained. One of the problems created by such a screening procedure was the increased difficulty of achieving a clear and simple identification of the factors extracted. In the present analysis we have been much more liberal in our selection procedures and, in effect, have retained any variable that either showed some relation to some aspect of fertility or which promised to contribute to clar-

[1] To be more exact, the criteria actually employed in the first phase were that the variable should show at least a ±.15 correlation with number of children desired, interval between marriage and the second birth or fertility-planning success in any one of the three religious groups.

ifying the factor structure. The result was that we have retained 39 "independent"[2] variables in addition to 4 fertility variables. The 43 variables fall into 5 nominal classes. The first 4 variables, as just indicated, are measures of *fertility*. The second group comprises 16 measures of the *family's demographic and social characteristics*, ranging from age and number of siblings to wife's employment duration and marital adjustment. The next 7 variables involve *religiousness*. The *socio-economic* group is represented by 10 variables. A final group, which can be labeled *background* characteristics, includes education, rural-urban origin, and ethnic history. With but few exceptions, where a particular variable was measured in both interviews, the one measured in the first interview was selected for inclusion in this analysis. This decision rests on the premise that a primary interest in a longitudinal study is prediction.

Most of the individual variables have been included in the same form in which they were discussed in earlier chapters. Three of the variables have been recoded for purposes of correlation analysis. The variable "urban background" runs from a low score of all rural through three intermediate mixed classes to a high score of all urban. The three-category "ethnic background" variable has a different content for each religious group. In each case the ordering is determined by the observed association with fertility. Catholics, for example, are classified Italian, Other, and Irish in that order.[3] And finally, a measure of the effect of the recession is also ordered in the direction of observed association with fertility, going from anxiety or actually reduced income to no effects at all, to unemployment. The ordering of most of the other variables is clear from their labels although some ambiguity or reverse coding occasionally occurs. These are noted in footnotes in the tables.

One further decision which deserves mention was also made. We could have conducted the analysis for each of the five religious classifications used in the preceding chapters. In view of the important differences found between the Active and Other members of the Protestant and Catholic religions there would seem to be good reason for such a procedure. However, for several reasons the decision was made to use only the three conventional categories. The first reason for using three rather than five classifications is to increase the comparability with the multivariate analyses in the first phase of the study. Secondly, it has the additional salutary advantage of increasing the sizes of the subsamples. And thirdly,

[2] The designation "independent" in this context has a substantive but not a mathematical meaning.

[3] For Protestants the ordering is Other, British, and German and Irish combined (mostly German). For Jews the classification is Slavic, Other, and German.

since part of our interest is in estimating how much of the variance of fertility we can explain, retention of the five categories would have the effect of substantially decreasing the within-group variance. Our multivariate prediction of fertility is already reduced by the use of religion as a control rather than a variable.

THE FERTILITY VARIATION EXPLAINED

Our first interest is in answering the question of how successful the variables included in this study have been in accounting for the variation in the number of pregnancies occurring since the second birth. Among the variables included are the number of children desired by the wife as stated six months after the birth of her second child, the interval between marriage and the birth of the second child, and the success in planning both children as well as the sociological and demographic variables. This approach is similar to that used in Chapter VII where multiple correlation analysis was employed to measure the capacity of these antecedent fertility variables for predicting fertility in the three and one-half year period following the second birth. The present approach differs in including many more variables as well as in focusing attention on the comparison of the factors affecting fertility for each religious grouping.[4]

Although some arbitrariness is involved in the decision of how many factors to retain as "significant," examination of the size of each latent root extracted and application of a conventional rule led to the retention of 12 factors from each 43 variable correlation matrix.[5] The proportion of the variance of the number of pregnancies since the second birth accounted for by these 12 factors is virtually the same for each religious grouping (see the communalities[6] symbolized by h^2 for the first variable in Tables 108, 109, and 110. For Protestants the estimate is 42 per cent, for Catholics 40 per cent, and for Jews 42 per cent. The outstanding fact is the similarity of these values, in contrast to the first phase of the study, where we

---

[4] The context of "prediction" in which the analysis is set is not wholly legitimate in the sense that some of the variables included may be more of a consequence than an antecedent to fertility.

[5] The principal-axes solution was used to factor the matrix of Pearsonian correlation coefficients. Humphrey's rule was employed to determine the number of factors to be retained. This rule states that if the product of the two highest loadings does not exceed twice the standard error of the correlation coefficient, the factor is probably not significant.

Each of the three matrices was factored iteratively between five and seven times to achieve stability of the communality estimates.

[6] The term communality (h^2) refers to the proportion of the total common-factor variance of any variable accounted for by all factors extracted. Arithmetically, h^2 is equal to the sum of the squares of the loadings of the particular variable in each factor.

TABLE 108

Protestants: Rotated Factor Matrix[a]

Variable	1	2	3	4	5	6	7	8	9	10	11	12	h²
Number of pregnancies since second birth	.38	.32	-.20	-.19	-.19	-.16	.14	.08	-.05	.03	.00	.00	.42
Interval marriage to second birth	-.09	-.93	.05	.00	.08	.25	-.05	-.07	-.06	.00	.04	.02	.95
Number of children desired after second birth	.73	.15	-.08	-.20	.00	-.11	-.08	.00	.12	.06	-.04	.01	.64
Fertility-planning success to second birth	.05	.29	-.21	-.03	.03	-.14	.12	.00	.12	.06	.09	-.12	.21
Sex identity of first two children	.32	.06	-.06	-.09	.06	-.06	.00	.29	.04	.03	-.10	-.07	.22
Age of wife	-.13	-.67	.00	.56	-.05	.18	-.07	.01	.07	-.06	-.11	.06	.83
Age of husband	-.04	-.67	.02	.63	.09	.12	.00	.07	.06	.07	.09	-.08	.89
Age at marriage of wife	-.08	-.12	-.01	.78	-.10	.00	-.09	.08	.28	.10	.16	.10	.79
Age at marriage of husband	.13	-.12	.04	.84	-.01	-.02	.02	-.03	.21	.08	.11	-.04	.80
Number of wife's siblings	.22	.06	.01	.01	.09	-.09	.01	-.15	-.36	-.08	.11	-.05	.24
Number of husband's siblings	.19	.01	.05	.15	.03	-.04	.03	.02	-.36	-.10	.15	.06	.23
Wife's employment to second birth	.04	-.68	-.03	.01	-.04	.16	-.03	.01	.00	.31	-.01	-.02	.58
Wife's future work intentions[b]	.00	.03	.02	.10	-.01	.10	-.04	.03	-.06	.63	-.05	.00	.43
Timing of future employment	-.01	-.12	.03	.01	.02	-.12	-.06	.02	-.04	.54	.00	-.09	.33
Extent of organizational participation	.00	-.26	.14	.06	.08	.08	-.35	-.04	.39	.02	-.12	.06	.40
Visit friends or relatives	.07	.00	-.14	.09	.05	-.09	.01	.04	-.33	-.05	-.11	.08	.17
General husband-wife agreement	.06	-.01	.58	.16	.01	.19	.25	.07	.16	.02	.03	-.04	.50
Agreement on fertility	-.09	-.05	.53	.01	.04	.15	-.06	-.12	.01	-.04	-.03	.08	.34
Marital adjustment	-.19	-.08	.38	.01	-.12	.04	-.15	.18	.20	.05	.16	-.06	.33
Adjustment to mother role	.10	-.07	.23	-.08	-.09	-.02	.10	.08	.02	.11	.04	.15	.14
Church attendance of wife (1957)[b]	.01	.04	-.01	.01	.05	.02	.78	-.06	.00	-.01	-.08	.03	.63
Church attendance of husband (1957)[b]	.05	-.01	.05	-.03	.05	.00	.82	-.03	-.02	-.02	-.13	-.03	.69
Informal religious orientation[b]	.03	.11	-.12	.03	.06	-.01	.55	-.11	-.09	.10	-.03	.20	.41
Education in religious schools, wife	.12	.04	.01	.00	.11	.00	-.09	-.06	.07	-.15	-.22	-.49	.35
Education in religious schools, husband	.04	.05	.02	-.04	-.05	-.10	-.15	.09	.02	-.10	-.33	-.36	.30
Church attendance of wife (1960)[b]	-.06	.05	-.10	-.11	-.09	-.05	.63	.08	-.10	.01	.17	-.06	.48
Church attendance of husband (1960)[b]	-.05	-.04	-.08	-.05	-.06	-.06	.76	.08	-.15	-.01	.18	-.02	.66

(continued)

TABLE 108 (concluded)

Variable	1	2	3	4	5	6	7	8	9	10	11	12	h²
Husband's 1956 earnings	-.01	-.10	.07	.20	.06	.80	-.03	-.02	.23	.03	.01	-.02	.76
Income change, marriage to second birth	-.01	-.34	-.04	-.08	.01	.62	-.03	.05	.07	-.04	.04	-.02	.52
Feelings of economic security	-.06	-.07	.15	.08	.05	.48	-.11	.43	.25	.06	.05	-.03	.54
Relevance of finances[b]	.32	-.09	.07	.13	.15	-.02	-.03	-.19	-.01	.03	.14	.12	.22
Occupational prestige	.04	-.15	-.06	.15	.04	.27	-.05	-.03	.71	.08	.05	.00	.64
Perception of husband's opportunities[b]	-.08	-.01	.03	.08	-.07	-.28	.12	-.37	.42	.03	.03	-.07	.43
Wife's drive to get ahead	.06	-.06	-.10	.05	-.06	.05	.10	-.01	.18	.02	.03	.09	.08
Husband's 1959 earnings	.10	-.06	.07	.26	-.20	.59	.00	-.10	.46	.13	-.05	.16	.73
Aspiration for children's education	-.01	.01	.11	-.03	-.15	.01	.05	.03	.39	-.03	-.01	-.08	.20
Education of wife	.00	-.08	.06	.20	-.05	.13	-.09	.09	.74	-.15	-.09	-.02	.66
Education of husband	-.11	-.05	.02	.16	.07	.03	.03	.05	.82	.01	.01	.02	.74
Rural-urban background of wife	.02	-.05	-.07	.07	-.09	-.05	.00	-.04	.09	.10	-.46	-.06	.27
Rural-urban background of husband	.01	-.10	-.02	-.09	-.31	.08	-.03	.01	.14	.04	-.53	.07	.32
Ethnic background of wife	.01	-.07	-.11	-.11	-.33	.07	-.03	-.07	-.09	.08	.07	.23	.19
Ethnic background of husband	.03	-.07	.11	.00	-.19	-.13	.05	-.17	-.01	.04	.01	-.29	.23
Effect of recession	.09	.12	.01	.00	-.19	-.13	.05	-.17	-.21	-.17	-.08	.21	.23

[a] Rotated to simple structure by the quartimax criterion, excluding the first four variables. (See footnote 7.)

[b] Variable is reverse coded. A plus value should be interpreted as low on the scale.

⟨ 213 ⟩

TABLE 109

Catholics: Rotated Factor Matrix[a]

Variable	1	2	3	4	5	6	7	8	9	10	11	12	h^2
Number of pregnancies since second birth	.38	-.36	.21	.16	-.13	-.12	.10	.05	-.04	.03	-.03	-.02	.40
Interval marriage to second birth	-.15	.91	-.16	-.05	.16	.02	-.11	-.03	-.16	.05	-.08	-.06	.95
Number of children desired after second birth	.58	-.30	.17	.33	-.17	.12	.17	.06	.08	.08	-.10	.00	.66
Fertility-planning success to second birth	.11	-.21	.08	.11	-.09	.11	.21	.01	.19	-.06	-.01	.03	.18
Sex identity of first two children	.18	-.08	.03	-.01	-.04	.05	-.05	.07	-.02	-.12	.15	-.05	.09
Age of wife	.03	.55	.00	.01	.74	-.16	-.04	-.01	-.04	.04	.00	-.02	.89
Age of husband	-.12	.48	-.07	.05	.77	.11	.00	-.04	-.04	-.01	-.03	-.04	.86
Age at marriage of wife	.16	.03	.18	.04	.79	-.10	.02	-.05	.04	.02	.05	.01	.71
Age at marriage of husband	-.04	-.03	.07	.00	.85	.18	.06	.07	.07	-.01	.02	-.01	.77
Number of wife's siblings	.13	-.02	-.29	.02	.14	-.13	-.09	.11	.09	-.08	-.08	-.14	.20
Number of husband's siblings	.05	-.05	-.26	.16	.16	.18	-.08	.06	.10	-.06	-.04	-.24	.21
Wife's employment to second birth	.00	.65	-.05	-.11	.03	.06	-.01	-.12	.23	.02	-.03	-.04	.51
Wife's future work intentions[b]	.05	-.09	.11	.09	.05	.05	-.03	.13	.59	.02	.05	.04	.41
Timing of future employment	-.08	.16	-.07	-.11	-.02	.06	.03	-.20	.50	-.05	-.06	.12	.36
Extent of organizational participation	.05	.16	.19	.09	.09	.14	.13	.15	-.04	-.01	.02	.03	.14
Visit friends or relatives	.04	-.03	-.28	-.01	.14	-.08	.10	-.11	-.01	-.08	.12	-.16	.16
General husband-wife agreement	-.05	.01	.11	.15	.03	.12	.01	.11	-.03	.71	.10	-.04	.59
Agreement on fertility	-.11	.03	.04	.03	.04	-.04	.02	.07	.01	.61	.04	.04	.40
Marital adjustment	-.10	.03	.07	.14	.11	.28	.06	-.06	.16	.23	.06	.01	.20
Adjustment to mother role	.06	.05	-.11	.11	-.06	-.17	-.01	.00	.04	.15	.12	.01	.11
Church attendance of wife (1957)[b]	-.02	-.04	-.06	.82	-.06	.02	-.04	-.02	-.06	-.03	.25	.00	.75
Church attendance of husband (1957)[b]	.01	.00	-.07	.77	-.03	-.01	-.08	.04	.05	-.02	.33	-.08	.72
Informal religious orientation[b]	-.07	.03	-.13	.50	-.16	-.14	.10	.02	.05	-.05	.03	-.03	.34
Education in religious schools, wife	.01	-.10	.07	.41	.07	.04	.35	.06	-.13	-.11	.27	-.03	.45
Education in religious schools, husband	.06	-.07	.09	.28	.03	-.04	.32	.01	.00	-.01	.21	.21	.28
Church attendance of wife (1960)[b]	.04	.00	-.04	-.76	-.01	-.01	.02	-.12	-.08	.03	.10	.18	.61
Church attendance of husband (1960)[b]	-.01	-.02	-.09	-.70	.04	.02	-.04	-.03	.07	-.01	-.55	.07	.81

(continued)

TABLE 109 (concluded)

Variable	1	2	3	4	5	6	7	8	9	10	11	12	h^2
Husband's 1956 earnings	−.04	.10	.18	.05	.09	.01	.06	.86	−.04	.01	.02	.00	.80
Income change, marriage to second birth	−.04	.35	−.06	−.04	−.09	−.14	−.03	.47	−.02	.06	−.08	.00	.39
Feelings of economic security	−.02	.01	.19	.11	−.03	.32	.03	.42	−.07	.15	.02	−.05	.36
Relevance of finances[b]	.44	−.09	.14	.13	−.01	.03	.10	.15	−.13	.10	.04	.05	.31
Occupational prestige	−.03	.01	.57	.06	.05	−.02	.03	.28	−.01	.09	.06	−.03	.42
Perception of husband's opportunities[b]	.10	.11	−.41	−.14	.12	−.09	.01	−.19	.02	−.13	.04	−.08	.30
Wife's drive to get ahead	−.08	−.04	.10	−.04	.00	−.18	−.06	−.06	.07	−.07	.09	−.10	.09
Husband's 1959 earnings	−.01	−.03	.44	−.01	.06	.00	−.01	.55	−.08	.10	−.07	−.01	.52
Aspiration for children's education	.03	.07	.25	.15	.00	.01	−.08	.01	.05	.07	−.04	−.09	.11
Education of wife	.16	−.03	.53	.09	.12	.18	.13	.21	.19	−.03	.06	.08	.47
Education of husband	.01	.00	.70	.16	.10	−.03	.08	.21	−.02	.04	.04	.04	.58
Rural-urban background of wife	.02	−.06	.00	.10	−.07	.09	.07	.04	.06	−.01	.01	.59	.38
Rural-urban background of husband	−.01	−.06	.12	.12	−.10	−.07	−.02	−.05	−.02	−.01	.12	.63	.47
Ethnic background of wife	.01	−.02	.18	.19	−.02	.07	.59	.05	−.09	.01	−.11	−.06	.44
Ethnic background of husband	.00	.00	.00	.15	−.01	−.04	.70	.10	.11	.00	.14	.01	.55
Effect of recession	−.01	−.02	−.14	.04	−.07	.04	−.09	.00	.11	.02	.06	.00	.05

[a] Rotated to simple structure by the quartimax criterion, excluding the first four variables. (See footnote 7.)
[b] Variable is reverse coded. A plus value should be interpreted as low on the scale.

TABLE 110

Jews: Rotated Factor Matrix[a]

Variable	1	2	3	4	5	6	7	8	9	10	11	12	h²
Number of pregnancies since second birth	.42	.30	−.23	.15	.15	−.15	−.10	.09	.06	.05	.03	.03	.42
Interval marriage to second birth	−.06	−.12	−.01	.85	.11	.00	−.03	−.04	−.06	−.10	−.03	.00	.75
Number of children desired after second birth	.56	.10	−.04	.17	.17	.08	−.15	.40	.06	−.01	−.13	−.09	.60
Fertility-planning success to second birth	−.03	−.12	.31	.37	−.01	.31	−.15	.22	.01	.10	.19	.22	.51
Sex identity of first two children	.03	−.27	.31	.12	−.06	−.14	.01	.03	.06	.13	−.17	.18	.29
Age of wife	−.08	.04	.06	−.54	−.08	−.24	.72	.14	−.09	.01	.03	−.08	.92
Age of husband	.03	−.08	−.03	−.36	−.11	.11	.84	.08	−.01	.01	−.04	−.05	.88
Age at marriage of wife	.00	.06	.00	−.05	.18	.17	.82	.01	−.04	.04	.00	.01	.74
Age at marriage of husband	.03	−.06	−.07	.08	.04	.13	.90	.20	.09	.07	.07	.05	.90
Number of wife's siblings	−.01	−.13	.10	−.04	.55	.02	.31	.27	−.10	−.01	.08	−.05	.52
Number of husband's siblings	.23	−.10	−.04	.08	.23	.14	.24	.34	−.13	.24	.01	−.06	.40
Wife's employment to second birth	.00	−.02	−.09	.71	.02	.07	−.05	.06	−.12	.14	−.07	.00	.56
Wife's future work intentions[b]	.14	.07	−.05	.29	.03	.00	−.08	.21	.32	.51	.02	.00	.53
Timing of future employment	−.05	−.04	.21	−.26	.12	.01	.13	.18	.13	.66	.07	.11	.64
Extent of organizational participation	−.16	−.02	.24	.02	.17	.08	.05	.45	.12	−.19	.11	.13	.40
Visit friends or relatives	.02	.01	.02	−.10	.11	.48	.08	−.15	.23	.13	−.09	.18	.39
General husband-wife agreement	.04	−.12	.03	.05	.04	.01	.13	−.03	.20	.04	.06	.85	.81
Agreement on fertility	−.06	.15	.04	−.08	−.06	−.07	.13	.02	−.11	−.07	.02	.68	.54
Marital adjustment	.29	.14	.09	.13	−.02	.16	.02	−.03	.26	−.11	.28	.20	.36
Adjustment to mother role	.05	.02	−.09	.04	.12	.13	−.13	−.22	.18	.21	.15	.15	.23
Church attendance of wife (1957)[b]	.11	.42	.73	.01	.02	.20	−.08	.03	.09	.01	.05	−.06	.78
Church attendance of husband (1957)[b]	−.18	.35	.68	.01	−.05	.14	.00	−.06	.17	−.04	.03	.07	.68
Informal religious orientation[b]	.12	.13	.53	.06	−.14	−.09	.08	−.27	.06	−.09	.17	.15	.48
Education in religious schools, wife	−.03	.15	.12	.09	.16	.11	−.03	−.04	.02	−.19	−.10	.01	.13
Education in religious schools, husband	−.04	.01	−.06	.27	.11	.37	−.12	.17	−.19	.04	.17	−.03	.33
Church attendance of wife (1960)[b]	.05	−.44	.75	.00	.01	.00	.07	.10	.00	−.25	.01	.04	.83
Church attendance of husband (1960)[b]	−.11	−.25	.66	.00	.09	.09	−.03	.09	.00	−.32	−.02	−.02	.64

(continued)

TABLE 110 (concluded)

Variable	1	2	3	4	5	6	7	8	9	10	11	12	h^2
Husband's 1956 earnings	-.03	.06	.08	.05	-.07	.06	.14	.14	.88	-.09	.10	.04	.86
Income change, marriage to second birth	.05	.08	.08	-.42	.02	-.02	-.19	.02	.52	.00	-.01	.00	.49
Feelings of economic security	.13	-.05	.06	.01	.14	.24	-.16	.05	.64	-.04	.17	.06	.58
Relevance of finances[b]	.05	.26	.07	-.05	.22	-.10	.25	.22	-.06	.15	.04	.02	.27
Occupational prestige	.10	.03	.06	.00	-.07	-.12	-.02	.66	.25	.10	.07	-.05	.54
Perception of husband's opportunities[b]	.01	.05	-.10	.01	-.28	-.10	.18	-.20	.38	-.05	-.36	-.18	.49
Wife's drive to get ahead	-.28	-.04	.01	.11	.07	-.04	.19	-.12	.06	.06	-.01	-.07	.16
Husband's 1959 earnings	-.07	.07	.04	.03	.00	-.10	.19	.23	.89	.02	-.17	.06	.92
Aspiration for children's education	-.37	-.09	.01	.04	.06	-.06	-.09	.12	-.01	.21	.26	-.04	.29
Education of wife	-.01	-.05	.03	.04	.16	.06	.07	.69	.15	.10	-.02	.08	.56
Education of husband	.04	-.06	-.04	-.08	-.13	-.03	.15	.82	.29	.04	.03	-.07	.82
Rural-urban background of wife	.09	-.07	-.08	.21	-.11	-.13	-.28	.02	.03	.17	.49	.06	.45
Rural-urban background of husband	-.07	.14	-.03	.07	-.01	-.01	-.08	.10	-.04	-.18	.65	.11	.51
Ethnic background of wife	.05	.20	-.06	.04	.03	.06	-.09	.20	-.06	-.25	.14	.04	.19
Ethnic background of husband	.05	.29	-.06	.14	-.24	.01	-.06	.00	-.02	-.24	.15	.43	.43
Effect of recession	-.28	.33	-.01	-.08	.33	-.09	-.07	-.08	-.04	-.11	.03	-.06	.34

[a] Rotated to simple structure by the quartimax criterion, excluding the first four variables. (See footnote 7.)
[b] Variable is reverse coded. A plus value should be interpreted as low on the scale.

⟨ 217 ⟩

noted least success in explaining the variation of fertility among Protestants. The explanation, we believe, lies in the fact that a different variable is being analyzed now. In the first phase, we emphasized the number of children desired by the wife for which the communalities estimated were .48 for Protestants, .64 for Catholics, and .55 for Jews. The fact that a number of additional pregnancies over the three-year period is apparently equally explainable for couples of all three major religious categories is not inconsistent with the earlier finding that the number of children desired, or for that matter any of the other fertility antecedents, is not equally predictable.

FACTORS RELEVANT TO FERTILITY

This quantitative similarity in predictability does not imply that the same kinds of factors operate or that they are of equal importance in determining fertility in each group. In Tables 108–110 the rotated factor matrices are presented with factors numbered in order of their statistical importance for fertility.[7] For each religious group, the factor containing the highest loading on desired family size includes a substantial portion of the variation of fertility ranging from 14 to 18 per cent of the *total* variance and from 34 to 42 per cent of the *explained* variance[8] (see Factor 1 in each matrix). The other variables included in this factor are the ones reported in the first phase as the main correlates of number of children desired.[9]

---

[7] The basic rotations used follow the quartimax criterion for simple structure. This solution maximizes the fourth moment of the distribution of factor loadings. The rotated factor matrices in Tables 1–3 include two or three additional rotations for the purpose of achieving a structure that would have some resemblance to the previous bivariate analyses. Actually, we undertook two sets of simple structure rotations. In the first set, the variable "number of pregnancies since the second birth" was suppressed, that is its factor loadings did not enter into the mathematical solution for simple structure but were rotated proportionately. In the second set, the values for the other 3 fertility variables—interval from marriage to second birth, the number of children desired, and fertility-planning success since marriage—were also suppressed. The differences in factor structure turned out to be negligible so that only one set (the latter) is reproduced here.

[8] The proportion of the total variance is calculated by squaring the loading of number of pregnancies on the factor in question, and the proportion of explained variance is calculated by dividing the square of the loading by the communality of the variable.

[9] The other variables appearing in Factor 1 for Protestants is the sex composition of the first two children and the perceived relevance of finances. For Catholics, the supplementary loading in Factor 2 is the perceived relevance of finances, and for Jews it is level of aspirations for the children's education. Other factors containing portions of the variance of desired family size (Factor 4 for Protestants, Factors 2 and 4 for Catholics and Factor 8 for Jews) include the remaining correlates of desired family size discussed in the first analysis. See C. F. Westoff, R. G. Potter, Jr., P. C. Sagi, E. G. Mishler, *Family Growth in Metropolitan America*, Princeton University Press, Princeton, N.J., 1961, pp. 327–328.

For Protestants and Catholics the other factor of importance for fertility equal to that of desired family size is defined primarily by the variable of marriage duration and the variance shared with age and other measures of time, such as the duration of the wife's employment since marriage and income change from marriage to the birth of the second child (see Factor 2 for Protestants and Catholics). For Jews, however, this factor of marriage duration (Factor 4) is of considerably lesser importance in determining fertility, containing as it does about 2 per cent of the variance of fertility. One reason why marriage duration is of more limited importance may be the fact that Jews desire fewer children on the average than either Protestants or Catholics and practice contraception more effectively, and thus time is of less significance.

The other factors of statistical importance for Jewish fertility appear to relate to the religious area. Factor 2, although weakly defined, seems to relate to change in attendance at religious services during the period between the birth of the second child and the second interview. The general pattern is for higher fertility to be associated with an increase in attendance, a pattern inferred from the opposite signs of the loadings on the factor at the two different time periods.[10] Factor 3 is much more clearly defined as religiousness, containing the common variance of the frequency of attendance at religious services and a measure of informal orientation. The factor implies higher fertility with greater religiousness. The remaining factors of some significance for fertility relate to the number of siblings, particularly those of the wife (Factor 5), age at marriage and age (Factor 7), social class (Factor 9), and Factor 6 which is too poorly defined to warrant speculations about its content. We must of course continually bear in mind the fact that the Jewish sample is numerically small (110 couples) and that some statistical instability certainly exists.

As discussed above, the main factors accounting for the fertility of Protestants and Catholics involve desired family size and marriage duration (defined in our sample as the interval between marriage and the birth of the second child). The two factors collectively account for nearly 25 per cent of the total variance and 58 per cent of the explained variance of Protestant fertility, while for Catholics the two factors account for 27 per cent of the total variance and 68 per cent of the explained variance of fertility. Limiting our attention to the other factors containing at least 1 per cent of the total variance of fertility, we see that there are five such additional fac-

[10] Church attendance is coded inversely so that a positive sign means low frequency of attendance.

tors for Protestants collectively which account for about 16 per cent of the total variance and about 40 per cent of the explained variance, and five such factors for Catholics, accounting for 11 and 28 per cent of the total and explained variance respectively.

In three instances—age, ethnic background and religiousness— the factors are the same for Protestants (4, 5, and 7) as for Catholics (5, 7, and 4) except, as we have seen in prior analyses, religiousness means higher fertility among Catholics but lower fertility among Protestants. The factor containing the common variance of age at marriage and the related portion of the variance of current age is of course (as all factors are) independent of the factor defined by marriage duration and current age and, at least for Protestants and Catholics, the marriage duration factor is of much greater importance for fertility than the age at marriage factor.

Although weakly defined, the ethnic factor (5) for Protestants reflects the tendency noticed in Chapter VIII for higher fertility to be related to German background. The comparable factor for Catholics is of greater theoretical significance in view of our earlier interest in the interrelations among Irish background, religiousness, Catholic education, and fertility. Factor 7 contains a very large proportion of the explained variation (80 to 90 per cent for wives and husbands respectively) of ethnic origin which was coded 0 for Italian, 1 for Other, and 2 for Irish. The next highest loadings are for extent of education in the Catholic schools. There are no significant loadings on church attendance or informal religious orientation. In brief, the factor contains that portion of the correlation between ethnic background and education in Catholic schools which is associated with fertility but not with religiousness and, as the loading on fertility (.10) indicates, this is not very much. The fact is, however, that the loading of fertility on the religiousness factor (Factor 4) is not much higher (.16) and a slight rotation could equalize the distribution of this variance. The rotation would increase the loading of fertility, Catholic education and ethnic background on Factor 7 while decreasing their loadings on Factor 4, but this would entail a compromise on the now pure separation of church attendance and informal religious orientation. All of this simply underscores the joint connection of these variables with fertility.

The remaining factors having some, though limited, relevance for fertility are different for Protestants and Catholics. For Protestants, the marital accord factor (3) and an economic factor (6) seem to play a role but there was no particular evidence presented in Chapter XII which lends any confidence to the marital accord result. For Catholics a social class factor (3) operates to a greater extent than among Protestants (9). The remaining factor (6) of relevance to fertility among Catholics is very poorly defined and probably reflects mainly statistical unreliability.

Factors Not Relevant to Fertility

It is instructive to look at the content of the factors that have little or no bearing on fertility. Limiting our attention to factors which are well defined and which include less than one per cent of the variance of fertility, there are several factors common to all three religious groups. Two of these are the wife-working factor (Factors 10, 9, and 10 for Protestants, Catholics and Jews respectively) and the rural-urban factor (Factors 11, 12, and 11). The absence of any relationship between rural and urban background and fertility when religion is held constant was emphasized in Chapter XII. The absence of any independent relation of the wife's work history and her future work plans and fertility does not mean that there is no intrinsic association between the wife's participation in the labor force and her fertility, but rather that the association is absorbed in the factor of marriage duration. In other words, the length of time worked by the wife prior to the birth of the second child is associated with fertility in the complex of variables affecting the interval between marriage and the second birth, and indirectly the fertility of couples after that event.

Among Catholics and Jews, neither the economic (8, 9) nor the marital accord factors (10, 12) appear to have any connection with fertility. That they do seem to be involved with the fertility of Protestants may be either simply fortuitous as is the suspicion in the case of the marital accord relationship or genuine as is the hunch for the economic factor.

The Fertility Factors

There are two basic approaches to the identification (in factor analysis) of the factors affecting fertility. The first approach, which we have just utilized, is an attempt to achieve "simple structure" among the "independent" variables in the matrix. By simple structure is meant achieving the clearest possible identification of factors by maximizing the separation of the clusters of intercorrelations. This objective is translated mathematically into criteria which maximize the fourth moment of the distribution of factor loadings in each factor by a rather laborious procedure of successive rotations. In this first approach we allow the associated variance of the fertility variables to be rotated proportionately without, however, entering into the mathematical solution for simple structure.

The second approach is to concentrate on the structure of the fertility variables themselves, and try to achieve some type of simple structure or some meaningful separation of the four variables. One possibility would be to rotate all of the variance of the number of pregnancies into a single factor and let the values of all other variables on this factor be determined by this rotation. The difficulty with this seemingly direct approach is that it does no more than produce a transformation of the original correlations of each variable with fertility. A more rewarding procedure and the one actually followed here is to derive four factors containing all of the common-factor variance of the four fertility variables. However, there is a decision required about what ordering of the four variables is desired among the four factors with 24 ($n!$) different arrangements being possible. The decision was to order the variables in the following sequence:[11] number of children desired following the second child, fertility-planning success from marriage to the second birth, the interval between marriage and the second birth, and finally the number of pregnancies since the second birth. The main advantage of this particular ordering is that actual fertility since the second child is located in the final position being preceded by variables which are genuinely antecedent in time. Thus, we loaded all of the common-factor variance of the number of children desired into Factor I along with all of the variance held in common with this variable and all other variables. Factor II was then defined by all of the variance of fertility-planning success and the correlated portions of all other variables which are not common with Factor I. Factor III, with no loadings on the first two variables, is composed of all the remaining variance of the interval from marriage to the second pregnancy not in the first two factors. The last factor,[12] IV, has the interesting property of containing all of the variance of number of pregnancies remaining after the extraction of that portion of its variance held in common with the first three variables. This factor analytic procedure permits us to examine the structure

[11] The technique used is the diagonal method of factoring the original correlation matrices relying on the communalities estimated iteratively in the preceding principal-axes solution. Since the diagonal method is extremely sensitive to and dependent upon the communality estimates, we used the communalities for all positive roots. Thus the values of h^2 appearing in Table 4 are slightly higher than those in Tables 1–3 where the communalities are equal to the sum of the squares of the loadings on each of the 12 factors with the largest positive roots.

[12] Actually there are eight remaining factors which are completely independent of the four fertility variables located exclusively in the first four factors.

of these individual factors within a meaningful time sequence and to make inter-religion comparisons of the factors affecting fertility.

Perhaps the most interesting factor is Factor IV (see Table 111) which contains the residual variance of fertility that is not common with any of the preceding fertility variables. For Protestants, a total of 18 per cent of the total common-factor variance and 38 per cent of the explained variance of the number of pregnancies is contained in this factor. For Catholics this is about 10 and 20 per cent respectively and for Jews Factor IV contains 23 and 46 per cent of the two types of variance.

The fact that a significant portion of the variance of number of pregnancies is independent of the previous three fertility variables is a reasonable proposition when we realize that changes in the number of children desired did occur and that the index of fertility-planning success (at best not a highly reliable measurement as indicated in Appendix C) for the first two births is not a good predictor[13] of success in planning the next pregnancy. Moreover, the interval of the time of observation terminated at three and a half years; changes in fecundity could have occurred and simple chance of conception is an element that cannot be ignored. The structure of this factor for each of the three groups is not particularly enlightening, perhaps because the existence of the factor may in part reflect the type of chance element introduced by initially selecting variables partly in terms of their correlation with fertility. Another reason is that the factor seems to include portions of correlations in which fertility may be playing more of a causal role, such as the extent of organizational participation which one would expect to decline with the arrival of a new infant in the household. Another variable of this kind may be the future work orientations of the wife.

The other factor of critical significance for number of pregnancies is of course the factor (I) containing all of the variance of desired family size and the associated variance of fertility-planning success and the length of the first two birth intervals. For Protestants and especially for Catholics this is the most important factor for fertility. For Protestants, Factor I contains 22 per cent of the total variance of number of pregnancies and 46 per cent of the explained variance. The Catholic picture reveals 36 per cent of the total or 75 per cent of the explained variance of fertility located in this factor. The Jewish factor structure discloses an almost equal amount (24 per cent of the total and 48 per cent of the explained variance) located in Factor I and in Factor IV.

[13] The correlation is .21.

TABLE 111

Four Factors Including All Common-Factor Variance of Number of Children Desired, Fertility-Planning Success, Interval from Marriage to Second Birth, and Number of Pregnancies since the Second Birth

Variable	PROTESTANTS					CATHOLICS					JEWS				
	I	II	III	IV	h²	I	II	III	IV	h²	I	II	III	IV	h²
Number of children desired after second birth	.82	.00	.00	.00	.67	.84	.00	.00	.00	.70	.81	.00	.00	.00	.65
Fertility-planning success to second birth	.12	.52	.00	.00	.28	.25	.43	.00	.00	.25	– .11	.76	.00	.00	.59
Interval from marriage to second birth	– .31	– .55	.76	.00	.96	– .51	– .45	.72	.00	.98	– .21	– .40	.78	.00	.81
Number of pregnancies since second birth	.47	.15	– .22	.43	.48	.60	.02	– .16	.31	.47	.49	– .02	– .18	.48	.50
Sex identity of first two children	.34	.11	.04	.02	.27	.12	– .12	– .17	– .03	.17	– .02	.24	.06	– .08	.39
Age of wife	– .38	.49	.40	– .16	.88	– .37	.19	.48	.03	.93	– .37	.26	.35	.10	.96
Age of husband	– .24	– .34	.53	– .17	.93	– .39	.29	.43	.05	.92	– .39	.20	.20	.11	.93
Age at marriage of wife	– .21	– .20	– .10	– .27	.83	– .04	– .05	.02	.05	.77	– .16	– .16	– .23	.00	.81
Age at marriage of husband	– .09	– .08	.01	– .23	.85	– .11	– .04	.02	– .01	.82	– .28	– .28	.00	– .21	.94
Number of wife's siblings	.16	.22	.19	.10	.32	– .02	.02	.10	.00	.27	.01	.01	.04	.08	.60
Number of husband's siblings	.06	– .02	.01	.12	.30	– .02	– .06	.02	– .24	.26	.09	– .10	– .10	– .01	.46
Wife's employment to second birth[a]	– .15	– .42	.49	.06	.62	– .27	– .03	.62	– .04	.54	– .16	– .38	.50	.29	.62
Wife's future work intentions[a]	.01	.07	.07	– .10	.46	.09	.23	– .09	– .03	.45	.11	.20	– .15	.16	.64
Timing of future employment	– .04	– .04	.05	– .21	.40	– .07	.12	.15	– .56	.42	.00	.03	.19	– .11	.71
Extent of organizational participation	.02	– .50	.03	– .42	.46	.09	– .18	.09	– .29	.22	.19	– .25	– .09	– .18	.50
Visit friends or relatives	.01	.15	.11	.04	.22	– .07	– .01	.03	– .09	.23	– .06	– .14	– .03	– .18	.48
General husband-wife agreement	– .04	– .27	– .10	– .32	.56	.10	– .13	.03	– .20	.62	– .10	– .20	– .22	.07	.85
Agreement on fertility	– .13	– .34	– .14	– .36	.40	.01	– .22	– .03	– .04	.44	– .18	– .29	– .05	.11	.60
Marital adjustment	.12	– .27	– .04	– .07	.38	.15	– .14	.02	– .26	.28	.17	.11	– .05	– .09	.45
Adjustment to mother role	.13	– .32	– .12	– .19	.20	.13	– .12	.09	– .10	.18	.00	.03	.04	– .02	.37
Church attendance of wife (1957)[a]	– .05	.27	.08	.24	.68	– .34	.03	– .20	.18	.79	.17	.21	.10	– .24	.83
Church attendance of husband (1957)[a]	– .08	.24	.11	.32	.75	– .29	– .02	– .12	.07	.77	– .08	.13	.01	– .15	.75
Informal religious orientation[a]	– .03	.16	– .08	.26	.47	– .29	– .08	– .18	.07	.40	– .15	.30	.06	.17	.56
Education in religious schools, wife	.07	– .06	– .08	– .10	.41	.31	.07	.11	– .07	.51	.04	– .10	– .19	– .04	.27

(continued)

TABLE 111 (concluded)

Variable	PROTESTANTS					CATHOLICS					JEWS				
	I	II	III	IV	h^2	I	II	III	IV	h^2	I	II	III	IV	h^2
Education in religious schools, husband	.07	−.03	−.11	.00	.35	.24	.19	.09	.08	.34	.08	.45	−.02	.16	.44
Church attendance of wife (1960)[a]	−.05	.27	.06	.38	.56	−.28	−.09	−.21	.16	.66	−.03	.23	.20	−.53	.87
Church attendance of husband (1960)[a]	−.13	.25	.10	.39	.71	−.26	−.03	−.07	−.03	.83	−.05	.24	.11	−.47	.71
Husband's 1956 earnings	−.14	−.41	.02	−.20	.80	.06	−.12	.02	.07	.84	.09	−.03	−.14	−.06	.93
Income change, marriage to second birth	−.09	−.27	.36	−.09	.56	−.16	.08	.37	.13	.44	.01	−.16	.32	.15	.58
Feelings of economic security	−.12	−.32	−.04	−.19	.58	.14	−.11	−.04	−.19	.44	.15	.04	−.02	.06	.65
Relevance of finances[a]	.29	−.10	.13	−.25	.27	.43	.03	.09	.05	.37	.15	−.10	−.13	.04	.38
Occupational prestige	.06	−.30	.01	−.27	.68	.15	.10	.09	.21	.50	.37	−.04	.02	.15	.62
Perception of husband's opportunities[a]	−.13	.22	.06	.12	.48	−.18	−.14	.00	−.22	.39	−.14	−.03	.03	.17	.56
Wife's drive to get ahead	.03	−.02	.06	.21	.17	−.10	.19	−.02	.18	.16	−.22	.02	−.13	−.20	.29
Husband's 1959 earnings	.00	−.32	.02	−.28	.79	.15	−.04	.00	.10	.57	.19	.02	−.03	.03	.99
Aspiration for children's education	.06	−.12	−.12	−.15	.26	.09	−.06	.02	.23	.19	−.28	.12	−.01	.09	.36
Education of wife	.04	−.33	−.17	−.24	.70	.33	.07	.02	−.08	.55	−.39	−.19	−.10	−.17	.63
Education of husband	.06	−.31	−.10	−.37	.77	.23	.02	−.01	.14	.63	.37	−.20	.01	.31	.87
Rural-urban background of wife	−.07	−.09	−.08	−.09	.34	.12	.16	.03	−.02	.43	.06	.23	−.09	.32	.54
Rural-urban background of husband	.11	−.12	−.08	−.04	.39	.08	.09	−.08	−.06	.50	−.06	.04	−.07	.26	.58
Ethnic background of wife	−.03	.03	.11	.16	.24	.25	.19	.15	.14	.48	.09	.02	.00	.06	.34
Ethnic background of husband	.06	.03	.12	.13	.28	.19	.36	.21	−.03	.58	.02	−.09	−.20	.16	.51
Effect of recession	.05	.02	−.15	.16	.31	−.01	−.01	−.04	−.11	.12	−.15	−.01	.00	.30	.42

[a] Variable is reverse coded. A plus value should be interpreted as low on the scale.

The content of Factor I presents the same pattern that we have seen both in the initial analysis of factors affecting desired family size[14] and in the earlier discussion in the present chapter. For Protestants, the constellation of variables affecting fertility through the avenue of desired family size are the sex distribution of the first two children, age, and relevance of finances. For Catholics, Factor I contains loadings on the perceived relevance of finance, the religious and ethnic component, education and age, and for Jews, the variables of education and age appear. Incidentally, this particular diagonal solution illuminates the role of current age in its effect on fertility. Its most potent influence is exerted on fertility through its association with desired family size and not through its connection with fertility-planning success independent of desired family size or through its connection with marriage duration (independent of either desired or fertility-planning success) or through any residual effect (such as fecundity) that age might exert on fertility independent of all three other variables.

The role of contraceptive effectiveness in affecting fertility is also illuminated. Factor II contains all of the variance of fertility-planning success remaining after the extraction of that portion of its variance shared with desired family size. The loading of actual fertility in Factor II is negligible but fertility does have high loadings on Factor I. This is another reaffirmation of the proposition first advanced in Chapter IV, namely that the association between contraceptive effectiveness and fertility is in large measure a function of desired family size.

Factor III contains most of the variance of the intervals between marriage and the second birth. This variance is independent of that appearing in Factors I and II which is associated with family-size desires and fertility-planning success. The loading of fertility in Factor III is small but implies a correlation of about $-.15$ between length of the interval and number of pregnancies that is independent of both family-size desires and fertility-planning success. The content of this factor is the element of time, weighted as it is with age, wife's employment duration, and amount of income change since marriage. What is the underlying basis of this association? Probably two processes are operating. First it probably reflects the correlation of fecundability and the rate of conception, with the more fecund having a higher rate and thus shorter birth intervals. Secondly, as we have noted, the measure of fertility-planning success is weak and it is possible that some of the variance of both birth intervals and number of pregnancies in Factor III should be located in the first two factors.

[14] Westoff *et al.*, *Family Growth in Metropolitan America*, pp. 327–328.

Factor Comparison of Religious Groups

The assumption underlying the separation of the three religious groups in this analysis has been that the factors affecting fertility have been different. We can now approach this problem with more precision and refinement of the concept of fertility. The type of question being posed is whether Protestants, for example, are more like Catholics or Jews in the factors affecting fertility with the latter variable being separated into the components of desired family size, fertility-planning success, the length of birth intervals, and a residual category. Our approach will be to examine the similarity of the structures of each of the four factors for each religious group.

In the first phase of the study we conducted a similar analysis of more limited dimensions of fertility with the conclusion that the greatest similarity exists between Protestants and Catholics. The data from the second phase now permit us to expand this question to include the four factors described above.

TABLE 112
Correlations of Factor Loadings between Religious Groups

| Religious Combination | Factor | | | |
	I	II	III	IV
Protestant and Catholic	.81	.47	.80	.27
Protestant and Jewish	.69	.71	.78	.02
Catholic and Jewish	.73	.48	.67	− .01

The correlations appearing in Table 112 in general support the hypotheses that Protestants and Catholics are more alike in the factors affecting their fertility than either is like the Jewish group[15] with one major exception. The exception is with reference to Factor II which contains the bulk of the variance of fertility-planning success in which there is a much higher correlation[16] between Protestants and Jews (.71) than between either of these groups and Catholics (.47 and .48 respectively). Part of the origin of this difference

[15] On the surface, this conclusion appears to contradict the main finding reported in Ronald Freedman, P. K. Whelpton, and John W. Smit, "Socio-Economic Factors in Religious Differentials in Fertility," *American Sociological Review*, 26 (August 1961), pp. 608–614. They reported that when Protestants and Catholics in their sample were matched with Jews on selected socio-economic characteristics that most of the Protestant-Jewish differences in fertility are eliminated but the differences with Catholics are increased. The explanation of this apparent contradiction is that matching the socioeconomic characteristics of Jews means that one is comparing Protestants and Catholics of higher occupational status, income and education. And, as we have seen, higher socio-economic status among Catholics implies higher fertility but among Protestants it means lower fertility thus bringing their fertility closer to that of the Jews.

[16] It should be emphasized that no basis exists for evaluating the significance of differences in these values.

is that religiousness and education relate to fertility-planning success in opposite ways for Protestants and Jews than for Catholics.

SUMMARY

The analysis presented in this chapter is designed to accomplish several objectives. The major purpose is to summarize by multivariate statistical analysis the extensive series of bivariate analyses conducted in the preceding chapters. We have been interested in particular in the comparative predictability of fertility for the three religious groups and in answering the question of how similar are the kinds of factors affecting the fertility of Protestant, Catholic, and Jewish couples. The technique of factor analysis was used in several forms to describe the underlying structure of the correlates of fertility, as they operate through the mechanisms of desired family size, fertility planning, and the length of birth intervals.

PART IV

SUMMARY

Chapter XVI. Summary of Major Findings

The publication of this book marks the completion of the second phase of the study. Although a third and final phase in which we could secure information on completed family size is eminently desirable and will very definitely be conducted, it seems worthwhile at this juncture to attempt some distillation of the results of our research to date. Since the first book did not contain such a summary we shall include here whatever is relevant from the first phase of the study. The chapter will take the form of an inventory of propositions about different aspects of human fertility based upon the research reported in both volumes.

The analyses of both this volume and the earlier one have been directed toward two main objectives. The first is to examine the degree to which number and spacing of births are controlled by fertility preferences—that is, desired family size and spacing preferences—with an accompanying effort made to learn more about the means and barriers to such control. Secondly, a broad range of social and psychological factors have been considered for their ability to discriminate, both individually and jointly, selected measures of birth intervals, desired family size, family-planning success, and fertility since first interview. In the present review, results will be presented as a series of propositions grouped around the two major interests just outlined.

It is perhaps unnecessary to point out the various limitations surrounding such propositions based as they are upon sample data of a special population at a particular time. Moreover, our analyses have often involved very small subsamples, a factor even further increasing the risks of erroneous inference. In addition to these reservations—standard in all such survey research—there is the additional complication that the fertility of many of the couples is not yet completed. Thus our reference must ordinarily be to behavior between marriage and a point in time approximately three and a half years past the second birth.

First phase results are based on lengthy interviews with a probability sample of 1,165 wives, together with mail questionnaires returned by most of these respondents and their husbands. The results of the second phase, analyzed in this volume, derive from a second set of interviews obtained from 905 wives of the original sample. The original panel of 1,165 members represented couples having a second birth in September of 1956, a few months before first interview, and at the time residing in one of the seven largest Standard Metropolitan Areas of this country. The respondents are further delimited by being native-white and English-speaking with marital histories uncomplicated by divorce, permanent separation, death, or extensive pregnancy wastage. The group reinterviewed is smaller—905 compared to 1,165—mainly because of difficulties encountered in relocating couples after three years and because of refusals. As a result the twice-interviewed respondents are biased in relation to the original panel. For instance, their education and income tend to be higher and they include disproportionately many Jews and few Catholics. Nevertheless, comparisons of respondents and nonrespondents based on first interview data indicate that statistical relationships are little affected by these biases. In view of these various limitations, therefore, the propositions advanced in the following pages are best viewed in the context of hypotheses which possess varying degrees of certitude. The general theme of our inventory is to assess what we now know about human fertility that we did not know (or knew with less certainty) before the study was conducted.

DEGREE OF FERTILITY CONTROL AND ITS MEANS AND BARRIERS

A number of results may be viewed as replications on a more specialized sample of findings from the 1955 Growth of American Families (GAF) Study of Freedman, Whelpton, and Campbell.

1. Most urban brides of this country enter first marriage while still in their late teens or early twenties—a generalization that appears to apply pretty much regardless of social class or religion.

2. Most of the two-child wives in the sample say they want two, three, or four children altogether, with under 10 per cent expressing a desire for five or more. This consensus on two to four children, obtained in both interviews, holds more consistently among social classes than among religious groups.

3. About half of the couples start practicing contraception before the first pregnancy and a large majority after the first birth. The few who do not, usually give subfecundity or religion as reason. Thus a fairly general consensus exists against having pregnancies as fast as biologically possible. Nevertheless contraception, if used, is interrupted or fails soon enough so that most birth intervals are four years or less.

This spacing, combined with young ages at marriage and preferences for two, three, or four children, means that most couples attain desired family size while still in their late 20's or early 30's and, as a result, face a "risk period"—perhaps averaging ten years or more when marriage lasts to menopause—during which they must practice highly effective birth control if they are to limit their families to desired size.

4. Another finding consistent with GAF results is the low effectiveness of contraception practiced during the first two birth intervals—a time when nearly all couples are practicing contraception to postpone rather than to prevent pregnancies.

In the analysis covering the first phase, rates of over 20 accidental pregnancies per 100 years of contraceptive exposure were calculated both for the interval between marriage and first birth and between the first and second birth. Nor did contraception seem to become more effective as one proceeded from the first to the second interval.

This lack of improvement is puzzling. Given youthful ages at marriage and preferences for two, three, or four children, such ineffective contraception projected over entire reproductive periods implies an average of two or more excess pregnancies per couple. Yet data from other sources plainly belie this projection. In particular, about three-quarters of the "relatively fecund" wives aged 35–39 from the GAF Study claimed to have successfully limited the number of their pregnancies. Even though these claims might be somewhat exaggerated, a high enough caliber of family limitation was indicated so that one wondered if effectiveness of contraception did not improve later in marriage when being used to prevent unwanted pregnancies rather than merely to space desired ones. Lacking this explanation, one could only posit wholesale reliance upon sterilization and induced abortion. While the 1955 GAF Study had shown sterilization to be an important element, the incidence indicated could not suffice as the explanation. Nor does it seem plausible to view induced abortion as the primary means of family limitation in this country.

A reanalysis of the contraceptive experience of the first two birth intervals, together with an analysis of contraceptive experience following second birth, has led to altered conclusions about the trend of contraceptive effectiveness with increasing marriage duration. By considering only the first 12 months of experience in any birth interval, and recomputing rates of accidental pregnancy on this basis, it is revealed that the fraction of high-risk couples practicing ineffectual contraception is definitely higher in the first interval following marriage than in the interval following first birth. (For a discussion of methodological aspects, see Appendix D, "Measurement of Contraceptive Effectiveness.") The incidence of early accidental pregnancy continues to decline when one proceeds to the interval following second birth. Even more striking, however, is the relationship between contraceptive effectiveness and the number of additional children desired, a relationship which leads to the following proposition:

5. As couples approach desired family size, the effectiveness with which they practice contraception increases sharply—so much so that this improved contraception would appear to be a substantial factor in the family limitation being attained in this country.

A more decisive confirmation of this proposition can be achieved if the sample is interviewed again after additional experience.

Besides high rates of accidental pregnancy, there are several other signs that many couples are not motivated to try to achieve their most efficient contraception before reaching desired family size. For example, barely half of the wives reported reliability as a main reason for adopting the method then in use. Similarly, many of the reasons given for postponing use of contraception are unrelated to spacing objectives.

6. As a consequence, studies not distinguishing between contraception used for family limitation and contraception used for spacing are likely to underestimate the ultimate use-effectiveness of a given method.

By the same token a comparison of two methods based on experience from a single birth interval will be biased if the users of one method are nearer their family size objectives than users of the other. A case in point is the rhythm method, favored by Catholics, as opposed to diaphragm and jelly or condom, favored by Protestants and Jews because the latter two groups prefer fewer children on the average than do Catholics.

The improvement in contraceptive control with increasing marriage duration is clearly not a matter of couples shifting from ineffective to effective methods of contraception inasmuch as the composition of methods used after the second birth is much the same as between marriage and first birth. Moreover, the predominantly young ages of the wives precludes sharply declining fecundity as an explanation. Nor has any association been found between reported coital frequency and contraceptive effectiveness. In addition, there does not appear to be any important practice effect, wherein contraceptive skill increases with longer usage, since the relationship between effectiveness of contraception and number of additional children wanted remains strong among couples practicing contraception for the same number of intervals.

7. Rather, the chief mechanism in the improvement of contraception appears to be a greater regularity of practice.

The present study is the first to investigate how much couples know about the positioning of the fertile period within the monthly cycle and the relevance of this knowledge for contraception.

8. There is substantial variation in the extent and accuracy of women's knowledge of the ovulatory cycle.

Knowledge about the timing of ovulation in the monthly cycle does not appear to influence efficiency with contraception, except among those using the rhythm method.

9. On the average, Jewish couples practice more efficient contraception than do Protestants or Catholics. This differential depends heavily, though not entirely, upon the nearly exclusive reliance of Jewish couples upon condom and diaphragm and jelly as methods of contraception, together with their desiring fewer children and thus being closer to desired family size during the initial two birth intervals.

10. On the whole, spacing preferences appear to be quite vague. The wife's preferred spacing of second and third children is correlated only weakly with her husband's, suggesting that their spacing preferences, at least as formulated so soon after the second birth, are ill-defined and little discussed. Only half the wives at first interview expected their reported preference regarding the timing of the next child to be realized. Questions about previous birth intervals reveal that no narrow range of interval length was perceived as peculiarly advantageous while all other lengths were deemed too short or too long. Indeed, one suspects that many mothers, some months after a last childbirth, reach a point where they have not yet carried their thinking about another pregnancy so far as to interrupt contraception, yet would not be dismayed to find themselves pregnant. At such times they may take chances by omitting contraception that they would have resisted a few months earlier.

REGULATION OF BIRTH INTERVALS

11. Although most couples maintain a fairly close check on family size, control over the spacing of desired births is much looser.

In part, this slack regulation reflects vague spacing preferences and correspondingly perfunctory contraception. However it also reflects more involuntary factors: time lost to pregnancy wastage, separations (especially those connected with military service), and delays of conception after contraception is interrupted or in its absence.

12. The importance of these latter factors was dramatized in an analysis which showed that they accounted for a generous half of the variances of both the first and second birth intervals, whereas

purposive postponement of pregnancy, as measured by length of contraceptive practice, accounted for the lesser portion of these variances.

The present couples have not been very successful in their efforts to shorten conception delays by increasing their coital frequency during that portion of the monthly cycle they judge to be most fertile. Only about one-fifth of the wives report ever making such efforts and these tend to be women who have had or are having difficulty conceiving. Half of the group who try to speed conception are handicapped by incomplete or incorrect information about the positioning of the fertile period within the monthly cycle. Moreover, coital frequency appears to be only one of several factors determining a couple's typical monthly chance of conception when not using contraception.

13. Thus, even given clear-cut spacing objectives and efficient contraception, there are definite limits as to how far regulation of birth intervals can be carried.

14. On the average, those who deliberately interrupt contraception take 5 to 6 months to conceive, though there is wide variation in the length of time waited for conception. The length of time required to conceive for women who have not yet started contraception is curiously longer—averaging 10 months even in the interval following marriage when postpartum amenorrhea is not a factor. In an analysis not included in this volume or the previous one, it is shown that a portion of this differential arises from failures to recall that contraception was started before first pregnancy. Also contributing to the differential is the rationalizing of accidental pregnancies as planned pregnancies promptly conceived.

15. Wife's desired family size 6 months after the second birth has proved to be the strongest predictor of fertility over the next three years of all the data collected in the first interview. Several reasons for this are: her desired family size is found to remain rather stable (the correlation between desires expressed at the beginning and at the end of the three-year interval is .70), corroborating a result from a Detroit Area Study; husband and wife's desires are similar (correlation .66); and finally, contraception becomes more effective once desired family size is attained, so that relatively few of those desiring two have an unwanted third birth.

16. Contributing to the inverse correlation between length of birth intervals and *completed* family size, so thoroughly documented by Glass and Grebenik for Great Britain and more recently by the Census Bureau for the United States, is the inverse correlation between length of birth intervals and *desired* family size. Family-size

preferences are linked to birth spacing chiefly in two ways. Wives desiring larger families tend to plan shorter birth intervals as evidenced by more "nonuse of contraception" for reason of wanting another pregnancy as soon as possible and by earlier interruption of contraception after marriage or a childbirth. At the same time, wives desiring more children tend to practice less efficient contraception and more often forego use of it for reasons unrelated to spacing objectives.

17. Average length of the first two birth intervals has proved the strongest predictor, after desired family size, of the number of pregnancies during the three and one-half year period following the second birth. The predictive power depends on multiple bases, such as the positive correlation of consecutive conception delays, as well as the tendencies of couples desiring large families to seek shorter birth intervals than average and to practice contraception more casually during the initial birth intervals.

Social and Psychological Factors

Investigation into the social and psychological factors affecting fertility follows a line of inquiry begun with the Indianapolis Study. In many respects that study as well as our own represents a radical departure from the traditional concerns of demography where theory ordinarily rests at the macroscopic level of populations and societies and where research has ordinarily involved analyses of data collected by governmental agencies. Although some of our earlier interests were oriented toward personality and attitudinal levels of explanation, the most successful probes have been in the more conventional sociological areas of differential fertility where our classifications presumably reflect subcultural normative systems delineated by religious, educational, occupational, residential, and other dimensions. The so-called "micro" level is still presumably implied in our attempt to explain individual rather than group variations in fertility. Where the macro and micro levels part, however, is rather arbitrary and, in any event, is probably not a fruitful subject for concern. The question ultimately is one of scientific efficiency and strategy.

Religion

One of the main emphases in this study has been on the connections between religion and fertility. The influence of religion on various aspects of fertility requires in many instances separate analysis within each religious group. The following generalizations have emerged from our study of religion and fertility:

18. Religious preference, that is preference for the Protestant, Catholic, or Jewish faith, is the strongest of all major social characteristics in its influence on fertility. Catholic couples want the most and Jewish couples the fewest children with Protestants in an intermediate position.

19. The influence exerted by religion operates primarily through its effect on the number of children desired and only secondarily through fertility-planning success. To oversimplify somewhat, Catholics by and large appear to be having the larger families they want. Their comparatively ineffective fertility planning should be viewed mainly in terms of child-spacing. The assumption, based on findings discussed earlier, is that once their larger family ambitions are realized their success in controlling family size improves. At the opposite extreme are the Jewish couples who want the fewest number of children on the average and whose fertility planning is extremely successful.

20. The fertility of Protestant-Catholic marriages is best understood not in terms of which spouse is Catholic but by whether the marriage was performed under the auspices of the Catholic Church.

21. Religiousness, as measured by indices of both formal and informal behavior, relates to fertility in opposite ways for Protestants and Catholics. As expected, the more religious Catholics desire and have more children. On the other hand, the more religious Protestants—possibly because of the increasing dissemination of a moral theme of responsible parenthood—tend to have fewer children. The pattern for Jewish couples is more puzzling and defies simple summary.

22. Protestants and Catholics appear to be more alike in the kinds of factors affecting their fertility than either is like the Jewish group. One clear exception to this generalization, however, is the structure of factors affecting fertility—planning success in which Protestants and Jews are most alike.

Because the Catholic religion has much more direct implications for fertility than Protestant or Jewish denominations, a considerable effort was invested in the study of internal variations in fertility among Catholic couples. This analysis produced the following generalizations:

23. Contrary to our own expectations, we found that only a small minority of Catholic women believe that their religion takes a position in favor of large families. Further research is necessary to isolate the social mechanisms by which a norm of high fertility is sustained.

24. Catholic education is one of the social mechanisms that

support a norm of large families but it seems to operate primarily at the college level, to some extent at the secondary school level, and not at all at the elementary school level. Although a process operates to select the more religious individuals into Catholic educational institutions, the education itself seems to exert an effect on fertility independent of this selectivity. There is certainly ground for research into the nature of the influence exerted since it probably functions at both formal and informal levels.

25. The ethnic origin of Catholics is also a factor affecting fertility although it is by no means independent of religiousness. Catholics of Irish heritage both want and have the most children.

Socio-Economic Status

Studies of the fertility of socio-economic classes of the population have been abundant in demography and constitute one of the main foundations of the sociologist's interest in the area of fertility. In recent years such research in the United States has revealed a definite contraction of class differences in fertility. Part of this contraction may be due to different relationships between socio-economic status and fertility for Protestants and Catholics.

26. Regardless of the measure (including subjective measures), fertility is negatively associated with the socio-economic status of Protestants and positively related to the socio-economic status of Catholics although in neither case is the relationship strong.

There are several important implications of this finding which are discussed in the summary of Chapter X.

27. Socio-economic status is less strongly related to fertility than is religion—a generalization that is valid even considering the opposite directions of association in the two major religious groups.

Another line of research pursued in this study was prompted in large part by Goldberg's reanalysis of Indianapolis Study data and data from other more recent studies. His observation is that the socio-economic differential in fertility may be largely a reflection of rural-urban differences in the background of the different socio-economic classes. Our analysis confirms this hypothesis in part:

28. In the Protestant population, the negative association of fertility with socio-economic status diminishes and tends to become positive among couples with several generations of urban living. Among Catholics, however, the positive relationship is maintained at approximately the same magnitude for all classes regardless of rural or urban heritage.

One of the outstanding findings of the Indianapolis Study (of Protestant couples) was that the relationship between socio-economic status and fertility was negative for the total sample but positive for couples who had planned their fertility successfully. This finding was important for what it implied about the future relationship between the two variables as contraception becomes more popular and more effective. Our study confirmed this finding among Protestants as well:

29. The correlation between socio-economic status and fertility is negative for all Protestant couples but is positive among couples who have been successful in planning all pregnancies so far. Among Catholics the correlation is positive in the total sample as well as among successful planners.

30. The relationship between socio-economic status and the extent of planning fertility successfully also follows an opposite pattern for the two religious groups. For example, among Protestants the relationship between education and fertility-planning success is positive while among Catholics it is negative. The explanation for this apparent paradox is the concentration of Catholics who attended college in the Catholic higher educational system. When the association is examined for Catholics whose education is secular the same pattern is found as for Protestants. This clearly requires an important qualification in the traditional generalizations about the relation of education to family planning.

SOCIAL MOBILITY

Probably no hypothesis received more attention in this study than that connecting fertility with social mobility, a variable that was measured in numerous different forms. There is very little more that can be added to a conclusion of essentially no relationship:

31. Social mobility appears to have little if any relation with fertility. There are some indications, as for the socio-economic dimension itself, that what little association exists follows opposite directions for Protestants and Catholics.

This conclusion includes measurements of inter- and intragenerational occupational mobility, income change and levels of aspirations. It is certainly worth reflecting on the reasons for the failure of this hypothesis to show any validity. Of course one can blame the insensitivity and unreliability of the measurements employed and this factor should not be ignored. But our suspicion is that there are substantive rather than methodological reasons involved. In a society in which socio-economic status itself has diminished greatly in its importance for fertility it is perhaps understandable that movement from one status to another seems to have little significance.

Moreover as Freedman suggests, the original hypothesis of a negative correlation is linked to an outdated view of urban society.

"It assumes that the mobile family is one of many individualistic units which rationally restrict family commitments and costs in order to compete successfully in an impersonal and highly individualistic market. Such a model may be applicable to the transitional stage when an urban society is developing indigenous institutions and drawing large masses of immigrants from rural areas. In this situation large numbers of people are unaccustomed to urban institutions and without established precedents or rules to guide their careers. But in the contemporary American scene large numbers have been socialized as indigenous urbanites to expect social change. Change and mobility are an established part of the social structure. The large bureaucratic enterprises in which more and more people work institutionalize mobility. People learn to expect and plan for change within reasonable limits as part of the routine of life."[1]

MIGRATION AND RESIDENCE

The general hypothesis, supported by analysis of census data, is that migrants characteristically have lower fertility than nonmigrants. Analysis of relevant data from our sample does not support this hypothesis, but the limitations of our sample and its design are particularly problematic in this area.

32. The fertility of couples who moved during the three and a half year interval following the second birth was higher than those who did not move.

There are obvious difficulties in separating any causal sequences that may be involved. What is clear is that the couples who did move wanted more children initially and used contraception less effectively in the interim.

The significance for fertility of the rise of the suburbs in postwar America has frequently been a subject for speculation. The most interesting sociological question in this connection is whether the suburbs are in part a reflection of the increased demand for additional space occasioned by higher fertility, or whether suburban life actually fosters larger families. Actually, there is very little relationship evident at all:

33. Catholic fertility is not associated with residence at all, while among Protestants, the highest fertility appears to character-

[1] Ronald Freedman, "American Studies of Family Planning and Fertility: A Review of Major Trends and Issues," in Clyde V. Kiser, ed. *Research in Family Planning*, Princeton, Princeton University Press, 1962, pp. 225–226.

ize the residents of central cities although the association is probably explained by the joint connections with socio-economic status and fertility-planning success. The same explanation apparently prevails for the association between housing and fertility.

ECONOMIC RECESSION

Between the first round of interviews in 1957 and the second round conducted in 1960 an economic recession as well as a major steel strike occurred. We were the recipients quite fortuitously of an experimental opportunity to examine the effects of macroeconomic events on the fertility of individuals directly involved. The steel strike seems to have exerted no effect on fertility but the recession produced a twofold effect:

34. Two main negative effects were distinguished: a reduction in income without unemployment, and unemployment. The former experience was characterized by lower fertility while the unemployed group actually appeared to have experienced somewhat higher fertility than the bulk of the sample unaffected by the recession. The latter part of this relationship was interpreted in terms of planning capabilities underlying both economic and fertility behavior.

PERSONALITY

Although no detailed discussion of personality characteristics is included in this present report, a comprehensive analysis of the relationships of fertility with each personality characteristic measured was conducted and, as indicated in the introductory chapter, no consequential associations were found. The personality characteristics included are: generalized manifest anxiety, nurturance needs, ability to delay gratification of impulses, self-awareness, compulsiveness, ambiguity tolerance, cooperativeness, and need achievement.

35. There seem to be no significant associations of fertility or fertility-planning success with the various measures of personality characteristics originally included in this study. It is not clear whether this negative result is due to the difficulties of measuring the personality dimensions or to lack of validity of our initial hypotheses.

SOCIAL RELATIONSHIPS WITHIN THE FAMILY

Under this broad heading we examined such diverse facets of relationships and attitudes descriptive of the wife and family as the wife's adjustment to marriage, her adjustment to the role of mother, liking for children, accommodations between spouses, problems with children, visiting patterns, wife's social participation, her employment experience, her employment plans, patterns of help available to the wife, and areas of husband-wife dominance. Five themes relate one or more of these variables to the number of children desired, the number of pregnancies following the second live birth, and success in planning fertility. These themes are: fertility as a value competes with career or employment interests; fertility affects fertility—that reactions to the first two births affect attitudes toward future fertility; male-dominated families or families with roles defined in a traditional manner tend to be characterized by poor planning and larger families; the orientation to family and the ease with which a wife adjusts to and copes with the demands of marriage influences the number of children she desires and her fertility; and effective family planning is based upon accommodation, compromise, or agreement regarding the number of children desired as well as sexual behavior.

36. No clear support of a statistical nature was found for any of the hypotheses linking social relationships within the family with fertility.

This seems in keeping with what is becoming a dependable outcome when attempts are made to establish associations between family structure and fertility. Among the many possible explanations for these negative results is the multiplicity of the determinants of fertility that minimizes the observable effects of family attitudinal and structural variables when considered singly or in restricted combinations. Also, we may be overestimating the stability over time of such variables. Hence their relationship to fertility is transitory and difficult to capture. Finally, there is the persisting problem of measurement that must always be considered.

AGE AND AGE AT MARRIAGE

Age at marriage is correlated negatively with completed size of family. The mechanism determining the relation is complex, involving such variables as fecundity, contraceptive effectiveness, desired family size, and pregnancy wastage. Though the couples in this study have as yet some years to go before they are through their childbearing years, reasonable inferences are already possible about this determining mechanism. Though age at marriage is related weakly if at all with the number of children desired, it is related to a greater degree to planning success and through this relationship the younger the age at marriage, the more quickly are children acquired. The joint process of family growth and aging are summarized by the following proposition:

37. Regardless of age at marriage, those wives desiring larger families either plan shorter intervals or else neglect effective contraceptive techniques and thereby experience shorter intervals. Hence by this selection at the birth of a second child, the younger the age of the wife the more children she desires; at the same time the younger the wife at the birth of the second child, the greater is the likelihood of a pregnancy within a three and a half year interval after the birth of a second child.

38. Thus, the explanation of the age at marriage, completed family-size correlation appears to be both fecundity and the poorer contraceptive practice of younger couples. In a sense the correlation is not dependent on either relationship between current age and desired size of family or age at marriage and desired size of family.

Parental Family Size

The correlation between family size in successive generations is well documented. Other studies, however, have neglected religion, sex composition, and birth order as these may alter or explain this generational association. Though all couples in the present sample have not terminated childbearing, there is some evidence to support the following proposition:

39. The correlation of family size in successive generations is due in large measure to the heterogeneity of average fertility among religions persisting over two generations at least. That is, Catholics desire and have larger families than Jewish couples, and in the urban setting this difference has prevailed for at least two generations.

40. Neither sex composition nor birth order in the parental family appears related to fertility.

Sex Preference

A preference for a given sex composition among offspring has been inferred from several studies. These data are the first—to our knowledge—where the inference of a preference could be checked by the subsequent performance of couples. In brief:

41. There is a preference among couples for a representation of both sexes among their offspring.

42. This preference is translated into an adjustment of desired number of children to provide this representation.

Next Steps

Our current plans call for reinterviewing the couples in this sample once more as they approach the end of their reproductive life. Since the couples vary considerably in age we have worked out a plan to interview the wife as she passes a certain age and to continue interviewing over a period of five years. One important advantage of this scheme is that it will minimize the sample attrition that would otherwise occur if we prolonged the interval since the second interview to a total of eight years.

The primary objective of this final interview will be to secure data on completed family size with which we will be able to evaluate further the validity of the numerous propositions advanced in this chapter. For example, we will be able to examine further the bases for the improvement of contraception during the approximate ten-year risk period that ordinarily follows the achievement of desired family size. The third interview will also of course permit us to explore many of the new leads opened by the present analysis, such as those in the area of religion and fertility as well as offering an additional opportunity to continue our methodological inquiries (see Appendix C) into the reliability of survey data on family planning.

PART V
APPENDICES

Appendix A. The Interview Schedule

Judging from the number of requests for copies of the interview schedule used in the first phase of the study, there seems to be good reason for reproducing a copy of the most recent schedule in the present book. Since most of the questions on attitudes were printed in Appendix C of the first volume, and since the background questions are mostly the standard items used in any questionnaire, only the fertility and directly relevant items will be reproduced below. Moreover, since there is a great deal of repetition of questions with each pregnancy only one block will be included.

The Respondent Eligibility Form contains twelve questions designed both to fix for the interviewer the number of children the respondent has and to determine her eligibility for inclusion in the second phase of the study. Aside from cases of surgical sterilization determined from the first interview, the only other event that would classify the respondent as ineligible is marital separation due to divorce, separation, or death. This information (tabulated in Appendix B) is secured in Q's. 9–12.

The main part of the interview was then conducted with all eligible respondents.

RESPONDENT ELIGIBILITY FORM

Sample Number____

SUGGESTED INTRODUCTION: I'm ____ from National Analysts, a market research company. You will recall that I (we) talked to you about three years ago in connection with a study about how women feel about the growth of American families and some other aspects of American Family life. The study was being done for the Office of Population Research at Princeton University. I believe that you have recently received a letter telling you that I would call to talk to you again in connection with the same study. The Office of Population Research is interested in bringing their information about American family life up to date.

1. How many children do you now have?		8. How many pregnancies have you had since the birth of your second child?	
ENTER NUMBER			
2. Have you lost any children through death — that is, children born alive who later died?		ENTER NUMBER	
		9. Since we interviewed you three years ago, have you been divorced, permanently separated from your husband, or widowed?	
Yes	1		
(SKIP TO Q.4) No	2		
3. (IF "YES") When was that child born? Date of Birth:____ (MONTH & YEAR)		INELIGIBLE: COMPLETE OTHER SIDE OF THIS FORM AND THEN TERMINATE INTERVIEW	Divorced 1
			Separated 2
			Widowed 3
4. Are any of your children adopted?		ELIGIBLE: CONTINUE WITH QUESTIONNAIRE	None of These 4
Yes	1		
(SKIP TO Q.6) No	2	10. (IF "DIVORCED" OR "WIDOWED" OR "SEPARATED") In what month and year was that? MONTH_____ YEAR___	
5. (IF "YES") What is the birth date of that child? Date of Birth:____ (MONTH & YEAR)			
6. Have you ever had twins or triplets; include any you've had even if one child was stillborn?		11. (IF "DIVORCED" OR "WIDOWED" IN Q.9) Have you remarried?	
			Yes 1
Yes	1		No 2
No	2	12. In what month and year was that? MONTH_____ YEAR___	
7. How many pregnancies have you had altogether, including any that ended in a still birth or a miscarriage?			
ENTER NUMBER			
(IF "DIVORCED," "SEPARATED" OR "WIDOWED" IN Q.9, INELIGIBLE. TERMINATE INTERVIEW.)			

(WHEN INTERVIEW IS COMPLETED, ATTACH THIS FORM TO QUESTIONNAIRE. IF QUESTIONNAIRE IS NOT COMPLETED, THIS FORM MUST BE MAILED IN BY ITSELF. BE SURE IN ALL CASES TO FILL IN NAME AND NUMBER.)

Q's. 89–112* relate to the respondent's perceptions of problems she has had with her children, repetitions of questions asked in the first interview about marital adjustment, feelings of economic security, and her perceptions of her husband's job opportunities.

Q's. 113 to the conclusion with Q. 186* cover a wide variety of background information, most of which is quite conventional.

* Not shown.

INTERVIEW SCHEDULE

A STUDY OF AMERICAN FAMILY LIFE

(1960 Reinterview)

(ASK Q.1 IF RESPONDENT REPORTED THREE OR MORE CHILDREN IN Q.1 OF ELIGIBILITY FORM. IF ONE OR TWO CHILDREN, SKIP TO Q. 2)

1. Could you tell me, please, the birth dates of your children born <u>since</u> the birth of your second child? Let's start with the first one born alive after 1956. Was it a boy or a girl? Do not include adopted children.

THIRD CHILD:

Boy	1
Girl	2

_____ _____ _____
(MONTH)   (DAY)   (YEAR)

FOURTH CHILD:

Boy	1
Girl	2

_____ _____ _____
(MONTH)   (DAY)   (YEAR)

FIFTH CHILD:

Boy	1
Girl	2

_____ _____ _____
(MONTH)   (DAY)   (YEAR)

SIXTH CHILD:

Boy	1
Girl	2

_____ _____ _____
(MONTH)   (DAY)   (YEAR)

USE THIS SPACE TO EXPLAIN ANY MULTIPLE BIRTHS:

2. Are you pregnant now?

	Yes	1
(SKIP TO Q.4)	No	2
	Not sure	3

3. (IF "YES") How many months pregnant?

ENTER NUMBER	

4. Have you had any pregnancies that miscarried? Which pregnancies were they?

First pregnancy	1
Second pregnancy	2
Third pregnancy	3
Fourth pregnancy	4
Fifth pregnancy	5
Sixth pregnancy	6
(SKIP TO Q.6) No miscarriages	0

5. In what month and year did (first miscarriage) occur? (What month and year was second? Etc.)

	Month	Year
First miscarriage		
Second miscarriage		
Third miscarriage		
Fourth miscarriage		
Fifth miscarriage		
Sixth miscarriage		

6. Have you had any still births? Which pregnancies were they?

Third pregnancy	3
Fourth pregnancy	4
Fifth pregnancy	5
Sixth pregnancy	6
(SKIP TO Q.8) No still births	0

7. In what month and year did first still birth occur? (In what month and year did second still birth occur? Etc.)

	Month	Year
First still birth		
Second still birth		
Third still birth		
Fourth still birth		
Fifth still birth		
Sixth still birth		

8. Do you have any reason to believe that you are now in the menopause; that is, in the change of life?

Yes	1
No	2
Not sure	3

9. Would you say that a woman's chances of becoming pregnant are greater or less during menopause than they were before?

Greater in menopause	1
Less in menopause	2
No difference	3
Don't know	V

10. Have you and your husband ever had any physical trouble or health problems in your becoming pregnant?

| | Yes | 1 |
| (SKIP TO Q.14) | No | 2 |

11. (IF "YES" IN Q.10) Would you please describe that trouble?

12. (IF "YES" TO Q.10) Before which pregnancy did you realize that you had trouble becoming pregnant?

First	1
Second	2
Third	3
Fourth	4
Fifth	5
Sixth	6
Since last pregnancy	7

13. (IF "YES" TO Q.10) What is the situation now? Are there any reasons to believe that you would have trouble becoming pregnant again if you wanted to?

Yes	1
No	2
Uncertain	3

14. (ASK EVERYBODY) How many children do you want to have altogether, counting those you have now? ("If you were able to have more children" — USE THIS PHRASE WHERE APPROPRIATE)

ENTER NUMBER:

15. Do you feel sure that (NUMBER GIVEN IN Q.14) is the number you want or do you feel that you might want more or that you might want fewer?

Want more	1
Feel sure	2
Want fewer	3

16. Many husbands and wives really have different ideas even though they do talk it over and reach an agreement. How many children do you think your husband really wants altogether, counting those you have now?

ENTER NUMBER:

17. Have there ever been any times since the birth of your second child when you and your husband have not seen each other for as long as three months?

| | Yes | 1 |
| (SKIP TO Q.19) | No | 2 |

18. Can you tell me when each of these periods began and ended? Start with the first period of three months or longer when you didn't see each other — when did it begin? When did it end? How about the next period?

	Date Began		Date Ended	
	Month	Year	Month	Year
1st				
2nd				
3rd				

19. Many married couples use natural means, such as rhythm, or other means to space their children or to limit the size of their families. (HAND RESPONDENT CARD #1) In your own case, since your marriage have you and your husband ever used any of these methods? Would you just tell me whether you have or have not used any of the methods.

| (SKIP TO Q.21) | Yes | 1 |
| | No | 2 |

THE TEXT OF CARD #1 FOLLOWS

CARD 1

1. SAFE PERIOD—Rhythm method.
2. DOUCHE. (Washing one's self out soon after intercourse)
3. WITHDRAWAL. (Husband pulls out or withdraws before completion)
4. CONDOM—Rubber. (Husband uses sheath or prophylactic)
5. DIAPHRAGM. (With or without jelly)
6. JELLY OR CREAM ALONE. (Jelly or cream applied inside before intercourse)
7. SUPPOSITORIES.
8. FOAM TABLETS. (Or other foam material used alone)
9. PESSARY—cervical cap, stem, ring.
10. SPONGE METHOD. (Insertion of a small sudsy sponge)
11. BREAST FEEDING. (Continuing to nurse a baby in order to postpone pregnancy)
12. ABSTINENCE. (No sex relations at all until pregnancy is desired)
13. OTHER.

20. (IF "NO") What are the main reasons that you have never used any method? (NOW SKIP TO Q.74)		24. (HAND RESPONDENT CARD #2) Under which <u>one</u> of these circumstances did your first pregnancy occur? (CIRCLE <u>ONE</u> CHOICE ONLY.)	
FIRST PREGNANCY (USAGE DATA) 21. Now let's go back a bit in time — (REFER TO CARD #1) Did you or your husband ever use any of these methods before your first pregnancy?		1. While we were actually using some method and didn't want a pregnancy just then.	1
		2. When we took a chance and didn't use a method.	2
	Yes — 1	3. After we deliberately stopped using a method in order to have a child.	3
(SKIP TO Q.26)	No — 2	4. Some other circumstance. (SPECIFY):	4
22. Which method or methods did you use most frequently before your first pregnancy? You may call off the numbers if you like. _____ (ENTER NUMBERS)		(IF CHOICE "1," "3," OR "4" IN Q. 24, SKIP TO Q.27 SECOND PREGNANCY— (USAGE DATA)) (IF CHOICE "2" CONTINUE WITH Q.25)	
23. (IF TWO METHODS MENTIONED) Did you use these methods in combination or at different times?		25. (IF "TOOK A CHANCE" IN Q.24) Why did you take a chance and not use a method? (NOW SKIP TO Q.27)	
	In combination — 1	26. (ASK ONLY IF "NO" IN Q.21) What is the main reason that you did not use any method before your first pregnancy?	
	At different times — 2		

NOTE: Q's 27-32 are exact repetitions for the second pregnancy.

(INTERVIEWER: REFER TO Q.7 OF ELIGI-BILITY FORM. IF RESPONDENT HAS HAD ONLY TWO PREGNANCIES, SKIP TO IN-STRUCTIONS BEFORE Q.69, CURRENT USAGE. IF RESPONDENT HAS HAD 3 OR MORE PREGNANCIES, CONTINUE UNTIL YOU HAVE COVERED ALL.)	37. (IF "TOOK A CHANCE" IN Q.36) Why did you take a chance and not use a method? (SKIP TO Q.42 FOURTH PREGNANCY (USAGE DATA) IF APPROPRIATE. OTHERWISE SKIP TO Q.69 — CURRENT USAGE DATA)

THIRD PREGNANCY (USAGE DATA)

33. (REFER TO CARD #1) Did you and your husband ever use any of these methods during the time between your second and third pregnancies?

	Yes	1
(SKIP TO Q.40)	No	2

38. (ASK IF "STOPPED TO HAVE CHILD" IN Q.36) What made you and your husband decide to have another child?

34. Which method or methods did you use most frequently before your third pregnancy? You may call off the numbers if you like.

_____
(ENTER NUMBERS)

39. To the best of your memory, how many months was it before you became pregnant after you stopped using this method?

35. (IF TWO METHODS MENTIONED) Did you use these methods in combination or at different times?

In combination	1
At different times	2

_____
(MONTHS)

(SKIP TO Q.42 FOURTH PREGNANCY (USAGE DATA) IF APPROPRIATE. OTHERWISE SKIP TO Q.69 — CURRENT USAGE DATA)

36. (REFER TO CARD #2) Under which one of these circumstances did your third pregnancy occur?

1. While we were actually using some method and didn't want a pregnancy just then.	1
2. When we took a chance and didn't use a method.	2
3. After we deliberately stopped using a method in order to have a child.	3
4. Some other circumstance. (SPECIFY):	4

40. (ASK OF THOSE SAYING "NO" TO Q.33) What is the main reason that you did not use any method before your third pregnancy?

41. To the best of your memory, how many months was it before you became pregnant for the third time?

_____
(MONTHS)

(IF CHOICE 1, OR 4 IN Q.36, SKIP TO Q..42 FOURTH PREGNANCY (USAGE DATA) IF APPROPRIATE. OTHERWISE SKIP TO Q.69 (CURRENT USAGE DATA).)

(IF CHOICE 2 IN Q.36, ASK Q.37)
(IF CHOICE 3 IN Q.36, SKIP TO Q.38)

(IF NO FOURTH PREGNANCY, SKIP TO Q.69 — CURRENT USAGE DATA)

NOTE: Q's 42-68 are exact repetitions for possible subsequent pregnancies.

CURRENT USAGE DATA	ASK ALL RESPONDENTS
(ASK Q's. 69, 70 & 72 IF EVER USED ANY METHOD — "YES" TO Q.19) (IF "NO" TO Q.19, SKIP TO Q.74)	74. What is the usual length or your monthly menstrual cycle — that is, how many days is it, usually, from the time you begin to flow for one period to the time you begin to flow for the next period? (DRAW VERTICAL LINE "|" IN CHART IN Q.77 AFTER NUMBER OF DAYS GIVEN.)

69. (REFER TO CARD #1) Are you and your husband using any of these methods at the present time?

	Yes	1
(SKIP TO Q.73)	No	2

Don't know	VV

70. Which method or methods are you using most frequently? You may call off the numbers if you like.

_____

(ENTER NUMBERS)

75. Generally speaking, would you say your menstrual cycle is usually very regular, fairly regular, somewhat irregular, or very irregular?

Very regular	1
Fairly regular	2
Somewhat irregular	3
Very irregular	4

71. (IF TWO METHODS MENTIONED) Are you using these methods in combination or at different times?

In combination	1
At different times	2

76. How many days do you flow, usually, during your menstrual period? (PLACE AN "X" OVER NUMBER OF DAYS FLOW IN CHART BELOW STARTING WITH "1")

Don't know	V

72. Are there times when you skip using (this)(these) method(s) — would you say never, once in a while or quite often?

Never skip	1
Skip once in a while	2
Skip quite often	3

(NOW SKIP TO Q.74)

73. (IF "NO" TO Q.69 — NOT CURRENTLY USING ANY METHOD) What are the main reasons that you and your husband are not using any method at the present time?

77. (INDICATE COMPLETE CYCLE ON CHART) If this is the length of your menstrual cycle and these are the number of days you usually flow during your period, show me on this chart when you would have the greatest chance of becoming pregnant? (WAVE HAND BACK AND FORTH OVER CHART) (IF "DON'T KNOW" TO Q.74 SAY "If 28 days were the length of your cycle...") (IF "DON'T KNOW" TO Q.76 SAY, "If you usually flowed for five days during your period...") (CIRCLE DAYS INDICATED)

```
 1  2  3  4  5  6  7  8  9 10
11 12 13 14 15 16 17 18 19 20
21 22 23 24 25 26 27 28 29 30
31 32 33 34 35 36 37 38 39 40
41 42 43 44 45 46 47 48 49 50
```

(SKIP TO Q.81)	Don't know	VV

78. About when did you find out about the time during your cycle when your greatest chance of becoming pregnant occurs — before marriage, or after marriage?

	Before marriage	1
(SKIP TO Q.80)	After marriage	2

79. (IF "AFTER MARRIAGE" IN Q.78) Before which pregnancy did you find out about this or was it since your last pregnancy?	85. (ASK EVERYONE) In recent months about how frequently have you and your husband had intercourse? I mean on the average, of course. (RECORD TIMES AND UNIT OF TIME.)

79.	
First	1
Second	2
Third	3
Fourth	4
Fifth	5
Sixth	6
Since last pregnancy	7

80. (ASK EVERYONE EXCEPT THOSE SAYING "DON'T KNOW" TO Q.77) Tell me, as nearly as you can, from whom you got this information. (GET RELATIONSHIP TO RESPONDENT, NOT NAME.)

86. Would you say you ordinarily have intercourse at the same time of the week — that is, only on weekends or on certain predictable nights of the week?

	Yes	1
(SKIP TO Q.88)	No	2

81. (ASK EVERYONE) Have you ever tried to shorten the time it takes to get pregnant by having more frequent intercourse at some particular time of the month?

	Yes	1
(SKIP TO Q.83)	No	2

87. (IF "NO") Is there any pattern or regularity to the times you have intercourse as far as you are aware of? What is the pattern?

82. (IF "YES") Before which pregnancies?

First	1
Second	2
Third	3
Fourth	4
Fifth	5
Sixth	6
Since last pregnancy	7

83. (ASK EVERYONE) In order to avoid getting pregnant, have you ever tried to avoid intercourse at some particular time of the month?

	Yes	1
(SKIP TO Q.85)	No	2

88. (ASK EVERYONE) Do you think you could accurately predict when you will have intercourse next — I mean, do you think you could narrow it down to the day?

84. (IF "YES") Before which pregnancies?

First	1
Second	2
Third	3
Fourth	4
Fifth	5
Sixth	6
Since last pregnancy	7

Appendix B. Sampling

A. Contacting Respondents for Reinterview

To locate the respondents for a second interview, main reliance was placed on Post Office Form 3547. A piece of third-class mail—not in any way identified with the study—was sent to each respondent at her address as determined in the first interview. Form 3547 was requested for each mail-out. Supposedly this piece of mail would be delivered to the respondent if she still resided at the address given. Alternatively, it would be forwarded to her if she had moved to another address within the same post office district, while a Form 3547 would be returned to us with a forwarding address. Finally, if the respondent had moved to an address outside of the original post office district, the form would be returned to us with a forwarding address, but with the mail-out itself not forwarded.

Returns from the mail-out implied that only 270 respondents had moved from addresses recorded at first interview. For 74 of these cases no forwarding address was supplied. At this point a second procedure was brought into play. During the first interview every respondent had been asked for the names and addresses of three persons most apt to know where they would be living if they should move. By letters sent to these referents, addresses were obtained for 44 of the 74 unlocated by Post Office Form 3547. The 29 respondents still remaining unlocated, together with the 13 known already to be sterile, were then dropped from the sample list.

However, when interviewers attempted to contact the remaining 1,123 respondents, it was discovered that only 498 were living at listed addresses. To find correct addresses, telephone directories were consulted and inquiries made of neighbors, postmen, and local business men. By these means, the number of unlocated respondents (out of 1,123) was reduced from 625 to 289. Letters sent to the referents of these 289 respondents further reduced the list of missing addresses to 95. Thus in the end, failure to maintain closer contact with the panel during the three-year period between interviews entailed a loss of about 10 per cent in sample size.

In addition to the 13 classified as ineligible because of a known sterilization operation, 22 additional wives, upon being contacted, were found ineligible for such reasons as death, divorce, permanent separation, or widowhood. Enough call-backs were made to hold down the number of not-at-homes to 31 including several couples whose addresses were never satisfactorily verified. Interviews were sought with respondents who had moved out of the seven Standard Metropolitan Areas, though no attempt was made to interview one mother living out of the country and another residing in jail. Altogether, 998 were contacted, and of these 92, or 9 per cent, refused the interview. These field results are summarized in Table B-1.

TABLE B-1

Results of the Second Phase of Field Work: Classification of the Original Panel of 1,165 Couples

Number of Couples	Status at End of Field Work
905	Successfully reinterviewed
95	Moved but no new address could be obtained
31	Unable to locate or contact (includes persistently not at home and cases where address could not be verified)
1	Moved out of the United States
1	In prison
22	Ineligible because deceased, divorced, permanently separated, or widowed
13	Ineligible because of sterilizing operation reported during first interview
92	Refused
5	Ill
1,165	Total

B. Sampling Bias

Differences between the 905 couples reinterviewed and the 260 nonrespondents have been tested by means of chi square. With respect to a number of characteristics measured at the first interview the following differences prove nonsignificant:

Standard Metropolitan Area
Average birth interval
Husband's age
Wife's desired family size
Number of moves since marriage
Marriage adjustment
Change in income—marriage to second birth
Prestige rating of occupation
Intragenerational occupational mobility
Wife's drive to get ahead

On a number of characteristics, however, the 905 wives reinterviewed are definitely biased (see Table B-2). These differences are based only on the comparison of univariate distributions while the critical concern is with bivariate distributions. One wonders how well the correlations yielded by the remaining sample accord with those that might have been obtained if all movers had been contacted and nobody had refused the second interview. Correlations representing all possible pairs of relationships among 31 variables

TABLE B-2
Differences Found Significant by Chi Square at the .05 Level or Lower

Variable	Degrees of Freedom	Level of Significance	Mean Value	
			Respondents	Non-respondents
Fertility-planning success	3	.02–.05		
Per cent "successful" or "semi-successful" planners			61%	55%
Wife's age	9	.001	26.0	25.2
Wife's age at marriage	9	.01–.001	21.8	20.3
Religion	2	.01–.001		
Protestant			49%	44%
Catholic			39%	50%
Jewish			12%	6%
Per cent returned mail questionnaire	1	.01–.001	87%	58%
Occupational class	9	.01–.001		
White collar			51%	41%
Husband's 1956 income	9	.01–.001	$5,200	$4,700
Wife's economic security	5	.01–.001	3.8	3.5
Wife's Vocabulary				
Test score	9	.001	11.4	10.5
Wife's Education	9	.001		
Attended College			27%	18%
Graduated from high school			80%	63%
Husband's Education	9	.001		
Attended college			40%	23%

TABLE B-3
Distribution of Absolute Differences in Values of Correlation Coefficients[a] Computed for the Original Sample of 1,165 Couples and the Follow-up Sample of 905 Couples

Amount of Difference	Number of Differences	Per Cent Distribution	Cumulative Per Cent Distribution
.00	103	22.2	100.0
.01	177	38.1	77.8
.02	113	24.3	39.8
.03	55	11.3	15.5
.04	12	2.6	3.6
.05	4	0.9	1.1
.06	1	0.2	0.2
Total	465	100.1	—

[a] These coefficients relate to all possible pairs of relationships—31(30)/2 or 465—involving 31 variables measured at first interview.

collected at first interview have been computed for the original panel of 1,165 couples and for the 905 reinterviewed and the absolute differences between corresponding coefficients tabulated in Table B-3. Although one might maintain that some small differences are large relative to the small base of comparison, no differences of any practical significance exist.

Appendix C. The Reliability of Data on Fertility Planning[1]

As a result of the growing concern over rapid population growth in the world today, more and more studies are being made of the practice of family limitation. Generally such studies rely on the technique of survey research. Far too little information exists yet about the reliability of responses about family planning as collected by interview. For instance, one wonders how the reliability and accuracy of contraceptive data are affected when the husband is interrogated instead of the wife. Poti, Chakraborti, and Malaker have recently made a valuable contribution to this subject with their analysis based on a large Indian sample survey.[2]

The present paper is concerned with another type of reliability, namely, the consistency of responses given by the *same* respondents asked identical questions at two different times—at the first interview in 1957 and in the second interview conducted three years later. Duplicate questions were asked about their histories of family planning from marriage to second birth. These questions, embracing such aspects as number and outcome of pregnancies, use or nonuse of contraception, reasons for nonuse, and circumstance of each conception have made it possible to classify each respondent according to an index of fertility-planning success.

The present analysis, then, focuses on the test-retest reliability over a three-year period of this index of fertility-planning success together with each of its components. The nature of the sample and our survey were such that the reliabilities obtained may fairly be regarded as approximating upper limits, at least for present-day standards of survey technique.

The study was conducted under as ideal circumstances as could be expected. Moreover, the sample of mothers we interviewed—young, comparatively well-educated, urban and suburban residents—can reasonably be considered as representative of a group

---

[1] This discussion is reprinted with some modifications from the original article by Charles F. Westoff, Robert G. Potter, Jr., and Philip C. Sagi, "Some Estimates of the Reliability of Survey Data on Family Planning," *Population Studies*, 15 (July 1961), pp. 52–69. Changes from the original article are in a reduction of the introductory and background material and inclusion of an analysis of the impact of unreliability on the correlation between fertility-planning success and subsequent number of pregnancies.

[2] S. J. Poti, B. Chakraborti and C. R. Malaker, "Reliability of Data Relating to Contraceptive Practices," in Clyde V. Kiser (ed.), *Research in Family Planning*, Princeton, Princeton University Press, 1962, pp. 51–65.

sophisticated in the cultures of contraception, child-rearing, and sexual behavior. In other words, we should expect to find a high degree of reliability associated with their reports of fertility planning, especially in view of their relatively short and uncomplicated pregnancy histories at the time. Although one might theorize that this type of sophistication is no necessary index of reliability, and that ignorance and simple, limited experience might be a better basis, the most reasonable inference would seem to be that this sample probably sets an upper limit to the reliability of such data. This does not of course imply that any improvement would be impossible; on the contrary, one purpose of the present analysis is to determine what improvements in questioning techniques might be desirable. In spite of the sophisticated nature of the sample, several examples will be furnished in which distributions of responses based on the first interview closely match distributions based on the re-interviews but at the individual level many responses prove inconsistent. If this "hidden" unreliability applies to classifications of family planning success, it furnishes part of the explanation why such generally low levels of correlation have been found in previous work between these classifications and a broad spectrum of social and psychological variables.[3]

Components of Fertility Planning

In constructing a classification of family-planning success we faced a special problem. For purposes of multivariate analysis, it was crucial to be able to rank all couples along a single continuum of fertility planning, including those who reported no practice of contraception before their second birth. To achieve this end, each pregnancy (prior to second birth) of every couple was classified as "planned" or "unplanned." Based on these gradings, four levels of planning success were distinguished, ranging from "completely planned" (all pregnancies planned) to "completely unplanned" (no pregnancies planned).

A pregnancy was considered planned under three circumstances: (1) contraception deliberately stopped in order to conceive; (2) contraception not used because of a desire to have the pregnancy as soon as possible; (3) contraception not used because of assumed difficulty in conceiving. Concerning the last two circumstances it was reasoned that a woman, believing herself subfecund

[3] *Ibid.*, p. 329. See also Edgar F. Borgatta and Charles F. Westoff, "The Prediction of Total Fertility," P. K. Whelpton and Clyde V. Kiser, eds. *Social and Psychological Factors Affecting Fertility*, 5 vols., Milbank Memorial Fund, New York, 1947–58, v, pp. 1087–1123.

or anxious to have her next pregnancy as soon as possible, was behaving rationally with reference to her spacing desires if she did not use contraception. The corresponding circumstances for unplanned pregnancies were: (1) pregnancy occurred while using a method of contraception; (2) pregnancy occurred while taking a chance and omitting contraception; (3) contraception not used for such reasons as religious scruple, ignorance, fear, aesthetic aversion, not caring when pregnancy occurred, or not believing pregnancy would occur so soon. With regard to the third circumstance, women who did not use contraception for such reasons as religious scruple or dislike of contraception were, of course, behaving rationally with reference to their larger value systems; but with reference to the single value of child spacing they were behaving inconsistently; the reasons they gave for nonuse were irrelevant to their spacing interests. Indeed, their failure to delay pregnancy was more complete than in the case of those using contraception unsuccessfully.

Quite obviously several kinds of measurement enter into our index of fertility planning. The opportunities for compounded unreliability are large. For such a classification to have reliability it is important that respondents be able to recall consistently how many pregnancies they have had and not to confuse the order of these pregnancies. Then there is the deceptively simple problem of determining whether contraception was practiced in a particular interval. Accurate reporting of contraceptive usage is influenced presumably by such factors as the type of method used, the regularity and duration of its practice, the experience of success or failure with it, as well as attitudes bearing on which methods are to be defined as contraception or which are regarded as acceptable for use.[4]

Next, if no contraception is reported, then the reason for nonuse must be determined and, as we will see subsequently, these responses concerning motivation are probably the weakest link in our index. Finally, if use of a method is indicated, the circumstance of conception must be ascertained, that is, whether the conception occurred at a time when contraception was actually being used, at a time when the couple "took a chance" and did not use any method, or following the deliberate interruption of contraception in order to conceive.

These, then, are the components of our measure of fertility-planning success—components that are important in their own

---

[4] A discussion of the accuracy of reporting on use of contraception and some analysis of internal consistency is contained in Ronald Freedman, P. K. Whelpton, and Arthur A. Campbell, *Family Planning, Sterility and Population Growth*, New York, McGraw-Hill, 1959, Appendix E, pp. 469–477.

right as well as in the construction of a summary index. The following sections will review the reliability of each component and conclude with an evaluation of the reliability of the summary index of fertility-planning success.

DISCREPANCIES IN PREGNANCY HISTORIES

Despite the simplicity of pregnancy histories up to the time of the first interview—all couples had only two live births with a maximum of three pregnancies—there are a number of discrepancies in these histories resulting from differences in reports by women who had experienced a miscarriage. Women reporting only one pregnancy aborting during the first five months of pregnancy were considered eligible for inclusion in the study; women with more than one such miscarriage or with a pregnancy aborting after five months were not included.

The relevant questions asked in the first interview were:

"How many pregnancies have you had, if any, that miscarried *before* five months?"[5]

If the answer was one such pregnancy (more than one made the respondent ineligible), the woman was subsequently asked:

"Which pregnancy was that? Your first, second, or third?"

and

"In what month and year did this miscarriage happen?"

Essentially the same questions were repeated in the second interview.

In the first interview, 131 or 14.5 per cent of the 905 respondents reported a miscarriage and 13.4 per cent recalled a miscarriage for the same period when questioned in the second interview. Thus the two aggregate estimates agree fairly well. The individual comparisons, however, reveal a number of different types of inconsistency. Most of the discrepancies recorded in Table C-1 involve inconsistencies only in the date (month) of the miscarriage.[6] These inconsistencies can undoubtedly be attributed to the lack of importance attached to the event of an early miscarriage compared to that associated with a live birth.

Almost all the remaining discrepancies, comprising 4.4 per cent of the total sample, involve an inconsistency in the number of mis-

[5] This followed a question: "Have you ever had any stillbirths, that is, babies born dead or pregnancies that miscarried *after* five months?"

[6] See Percy G. Gray, "The Memory Factor in Social Surveys," *Journal of the American Statistical Association*, vol. I, No. 270 (June 1955), pp. 344–363 for analogous findings of the comparison of recall of dates and events.

carriages reported. These discrepancies include nearly one-third of all the respondents who reported a miscarriage in either or both interviews.[7] This is an important error, and has significant implications for estimates of contraceptive effectiveness and fertility-planning success as well as the measurement of fecundity, time required for conception, and pregnancy wastage.

TABLE C-1
Discrepancies in Pregnancy Histories

Type of pregnancy history and discrepancy	Number	Percentage
Total sample	905	100
History does not include miscarriage	774	85.5
History includes miscarriage, no discrepancy	30	3.3
Discrepancy in reported month of miscarriage	59	6.5
Discrepancy in order of miscarriage	2	0.2
Discrepancy in number of miscarriages	40	4.4
History includes a miscarriage	131	100
No discrepancy	30	22.9
Discrepancy in reported month of miscarriage	59	45.0
Discrepancy in order of miscarriage	2	1.5
Discrepancy in number of miscarriages	40	30.5

The lesson would seem clear that no great reliability can be expected from reports of miscarriages. Perhaps additional questions could be included profitably that might serve to identify cases where the woman is not positive that a pregnancy has occurred, which is probably the main source of the error. Beyond this, little optimism seems justified particularly if one thinks in terms of more general samples including longer and more complicated pregnancy histories.

In order to avoid confusion in classifying types of inconsistencies, the following discussion will exclude temporarily the 4.4 per cent who reported different numbers of miscarriages and the 0.2 per cent who were inconsistent on the order but not the number of that pregnancy.

USE OF CONTRACEPTION

Regarding use of contraception the following initial question was asked of each respondent:

[7] Every attempt was made to reconcile inconsistencies by searching both interviews for clues. The numbers reported here should therefore be regarded as the really hard-core inconsistencies.

"Many married couples use natural means such as rhythm or use other means to space their children or to limit the size of their families. In your own case, since your marriage have you and your husband *ever* used any of these methods? Would you just tell me whether you have or have not used *any* of these methods?"

Meanwhile the respondent had been handed a card containing a list of thirteen methods of contraception.[8] If the answer was "yes," a shorter version of the same question was then repeated for each pregnancy interval.

In the first interview 55 per cent of the women reported that they had used some form of contraception after marriage prior to their first pregnancy (Table C-2). At the second interview, three years later, the proportion reporting contraception during this first interval was virtually the same—54 per cent. This close aggregate correspondence masks the fact that 20 per cent of the total sample gave contradictory reports: 10 per cent reported contraception in the first but not the second interview and the same proportion in the second interview reported using contraception but did not in their first report.

TABLE C-2
Reliability of Reporting Use and Nonuse of Contraception

Reliability of Reporting	First Interval		Second interval	
	Frequency	Percentage	Frequency	Percentage
Use of contraception reported in both interviews	386	44.7	628	72.8
Use reported in first interview, nonuse in second	89	10.3	67	7.8
Nonuse reported in first interview, used in second	83	9.6	63	7.3
Nonuse reported in both interviews	305	35.3	105	12.2
Total	863	100	863	100

In the second pregnancy interval, which was longer in duration and closer in time to the interview, 80 per cent reported in each interview having used contraception. The total inconsistency here amounted to 15 per cent and again the error was evenly divided in each direction.

Probably one source of this unreliability is the procedure followed of giving the respondent an easy opportunity to answer "no"

[8] These methods were identified by a number of synonyms including vernacular expressions in order to minimize any misunderstanding.

to the question of whether she ever used any method since her marriage. Future surveys should place the burden of denial upon the respondent in each successive pregnancy interval rather than permitting her to answer "no" to a single introductory question.

Another source of unreliability is uncertainty and vacillation on the part of the respondent concerning whether techniques such as rhythm, withdrawal or douching should be viewed as contraception. As will be shown in the next section, women who mention any of these three methods in the first interview are especially liable to report something else in the second interview—either another method or no method at all.

METHOD OF CONTRACEPTION

Type of contraceptive method furnishes a rather dramatic instance of close agreement at the aggregate level but frequent discrepancies in the reports of individuals. The distributions of methods reported in the first interview are essentially those reported in the re-interviews, both with respect to contraception before first pregnancy and contraception before second and third pregnancies.

TABLE C-3

Consistency of Responses about Type of Contraceptive Method Used before First Pregnancy

Method of Contraception Reported in First Interview	Number of Users	Percentages Reporting in Second Interview			
		Use of Same Method	Use of Different Method	Use of No Method	Total
Diaphragm and jelly	75	73.3	21.3	5.3	100
Condom	165	68.5	14.6	17.0	100
Other (mostly jelly)[a]	26	57.7	23.1	19.2	100
Rhythm	64	46.9	12.5	40.6	100
Withdrawal	19	31.6	36.8	31.6	100
Two or more methods combined or alternated	99	31.3	59.6	9.1	100
Douche	25	20.0	36.0	44.0	100
Total	473	53.9	27.3	18.8	100

[a] Mostly jelly alone; secondarily suppository or abstinence.

Moreover, the same result is obtained even if the distributions are modified to include non-use of contraception as an additional category.[9]

Regarding individual consistency, Tables C-3 and C-4 show that among respondents reporting use of a method in the first inter-

[9] Four chi square values (based on 8 or 9 degrees of freedom) all proved non-significant.

view barely more than half mention the same method three years later. The consistency level is only slightly higher for methods reported before second and third pregnancies[10] than for methods reported before first pregnancy.

TABLE C-4

Consistency of Responses about Type of Contraceptive Method Used before Second or Third Pregnancy

		Percentages Reporting in Second Interview			
Method of Contraception Reported in First Interview	Number of Users	Use of Same Method	Use of Different Method	Use of No Method	Total
Diaphragm and jelly	134	73.9	25.4	0.8	100
Condom	239	69.9	21.8	8.4	100
Other (mostly jelly)[a]	24	58.3	37.5	4.2	100
Rhythm	156	62.8	19.2	18.0	100
Withdrawal	37	40.5	51.4	8.1	100
Two or more methods combined or alternated	147	31.3	61.2	7.5	100
Douche	31	22.6	38.7	38.7	100
Total	768	58.1	32.0	9.9	100

[a] Mostly jelly alone; secondarily suppository or abstinence.

Consistency levels vary markedly among the different types of method. Highest reliabilities associate with diaphragm and jelly and with condom. If one of these two methods is mentioned in the first interview, then roughly 70 per cent mention it again in the second interview. Use of jelly alone is somewhat less consistently reported.

For reasons that are not readily apparent, the reliability of reports about the rhythm method varies with the pregnancy interval.[11] Use before first pregnancy is consistently recalled 47 per cent of the time as opposed to a significantly different 62 per cent before second and third pregnancies. Relatively lower reliabilities characterize reports about withdrawal, in large part because so many women initially reporting withdrawal change their report to a different method in the following interview. Low reliability also characterizes reports about combining or alternating two or more methods within the same pregnancy interval. Obviously it is more difficult to reconstruct accurately a grouping of methods than a single method. Reports about douching as a contraceptive show the least

[10] In Table 4 usage before second and third pregnancies is combined in order to increase cases in the seven categories of method being distinguished.

[11] The possibility that the groups using rhythm in the two intervals differed in educational composition was explored but no differences were found. It may mean that recency of recall is more critical for the rhythm method than for other methods.

reliability. Only a fifth of the women in the first interview reporting douching as their sole protection offer the same information in the second interview; more often they claim a different method or no method at all. Such a low reliability may reflect uncertainty on the part of many users whether to consider douching a contraceptive or merely a hygienic measure.

Essentially the same set of results is obtained when respondents are classified by type of method reported in the *second* interview, with first interview responses then categorized into same method, different method, or no method. Accordingly these additional tables are not included. When no method is reported in an interview, usually no method is reported in the other interview; but if a method is reported in the other interview, then more often than expected it is rhythm, douche, or withdrawal and less often than expected it is a combination or alternation of two or more methods.

CIRCUMSTANCES OF CONCEPTION

The reliability of reporting the circumstance of conception is affected by the reliability of reporting whether contraception was used during the interval. Since the questions on circumstance were asked only of women who reported using contraception, those who inconsistently reported use were necessarily found inconsistent on circumstance. Our analysis here will concentrate on both aspects of the problem—how unreliable is the reporting on circumstance of conception during an interval in which contraception is consistently reported, and what is the total extent of unreliability when both the dimensions of use and circumstance are incorporated.

If the respondent reported using contraception, say in the interval preceding the first pregnancy, she was subsequently asked after determining the method used:

"Under which *one* of these circumstances did your first pregnancy occur?"

The respondent was then handed a card which read:

(1) While we were actually using some method and didn't want a pregnancy just then.

(2) When we took a chance and didn't use a method.

(3) After we deliberately stopped using a method in order to have a child.

(4) Some other circumstance. (Specify.)

The respondent was instructed to select one of these categories and report the number to the interviewer.[12] Only a few gave re-

---

[12] At this juncture there is, of course, an opportunity for recording error, the amount of which we have no way of ascertaining.

sponses that could not be classified in the first three categories so we may ignore category 4. Categories 1 and 2 are defined as an unplanned pregnancy and category 3 as planned.

One of our concerns is whether there is any observable bias toward reporting pregnancies as planned, which were initially reported as unplanned. There does seem to be such a bias for the first interval (7.5 per cent change categories from unplanned to planned and 4 per cent change in the opposite direction) but this difference does not appear for the later interval. A stronger bias of this nature does occur in the reporting of reasons for non-use of contraception. In both pregnancy intervals, twice as high a proportion remember as planned a conception originally reported unplanned than recall the converse combination.

TABLE C-5

Reliability of Reporting Circumstances of Conception for Wives Reporting Consistently that Contraception Was Used

Circumstance Reported in First Interview	Circumstance Reported in Second Interview		
	Using	Chance	Interrupted
	FIRST CONCEPTION		(N = 386) Total
While using a method	8.0	2.6	2.1	12.7
Taking a chance	4.1	12.4	5.4	22.0
Deliberately interrupted use	1.6	2.3	61.4	65.3
Total	13.7	17.4	68.9	100
	SECOND CONCEPTION		(N = 616) Total
While using a method	10.4	3.9	1.6	15.9
Taking a chance	2.9	10.4	4.2	17.5
Deliberately interrupted use	2.9	4.5	59.1	66.5
Total	16.2	18.8	64.9	100

If we confine our attention to the women who reported using contraception in both interviews, the consistency of reporting the three categories above for the first birth interval is 82 per cent, if we ignore the differences between categories 1 and 2 and are content with the dichotomy "planned" and "unplanned," the consistency rises to nearly 89 per cent. This high degree of consistency is reflected for both intervals in the close aggregate correspondence of the distributions for the three circumstances between the interviews (see Table C-5).

If we consider the total sample and raise the question of how accurately we can reproduce the entire picture of fertility planning in the first birth interval, including use or nonuse of contraception as well as circumstance of conception for those who reported use, the answer is 75 per cent. This figure is an upper limit because it does not take into account either the consistency of reasons reported for nonuse which is relevant to the planning dimension or the difference between the two types of unplanned conceptions. With these two additional criteria incorporated, the consistency of events reported to precede the first pregnancy drops to 62 per cent. A final figure of 65 per cent, ignoring the difference between irregular practice and method failure, would seem to be a reasonable estimate of the proportion of couples (or pregnancies) which would be classified the same in the interval between marriage and first pregnancy on both the dimensions of use or nonuse of contraception and successful or unsuccessful planning.

For those who consistently reported practicing contraception in this interval, the consistency of reporting the circumstances of the second conception is 80 per cent for the three categories and 87 per cent if we settle for a "planned-unplanned" dichotomy (Table C-5). Combining the dimension of use and nonuse with whether the contraceptive circumstance was planned or unplanned reduces this to 72 per cent. Adding the further dimensions of reasons for nonuse and the more detailed three circumstances of conception reduces this to 67 per cent. A more reasonable final estimate of 70 per cent ignores this last distinction. This figure represents some improvement over the 65 per cent consistency estimate for the first interval but essentially it is very similar.

THE INDEX OF FERTILITY-PLANNING SUCCESS

Having considered the reliability of its components, we now turn to the index of fertility planning itself.

Four levels of planning success are being distinguished: "completely planned," "semi-planned," "semi-unplanned," and "completely unplanned." The classification of a pregnancy as "planned" or "unplanned" is that described earlier. Complete planning denotes that all pregnancies are planned prior to second birth, while the completely unplanned history is one in which no pregnancies prior to second birth are planned. Couples in the "semi-planned" category have planned their last pregnancy but failed to plan an earlier pregnancy. Most couples assigned the rank of "semi-unplanned" have planned the first pregnancy and failed to plan their last one; a few have planned their last pregnancy but failed to plan two earlier ones.

Every one of the 905 respondents was ranked according to this scheme initially on the basis of first interview data and then again independently on the basis of second interview data. The inter-relationships between the two sets of assignments are presented in Table C-6. As expected from previous results, a barely higher percentage of histories was classified as completely planned in the second interview than in the first (47 compared to 43 per cent).

TABLE C-6
The Consistency of Classifications of Fertility-Planning Success

| | PER CENT DISTRIBUTION—SECOND INTERVIEW | | | | |
| | *All Couples* ($N = 905$) | | | | |
FIRST INTERVIEW	Completely Planned	Semi-Planned	Semi-Unplanned	Completely Unplanned	Total
Completely planned	33.7	3.4	3.8	1.8	42.7
Semi-planned	6.1	8.2	0.6	3.1	17.9
Semi-unplanned	3.0	0.9	7.8	3.5	15.2
Completely unplanned	4.2	1.9	4.1	14.0	24.2
Total	47.0	14.4	16.2	22.4	100

Approximately two-thirds of the sample (64 per cent) are classified identically in the two classifications. Examination of frequencies lying off the main diagonal reveals a variety of error types. Most interesting are those located in the extreme disagreement categories—where all pregnancies were inconsistently reported.[13] The total of such cases adds to 54 (6 per cent) with 38 wives initially reporting all pregnancies as unplanned and subsequently as planned, and 16 wives in the converse position. In view of the extreme error involved and its implications for the correlations observed between fertility-planning success and other variables, a thorough examination of these cases seems advisable.

A clue to one common type of error is derived from an analysis by religion (Table C-7). Extreme disagreement is highest among Catholics, totalling 9 per cent, and they contribute approximately three-quarters of all such error instead of an expected one-half. This result focuses suspicion on the reporting of reasons for not using contraception—a type of exposure most common among Catholics. We returned to the actual interview schedules of each of the 54 wives involved in this extreme form of error, and the following

[13] At least as extreme a disagreement exists also for cases classified as semi-planned at one time and semi-unplanned at another since it also implies an inconsistency involving both pregnancies. Most of the total 13 cases involved in this type of discrepancy, however, had reported a third pregnancy (implying a miscarriage) so that the inconsistency mainly reflected the problem of incorporating this additional pregnancy into the classification.

profiles are illustrative of the more common types of such inconsistencies.

TABLE C-7

The Consistency of Classifications of Fertility-Planning Success, by Religion

Religion	Number	Identical Agreement	Degree of Consistency Extreme Disagreement	Other Disagreement	Total
Protestant	372	66.2	2.2	31.6	100
Catholic	423	57.7	9.5	32.8	100
Jewish	110	79.1	5.4	15.5	100
Total	905	63.7	6.0	30.3	100

Among Catholics the most frequent pattern did involve the discrepancies between reasons reported for not using contraception. The typical pattern was for the wife initially to reply that methods of family limitation were not used for religious reasons and to report in the second interview that the reason no method was used was that they wanted to have children as soon as possible. For example:

2150. First interview—"We don't plan the children. That's in our Maker's hands."

Second interview—"We wanted to have children, so there was no need to."

2088. First interview—"It's against our religion."

Second interview—The reason offered for using no method before the first pregnancy was: "Wanted children right away" and in the second interval: "Wanted to continue to have children to build our family."

1278. First interview—"We just never thought about it."

Second interview—"Because we wanted a baby" was the reason offered for using no method before the first pregnancy, and for the second interval, she explained that they "Wanted two children and not too far apart."

The converse pattern of initially ascribing nonuse to a desire for children and subsequently attributing it to religious motives also occurs but is a less common form of inconsistency.

These cases illustrate the weakness of a classification which depends on answers to an open-ended question. Part of the problem lies in the noncomparability to a respondent who is more verbal or who is interviewed by an interviewer who keeps probing for further considerations as opposed to a respondent who is less verbal or whose interviewer is content with short, direct answers. The only solution, if there is any, is to cross-examine the respondent with questions asking whether there are any additional reasons or perhaps provide some kind of a check list of reasons. There is probably no complete solution to the problem, but significant improvement can undoubtedly be achieved.

To test the hypothesis that the reliability of the fertility-planning index is substantially reduced by the problems of classifying motivations for not using contraception, we computed reliability coefficients for two subsamples: those who consistently reported not using a method in both intervals and those who consistently reported practice of contraception in both intervals. Our impressions were clearly confirmed: among the latter group of users, the coefficient of correlation between the indices of fertility-planning success is .75, while among the nonusers it drops to .45 (and even lower, to .38 among Catholics).[14] The largest single group omitted from this dichotomy are couples who used no method until after the birth of their first child and, as expected, the reliability coefficient of .65 observed for this group is intermediate between the purer types.

The remaining extreme errors involve couples who reported using a method at some time or other during the first two birth intervals. The following responses illustrate cases of reporting both pregnancies as unplanned in the first interview and planned on the second. These are Protestant women:

1494. First interview—The first pregnancy was reported to have occurred because her "husband didn't want me to use anything nor did he." The second conception occurred while using a condom and not wanting another child.

Second interview—No method was used before the first pregnancy because "we wanted a child" and she now also reports not using any method in the second interval because "we wanted a second child so we did nothing at all to prevent me from becoming pregnant."

3035. First interview—Reports not using any method prior to the first pregnancy because "I didn't know any better. I guess ignorance is the only answer." Second interval she recalled having alternated between the use of condom and withdrawal, and stated that her second pregnancy occurred when they "took a chance" because she "didn't think I could get pregnant with tipped ovaries." She added specifically that she didn't decide to have a child.

Second interview—No method was reported in the first interval because "I wanted a baby right away." The second

[14] There is no difference by religion in the reliability among users.

conception is now recalled to have followed the deliberate interruption of the use of condom.

3430. First interview—Never used any method in any interval. Why? "We just never have used anything I'm afraid. I might get cancer or something so we just don't use any."

Second interview—Reported using the condom in both intervals and deliberately interrupting its use to conceive.

These cases are rather glaring examples of unreliability, many of which have no apparent explanation. This last woman, who would appear to be an uneducated respondent, actually reported college attendance of one year.

The problems of some methods being close to no contraception, and ambivalence because of religion is illustrated in some of the following Catholic wives' reports:

4111. First interview—Withdrawal used in both intervals and stopped to have a child.

Second interview—Never used any method. Why? "Religion—we're Catholics."

7066. First interview—Rhythm used in both intervals and deliberately interrupted to conceive.

Second interview—No method used in either interval. In the first interval the reason offered was "Because we're Catholic" and in the second interval because we "wanted more children and we're trying to live up to our religion."

5291. First interview—used rhythm and reported that both pregnancies had occurred when they had taken a chance and not used any method.

Second interview—Reported using no contraception in the first interval because they "wanted to start a family right away" and also none before the second pregnancy because they "wanted children close together."

4105. First interview—never used any method. Why? "Didn't care when children came."

Second interview—interrupted use of rhythm to conceive both pregnancies.

2327. First interview—Never used any method. Why? "Don't believe in it. Believe that nature takes its course in such things."

Second interview—No method reported before first pregnancy because "we wanted to have a child as we were just married and had no reason not to have one." The second pregnancy was reported to have followed the interruption of douching in order to become pregnant.

There were other Catholic women in this extreme error category who used the rhythm method and who simply reported a different circumstance—from either "taking a chance" or "while using the method" to interrupting its use to conceive. And then there are wide differences which seem completely inexplicable:

1472. First interview—Never used, explaining that they simply "trust to luck."

Second interview—First conception followed deliberate interruption of using the condom; second conception occurred after they stopped practicing withdrawal.

1554. First interview—Used no contraception in first interval because they "wanted a child right away." In the second interval, they alternated use of condom and diaphragm and interrupted practice deliberately to conceive.

Second interview—"Just didn't" is the only reason offered for using no method in the first interval. No contraception at all is reported for the second interval with the explanation that there was "no reason—it didn't matter if we had a baby or not."

1726. First interview—used a condom before both first and second pregnancy, deliberately interrupting its use each time.

Second interview—reported no contraception used in the first interval because she "didn't expect to become pregnant so soon after marriage." The second pregnancy is now attributed to unsuccessful practice of rhythm.

The Jewish women in the sample showed the highest degree of perfect consistency in reporting fertility planning—79 per cent were classified in the identical categories at both times. However, compared to Protestants, they produced a higher proportion (5.4 compared to 2.2 per cent) of the extreme disagreement under discussion. Some examples follow, but there is no pattern evident.

1254. First interview—both pregnancies followed deliberate interruption of use of condom.

Second interview—both pregnancies now attributed to "taking a chance" and not using the condom. The set of circumstances in the first interval was explained: "Well, actually we were beginning to think about a child, so if I became pregnant we both felt it would not matter much." Taking a chance in the second interval was similarly explained: "Well, we felt it was two years, and it was time—but it did not matter too much."

The inconsistency here is clearly understandable, depending

perhaps on nothing more than the expansiveness of the respondent's mood at the time of the interview. Less obvious are the following reports which are from two Jewish respondents, although such inconsistencies are also characteristic of many Protestant and Catholic responses.

1843.   First interview—No method used in either interval because "my husband doesn't care for it."

Second interview—no method used before the first pregnancy because they "wanted a child immediately after marriage." The second pregnancy is now reported to have followed the deliberate cessation of withdrawal.

5206.   First interview—no method used in either interval because they "wanted a baby . . . and a second baby right away."

Second interview—the diaphragm used in both intervals with the first pregnancy occurring while "taking a chance" and the second while actually using the method.

CORRELATES OF UNRELIABILITY

We have already indicated (Table C-7) that the reliability of fertility-planning assignments varies appreciably by religion. Classifications of Jews have proved most reliable, and those for Catholics least reliable, with Protestants occupying an intermediate position. Two factors are operating to produce this differential. Catholics and Protestants rely more heavily than Jews on rhythm, withdrawal, and douche, the single methods with poorest records as to consistency of reporting. Then, too, Catholics have the greatest incidence of noncontraceptive exposure which entails classifications based on reasons for nonuse; and Protestants have a greater amount of this type of exposure than Jews.

We turn now to the question of whether there are any additional social characteristics that relate to consistency of reporting. The first direction we looked was toward education. The number of years that the wife spent in schools correlates with an index of consistency[15] at only .10. Other avenues explored were age, income, and duration of recall.[16] All of these produced weak and not independent correlational values ranging between .10 and .15.[17]

[15] An index of consistency was constructed for the purpose of this analysis which contains four categories combining the dimensions of use and circumstance.

[16] Length of recall to the second birth was constant at six or thirty-six months depending on the interview, while length of recall to first birth varied as a function of these controls plus the interval between first and second birth.

[17] The correlation between length of recall time and consistency is unexpectedly positive. This is probably due to the fact that long birth intervals are associated with being older, more educated and more successful in planning fertility.

Two other possible correlates were investigated. A considerable number of the interviewers had worked on both phases of the study and many respondents had been interviewed by the same person. One might expect that an interviewer who had worked on both phases would have accumulated further experience that might serve to reduce unreliability and that respondents who were being interviewed a second time by the same person might feel some pressure to avoid at least any conscious inconsistencies. In spite of the plausibility of the argument, however, no differences in consistency were uncovered. This, of course, strengthens our interpretation of the inconsistencies being due to respondent unreliability.

Similarly, one might expect that the more difficult respondent would produce more inconsistency but again no differences are evident when the consistency index is correlated with an interviewer's rating of the respondent's cooperativeness.

In summary, although statistically significant relationships with some variables have been found, there is nothing particularly instructive or of great practical value in the findings. The only implications, aside from the occasional suggestions for improving questions that we have noted in passing, are the rather obvious cautions that Catholics pose special problems in this area—problems not of initial cooperation but of definition, interpretation, and perhaps greater sensitivity—and that the less educated respondent is slightly[18] more apt to give unreliable responses.

The Effects of Inconsistency on Correlations

To what extent has the unreliability of our measure of fertility-planning success depressed the correlational values observed between this variable and other variables? Or to phrase it somewhat differently, can some substantial part of the comparative lack of success in explaining the variability of fertility planning be attributed to unreliability of measurement? We can, of course, only test one part of this question since we cannot estimate the reliability of the other variables and those such as income and number of children desired undoubtedly contain large components of unreliability.[19] We did repeat the same questions on number of children desired in

[18] Undoubtedly, the low correlation we report between education and reporting consistency is an underestimate of a stronger association that would probably obtain in a more heterogeneous population where illiteracy exists.

[19] See the analysis of the reliability of reports on family income in Robert Ferber, "On the Reliability of Responses Secured in Sample Surveys," *Journal of the American Statistical Association* Vol. L, No. 271 (September 1955), pp. 788–810. Also see Stephen B. Withey, "Reliability of Recall of Income," *Public Opinion Quarterly*, Vol. xviii, No. 2 (1954), pp. 197–204.

the second interview, for example, but some differences are due to genuine change during the three-year period.[20]

To test the partial effect[21] of unreliability on the correlations of the index of fertility-planning success with other variables, we selected those respondents who were classified identically on the index in both phases of the study. Keeping the religious groupings separate, the three samples are those reported in Table C-7 to have identical agreement in classifications. The differences we observe in the correlations between fertility-planning success and any other variable in these selected samples of consistent respondents and that observed for the original samples we infer is due to the reliability component.[22]

The variables selected for comparison are three initially revealing higher correlations with fertility-planning success: interval between marriage and second birth, number of children desired at the time of the first interview, and the wife's age. We have also included the number of pregnancies since the second birth because of its obvious theoretical significance. Comparisons of the original correlations with those computed among the subsamples of consistent respondents mostly reveal some increase in value. Thus, for the total sample the original correlation of the interval between marriage and second birth with the index of fertility-planning success is .34 while for those classified on the index consistently in both phases, the correlation increases to .41. By contrast, the correlation with the classification in the first phase among respondents who were inconsistent is .20. The corresponding differences among Protestants and Catholics[23] are shown in Table C-8 and similar differences are apparent for the two groups as well as for the variables. It would appear that unreliability has had some depressing effect on the correlations. However, in view of the fact that consistent respondents outnumber the inconsistent by nearly two to one, and seeing that even among the inconsistent respondents some correlation tends to persist, the most reasonable conclusion is that the low

[20] This correlation is .70.

[21] Because the individuals who are most reliable on fertility-planning success are probably also more consistent on the other variables, it is reasonable to assume that our estimated corrections for attenuation are between the maximum expected if both reliabilities were known and the minimum estimate resulting from an assumption of perfect reliability in the other variable.

[22] Other influences can operate as well, such as the increased sampling variability due to a reduction in sample size and changes in the distributions of the variables involved.

[23] Because nearly 80% of the 110 Jews are in the identical agreement category (Table C-7) and the highly skewed distributions on fertility-planning success, correlations for this group are not presented separately.

correlations of fertility-planning success with other variables are not due as much to unreliability as might have been expected. It seems certain that the factor of unreliability is not the main reason for the low correlations found with the other variables in the study.

TABLE C-8
Correlations[a] of the Index of Fertility-Planning Success[b] with Four Selected Variables

	Number of Wives	Interval Marriage to Second Birth	Number of Children Desired after Second Birth	Age of Wife	Number of Pregnancies Since Second Birth
All wives					
Total	905	.34	−.20	.24	−.18
Consistent	576	.41	−.24	.27	−.21
Inconsistent	329	.20	−.12	.13	−.13
Protestants					
Total	372	.32	−.10	.30	−.13
Consistent	246	.39	−.14	.33	−.16
Inconsistent	126	.16	.03	.16	−.04
Catholics					
Total	423	.33	−.21	.18	−.16
Consistent	244	.42	−.24	.22	−.20
Inconsistent	179	.19	−.17	.10	−.08

[a] Pearsonian product-moment correlations.
[b] Among inconsistent respondents, the correlations are with the index of fertility-planning success that was constructed from first interview data.

SUMMARY

This report has been concerned with assessing the reliability of interview data on family planning, a subject that is becoming increasingly important with the growing reliance of population studies on survey research techniques. The opportunity to examine the reliability of such data derives from a longitudinal study of fertility in the United States in which a sample of couples was interviewed initially six months after the birth of their second child and interviewed again three years later. In both of these interviews data were collected about experience prior to the second birth—number of pregnancies, the use or nonuse of contraception, reasons for nonuse, methods of contraception used, and circumstances of the conception. Given the simplicity of the pregnancy histories (a maximum of three pregnancies), the relatively sophisticated sample interviewed, and the intensive preparation of the research, the reliability of data on family planning reported in this paper is assumed to overestimate the reliability of such data collected under less favourable circumstances.

Discrepancies in pregnancy histories have been found in three-quarters of the group reporting a miscarriage. Most of these involve inconsistencies in the recall of the month of the miscarriage but nearly a third involve a discrepancy in the reported number of miscarriages.

The distribution of couples by use or nonuse of contraception in each birth interval is the same for both interviews, but this is the result of compensating error. In the interval between marriage and the first birth, 20 per cent give contradictory replies, half of whom are inconsistent in one direction and half in the other. Between the first birth and second pregnancy, about 15 per cent are inconsistent in reporting whether contraception was used and again the error is divided equally in both directions.

Essentially identical distributions of contraceptive methods are reported in the two interviews, although again among individual respondents, inconsistency is frequently found. Consistency levels vary markedly according to type of method, with greatest consistency associating with diaphragm and jelly or condom and lower reliabilities characterizing reports of rhythm, withdrawal, douching, or use of multiple methods during an interval.

Among couples who consistently reported practicing some method of contraception, the reliability of reporting whether the conception was planned is quite high—over 85 per cent consistency in both intervals together with a slight bias favoring the recall of a pregnancy as planned which was originally reported to be accidental.

Estimating the complete reproducibility of circumstances preceding a pregnancy involves combining the reliabilities of reporting use with those about the circumstances of conception and the classification of reasons for nonuse as planned or unplanned. Such complete reproducibility is met 65 per cent of the time for the first birth interval and 70 per cent of the time for the second birth interval. By far the most vulnerable link is the inconsistency of reporting reasons for nonuse.

This problem is highlighted in the analysis of the reliability of a summary index of fertility-planning success that classifies the total fertility-planning experience of each couple on a four-point scale. Approximately two-thirds of the couples are classified consistently. The verbatim responses of the 6 per cent who reported the planning of both pregnancies differently are reported illustratively, and the problem of consistency in connection with classifying the reasons for nonuse is clearly apparent.

Religion has proved to be important in differentiating levels of reliability on this subject of family planning. Catholics are assigned least consistently to the summary index of family planning, mainly because they used contraception less and thus were required to be consistent in reporting reasons for nonuse, but also because they were heavily concentrated among rhythm users, a method apparently too close to no contraception to be reliably reported. For analogous reasons assignments of Protestants to the index have proved less consistent than for Jews.

Except for religion the search for correlates of unreliability proved largely fruitless. Only slight associations are evident with amount of education, age and duration of recall.

The final section of this report examined the extent to which correlations between the index of fertility-planning success and other variables were being reduced by the unreliability of the index. A few estimates were included which indicated the amount of increase that could be expected with an improvement in reliability.

Appendix D. Measurement of Contraceptive Effectiveness

Couples practicing contraception vary in their monthly risk of accidental pregnancy. As a result, when an interval of contraceptive exposure, such as from marriage to first conception, is segmented into six-month subintervals and a pregnancy rate computed for every subinterval, one may expect to find these subinterval pregnancy rates declining successively. With the more accident-prone members progressively eliminated, there is left behind a more and more homogeneously low-risk group. Other things equal, the more varied are the risks at the start of the interval, the more rapidly will the subinterval pregnancy rates decline.

Among FGIMA couples, a wider variation in monthly risks of accidental pregnancy is found in the initial interval of contraceptive use, between marriage and first conception, than in the period following first birth. The comparison of subinterval pregnancy rates, given in Table D-1, shows this contrast. Following marriage, the subinterval pregnancy rates start higher and decline more steeply than they do in the period following first birth. However the preg-

TABLE D-1

Accidental Pregnancies per 100 Years of Contraceptive Exposure for Specified Divisions of the Intervals between Marriage and First Pregnancy and First Birth and Next Pregnancy

Months from Marriage (or First Birth)	Interval Marriage to First Pregnancy Number of Exposure Months	Failure Rate	Interval First Birth to Next Pregnancy[a] Number of Exposure Months	Failure Rate
0	522	(36.9)	751	8.0
1	484	49.6	737	21.2
2–6	2,019	34.5	3,382	29.8
7–12	1,757	33.3	3,301	24.0
13–18	1,230	11.7	2,363	20.8
19–24	859	19.6	1,601	12.7
25–36	1,054	13.1	1,859	10.3
37–48	464	7.8	1,052	9.1
49 Plus	369	9.8	1,609	14.9
Total	8,758	25.5	16,655	19.5

SOURCE: R. G. Potter, Jr., "Contraceptive Practice and Birth Intervals among Two Child White Couples in Metropolitan America," in *Thirty Years of Research in Human Fertility*, Milbank Memorial Fund, New York, 1959, p. 76.

[a] Only couples without miscarriages are included.

nancy rates converge to about the same value toward the end of both periods. Thus only near the start of the two intervals is there a marked contrast in the frequency of accidental pregnancy. Part of this difference is attributable to an imperfect removal of postpartum amenorrhea from the contraceptive "exposure" following first birth. Nevertheless it is fairly certain that the fraction of high-risk couples practicing irregular or incompetent contraception is higher during the first interval than the second. These high-risk couples, becoming pregnant rather quickly, materially influence only the initial few subinterval rates.

The situation just described may be a fairly common one. Most methods of contraception when correctly and consistently used reduce pregnancy risks to very low levels; but the same methods, when wrongly or erratically employed, admit of much higher risks. Accordingly an appreciable average risk on the part of a sample of couples is apt to mean a considerable hererogeneity of individual risks owing to a sizeable fraction of irregular or otherwise careless users of contraception. Moreover when a sample of couples improves its contraception, it may be chiefly by reduction of chance-taking, which leads to a reduced fraction of high-risk couples. It is important, therefore, that a measure of contraceptive effectiveness be sensitive to such changes in the proportion of high-risk couples.

If the frequency of accidental pregnancy is markedly higher at the start of one interval than another, this contrast is perhaps best brought out by two series of subinterval pregnancy rates such as given in Table D-1. The same contrast tends to be obscured if only two summary pregnancy rates, one for the entire first interval and one for the entire second interval, are computed. Nevertheless unless sample sizes are large, an approach based on subinterval pregnancy rates is not feasible and summary pregnancy rates become a practical necessity. Fortunately, as Table D-2 demonstrates, the tendency of summary pregnancy rates to obscure differences in the fraction of high-risk couples may be lessened by considering only the first few months of experience of each couple and ignoring their subsequent experience. That is, all contraceptive exposures, when they do not end sooner, are truncated at something like 12 months. If exposures are left untruncated, as in the pregnancy rates conventionally computed, then the very long exposures of a minority of couples may average down the two overall pregnancy rates and thereby largely hide even a large difference in pregnancy risk at the start of the two contraceptive experiences. Another advantage to be gained by truncating exposures is that it reduces bias resulting from unequal lengths of intended postponement of pregnancy. When one

TABLE D-2

Accidental Pregnancies per 100 Years of Contraceptive Exposure when Exposures are Truncated at Specified Points

Span of Observation Period	Interval Marriage to First Pregnancy Number of Exposure Months	Failure Rate	Interval First Birth to Next Pregnancy Number of Exposure Months	Failure Rate
2 months	1,006	42.4	1,488	14.5
6	3,025	37.1	4,870	25.1
12	4,782	35.7	8,171	24.7
18	6,012	30.8	10,534	23.8
24	6,871	29.4	12,135	22.3
36	7,925	27.3	13,994	20.8
48	8,389	26.2	15,046	19.9
No truncation	8,758	25.5	16,655	19.5

SOURCE: R. G. Potter, Jr., *op.cit.*, p. 80.

group seeks longer postponements than another, its pregnancy rate, if based on untruncated exposures, is biased downward by the fact that its successful contraceptors are contributing longer exposures than are the successful contraceptors of the other group who do not seek such long delays of pregnancy.

Summary pregnancy rates based on exposures truncated at 12 months have been used throughout Chapter IV. Truncation at 12 months has been adopted as a compromise, the feeling being that to truncate earlier would be to sacrifice too much information as well as to magnify any inadequacies in the removal of postpartum amenorrhea from contraceptive exposure.[1]

[1] See also C. Tietze and S. Lewit, "Recommended Procedures for the Study of the Use-Effectiveness of Contraceptive Methods," in *International Planned Parenthood Federation: Medical Handbook*, Part 1, *Conception Control*, London, pp. 55–61, 63–69.

Appendix E

Significance Levels of Correlation Coefficients

Coefficients of Correlation Required to Reject the Hypothesis $\rho = 0$ at 5 and 1 Per Cent Levels of Significance

| | Magnitude of r's by Levels of Significance | | Degrees of Freedom $(n - 2)$ |
	5%	1%	
Total sample	.07	.09	903
Protestant	.10	.13	370
Catholic	.10	.13	421
Jewish	.19	.25	108
Active:			
Protestant	.15	.20	172
Catholic	.19	.26	105
Other:			
Protestant	.14	.18	196
Catholic	.11	.15	314

Author Index

Subject Index

abortions, 233
adjustment to marriage
  birth intervals and, 187
  coital frequency and, 187
  fertility planning and, 184–86, 195
  fertility since second birth and, 185,
    196–97, 242–43
  hypotheses, 7, 182–84
  income and, 186
  measurement of, 195–96
  multivariate analyses, 220ff.
  number of children desired and,
    184–86, 197
adjustment to mother role
  birth intervals and, 187
  coital frequency and, 187
  fertility planning and, 184–86
  fertility since second birth and, 185,
    242–43
  hypotheses, 183–84
  number of childred desired and,
    184–85
age
  fecundity and, 198, 201
  fertility planning and, 199
  multivariate analyses, 219ff.
  number of children desired and,
    199–200
age at marriage and, 232
  birth intervals, 199–202
  family size, 198
  fertility planning, 199–202, 243–44
  fertility since second birth, 199–202,
    243–44
  multivariate analyses, 219ff.
  number of children desired, 199–202,
    243–44

birth intervals and
  adjustment to marriage, 187
  adjustment to mother role, 187
  age at marriage, 199–202
  birth spacing preferences, 21, 63, 235
  fertility since second birth, 71–72
  "intended" and "residual" com-
    ponents, 21–22, 56–57, 72, 235–36
  marriage duration, 12, 71–72, 219
  migration and, 171
  multivariate analyses, 75, 219ff.
  number of children desired, 44, 56–59,
    62–63, 72, 236–37
  occupational mobility, 242–44

parity, 12–15, 56
religion, 79, 89
see also, preferred birth intervals
birth order, 205

Catholics
  see religion, religiousness, education
chance taking
  see contraception, regularity of
children's problems
  fertility since second birth and, 193,
    242–43
  hypotheses 193–94
  measurement of, 193
church attendance
  change over time, 92, 93
  fertility planning and, 93
  fertility since second birth and, 93
  fertility trends of Catholics and, 130
  multivariate analyses, 219ff.
  number of children desired and, 92–93
  see religiousness
class
  see occupational class
cohort fertility trends, 130
coital frequency, 27, 32–34, 51–52, 187,
    234
coitus interruptus
  see withdrawal
communication between spouse
  see adjustment to marriage
commutation to work
  see residence
conception delay
  birth intervals, 4, 24
  coital frequency and, 27, 32–36, 236
  factors affecting, 26, 236
  ovulatory cycle, knowledge of, and,
    27–32, 36, 236
condom
  effectiveness of, 41
contraception
  acceptability, 38
  changes in, 49
  first use of, 232
  improvement of, 4, 23, 45–55, 233–34
  measurement of effectiveness, 283–85
  number of children desired and, 23–24,
    38–44, 49–50, 60, 64, 69, 234
  ovulatory cycle, knowledge of, 52–53,
    235
  reasons for nonuse, 60–61, 232